SUBMARINE!

The Australian Submarine Service in History

Paul Davidson

Connor Court Publishing

First Published in 2024 by Connor Court, Publishing Pty Ltd

Second edition, paperback, published in 2025 by Connor Court Publishing Pty Ltd

Copyright © Paul Daivdson, 2025

All rights reserved. Apart from any fair dealing for the purpose of private study, research, brief quotations embodied in critical articles or reviews as permitted under Australian Copyright Act (1968), no part of this work may be reproduced by electronic or other means without the written permission of the publisher.

Connor Court Publishing Pty Ltd
PO Box 7257
Redland Bay QLD 4165
sales@connorcourtpublishng.com.au

ISBN: 9781923224551 (paperback edition)

Printed in Australia

Cover Painting: AE2 and E14 in the Dardanelles used by permission of Marine artist Don Braben. With acknowledgement and appreciation to the United Service Club Brisbane

Dedicated to those who served and serve in submarines, in the cause of peace, and to my submariner friend Commodore Michael Dunne AM RAN (1944-2024).

CONTENTS

Foreword	7
Preface	11
Glossary	14
1 Early Development and World War One	17
2 Between the Two World Wars	51
3 World War II	63
4 The Cold War (1945-90) and Post-Cold War	171
5 Australian Submarine Service; Past, Present and Future	180
6 Nuclear-powered Submarines	209
7 The Future for Australian Submarines	152
8 The Perisher course and Australian Submarine Commanders	264
Reflections on Submarine Command	281
Bibliography	322
About the Author	330
Index	333

FOREWORD

Submarines and their history and development are very much to the fore and this new book entitled Submarine!: *The Australian Submarine Service in History* by Dr Paul Davidson is very welcome. There are several books setting out the history of our Australian submarines, including my own on Australian submarine history,[1] two on our first submarines AE1[2] and one on AE2 and her captain[3], one on the *Collins* class[4] and quite a few online sites covering different aspects of Australian submarine histories. None of these histories, however, provides the background setting of the Australian submarines against the development of submarines in the navies of our two main allies, the British Royal Navy and the United States Navy. This book does this admirably.

The subtitle he has chosen of *The Australian Submarine Service in History* accurately reflects the breadth of this book. The author opens the book with Chapter 1 setting out the background to the development of the first primitive submarines and the contemptuous attitude towards them by the

---

[1] White M. (2015). *Australian Submarines: A History*, 2nd ed, Australian Teachers of Media, St Kilda, Australia.

[2] Spurling, K. (2014). *The Mystery of AE1: Australia's Lost Submarine and Crew*. Missing Pages Publishers; Seal, G. (2014). Finding the Lost Submarine: The Mystery of AE1. *Journal of Australian Naval History*, vol. 5 no. 1, pp.53-70. Submarine Institute of Australia Inc.; Foster, J. (2006). AE1: *Entombed but not Forgotten*, Australian Military Publications. Loftus, NSW; Seal, G. (2013). *Century of Silent Service*. Boolarong Press, Brisbane.

[3] Brenchley, F. & Brenchley, E. (2001). *Stoker's Submarine*. Harper Collins, Sydney.

[4] Yule P & Woolner D, (2008), *The Collins Class Submarine Story: Steel, Spies and Spin*, Cambridge University Press, Port Melbourne.

chiefs of the greatest naval power of the time, the Royal Navy. Chapter 2 deals with the technological development, which was so important. Submarines have always had a small safety margin where one accident or failure could readily lead to the loss of the submarine and crew, which is not the case for most surface ships. As a result of the high risks, in nearly every case, the crews have been formed by volunteers and when "pressed" men were used it usually did not end well. The service reverted to recruiting volunteers.

Chapters 3 deals with the era of hot war in World War II (1939-1945), notable for the courage of submariners and improvisation of technologies, as well as much evolution of thought as to how best to use their capabilities both tactically and strategically.

Chapter 4 covers the more subtle but important Cold War (1950, 1960s and onwards). This included the period when I was serving at sea in submarines, in the 1960s. Both in the North Atlantic area where there was much tension about whether the USSR would invade the west and, if so, how the NATO submarine forces would oppose the Russian fleet as it sortied south around Russia and offshore from the Norwegian coast. Our squadron's operations included "mystery patrols" off Russia but in the main hostilities ensued on the rare occasions when our boats, or the Russians doing patrols in "our" waters, were detected. On the other hand, the submarine operations in the South-East Asian waters involved two hot wars for an Australian like me serving in a British submarine; the Vietnam war, in which Australia was involved but the UK was not, and the "Confrontation" in Borneo where both countries were involved in resisting the Indonesian invasion of Borneo. While Dr Davidson does not detail South-East Asian operations in the 1960s, his book gives a very valuable background for them.

From Chapter 5 to the end of the book the author returns to

the Australian story, with a brief descriptive section on the RN and USN and nuclear submarines in Chapter 6. The concept of nuclear propulsion is important for submarine operations because it enables them to be true submersibles Air-dependent submarines such as the *Collins* class with their diesel engines are vulnerable to detection while snorting because of their physical structure above the water (snort air intake and periscope) and their heat exhaust just below the surface heating up the water (very hot exhaust from very large and powerful diesel engines). Modern technology makes submarine batteries last longer and air independent systems (AIPs) do exist, but the AIPs do not allow full power for long periods that are needed to get to and from a distant patrol area – only the nuclear boats can do this. Further, the nuclear-powered boats carry a bigger weapons load, can carry more stores for extended patrol periods and provide greater comfort for the crews. The author deals with these issues nicely in Chapter 6. His Chapter 7 deals with AUKUS and the nuclear submarine issues by giving an excellent account of the current situation.

The book includes reflections by prominent Australian submarine commanders concerning the exercise of command in an isolated unit like a submarine on patrol, and aspects of the Commanding Officers Qualifying Course ("Perisher"), that they all have to pass to qualify for submarine command. The Chief of Navy, Vice Admiral Mark Hammond AO, illustrates the challenges of submarine command: "The ability to manage risk is critical… But in a submarine when you are deep and fast you don't know what you don't know…You are trusted by the crew's families, and by the government, to do the right thing. It's a great responsibility".[5] This reflects the heavy responsibility that the captain carries when isolated on patrols. This critical feature of submarine service has not been covered to this extent

---

[5] See Chapter 8.

in other works. Overall Dr Davidson has done a great service in researching and writing this book and I commend it to all who have an interest in the Australian Submarine Service and submarine warfare.

-- Dr Michael White OAM KC FRHSQ, B.Com, LLB (Qld), PhD (Bond); Cert Higher Ed, LLD (UQ), Adjunct Professor of Maritime Law, TC Beirne School of Law, University of Queensland. Lieutenant Commander (Retd) Royal Australian Navy Submarine Service

PREFACE

Tragically, the word 'Submarine!' was among the last words spoken by untold numbers of seafarers and innocent passengers in ships in the last century. Thousands of others never saw the enemy periscope stalking them, or saw the dreaded torpedo tracks heading towards them. This book acknowledges this brutal truth in the history of submarine warfare, as a background to discussing the past, present and possible future of the Australian Submarine Service in a world of proliferating numbers of submarines. I served as a staff officer Operational Analysis in the Submarine Branch (2017-18), but I am not a qualified "dolphins-wearing" submariner. At best I am an amateur naval historian. I have written this book because at the present time in Australia's history, perhaps more than at any other time, as we plan for a nuclear-powered fleet, we need to have an understanding how submarines have been used in naval warfare in the past, especially in World War II, and how Australia is continuing the heritage of its submarine service. The global significance of the submarine is well expressed by a naval historian over two decades ago:

> In less than a century the submarine has matched or overtaken, outlasted, or seen off the battleship, the aircraft carrier, the strategic bomber, even the land-based missile in its silos. The world is left with more than 700 submarines, 400 of which run on conventional diesel-electric power and nearly 300 powered by nuclear energy, including scores armed with nuclear ballistic

missiles.[6]

The conclusion can be only that the threat of subsurface warfare is likely to become more significant.[7] We need to keep in mind that sea-bed cables carry most of the world's ever-increasing internet traffic on which we have come to depend, and as an island nation reliant on the sea for our trade, we must understand how important the sea is to Australia.[8] Our national security and resilience are inextricably linked to the sea and our use of it. It is a major element in the study of war, and as such, in the history and future of submarines.

There have been many fine books written about submarines in wartime, such as *One Hundred Days*, by Rear Admiral Sandy Woodward RN, a submariner who became famous for leading the British forces in the Falklands War.[9] Dr Michael White lists others in a footnote in the Foreword to this book. Books and movies demonstrate the intrigue that surrounds the submarine. Titles such as *Above Us the Waves*, *The Hunt for the Red October* [10], *Das Boot*, and *HMS UNSEEN* [11] are the popular stuff of literature and movie legend. The elite crews who remained effective yet undetected contributed to their respected reputation in their countries as "The Silent Service". Many of us struggle to comprehend the courage and skill shown by individual commanders and crews such as Captain George Hunt DSO DSC RN.[12] We may wince at the costs and

---

[6] Van Der Vat (1994). *Stealth At Sea: The History of the Submarine*. Weidenfeld & Nicholson, London.

[7] Sweeney, M. (2023). Submarines will reign in a war with China. *Proceedings*, US Naval Institute. March, pp. 21-25.

[8] Shackleton, D. (2023). Personal communication.

[9] Woodward, S. (2003). *One Hundred Days*, Harper Collins, London.

[10] Clancy, T. (1984), *Hunt for the Red October*, Naval Institute Press, Annapolis.

[11] Robinson, P. (1999). *HMS Unseen*. W.F. Howes, Ltd, London.

[12] Dornan, P. (2010). *Diving Stations*, Pen & Sword Books Ltd, Barnsley.

challenges in building and crewing our submarines.[13] We may be intrigued by details of the technology in the Royal Navy's *Hunter Killers*.[14]

What we do not doubt is that the stealth and lethality of submarines make them very different from surface ships. Submarine warfare is different from surface warfare, and the people who sail in submarines are different. The tasks set them, the conditions they endure, and the dangers they face, mark them out. It's entirely possible that one day, regrettably, the survival of our nation and way of life may depend on them, and on their capability in deterring or defeating our enemies. Knowing something of the history of the submarine at war gives perspective to understanding the significance of current activities in relation to the Australian submarine Service in particular, and its place in the history of submarine warfare.

A note on the second edition

This second edition was not written because the first edition sold well. It did, but the motivation to write this edition was to update recent history, to give more context of the history of the war as well as submarine history, and to generally revise and expand on the relevant information that backgrounds the strategy of contemporary submarine warfare.

- Paul Davidson Brisbane 2025

---

[13] Yule, P & Woolner, D. (2008). *The Collins Class Story: Steel, Spies, and Spin*. Cambridge University Press, Melbourne.

[14] Ballantyne, I. (2013). *Hunter Killers*, Orion, London.

Glossary

AM	Member of the Order of Australia
AO	Officer of the Order of Australia
AOM	Medal of the Order of Australia
ASDIC	Antisubmarine Detection Investigation Committee. The name given to the device for sending an electronic vibration through water. It bounced back from another underwater mass such as a submarine and the time interval allowed calculation of range and bearing. ASDIC was the forerunner of SONAR.
ASW	Antisubmarine Warfare
CAPT	Captain. Senior Naval officer below the rank of Commodore ("1-star"). The term is often used without reference to rank, to refer to the Commanding Officer of a vessel.
CB	Companion of the Most Honorable Order of the Bath.
CDF	Chief of Defence Force. Currently a 4-star officer (General, Air Marshal or Admiral).
CDRE	Commodore. A 1-star Naval Officer, above the rank of Captain. Equivalent to an army Brigadier (BRIG) and an airforce Air Commodore (AIRCDRE).
CMDR	Commander. A Naval Officer one below the rank of Captain. Often colloquially referred to as a three ringer in respect of the gold braid rings worn on the shoulder epaulettes or on the sleeves. Equivalent to an Army Lieutenant Colonel (LTCOL) and an airforce Wing Commander (WCDR).
CN	Chief of Navy in the RAN (currently a VADM – a 3-star naval officer), equivalent to an Army Lieutenant General and an Airforce Air Marshal.
Commission	Officers and ships are commissioned into service by the Governor General.
DGSM	Director General Submarines (Head of RAN Submarine

	Profession).
DSO	Distinguished Service Order.
DSC	Distinguished Service Cross.
Dolphins	Qualification badge worn by submariners.
Fin	Free flooding superstructure containing the submarine's conning tower, masts and periscopes.
FOSM	Flag Officer Submarines (RADM). The senior uniformed rank in RN Submarine service – 2-star officer).
KBE	Knight Commander of the Most Excellent Order of the British Empire.
KCMG	Knight Grand Cross Most Distinguished Order of St Michael and St George
Knot	A measure of speed of 1.85 kms per hour. The singular abbreviation is kt. The plural is kts.
LCDR	Lieutenant Commander. A rank one below Commander, often colloquially referred to as "a two-and-a half" in respect of the two thick and one thin gold braid rings worn on the shoulder epaulettes or sleeve. Equivalent to an army Major (MAJ) and an airforce Squadron Leader (SQNLDR).
Nm	Nautical mile unit of distance at sea (1,852 metres).
LEUT	Lieutenant A junior officer rank one below Lieutenant Commander, often colloquially referred to as "a two ringer" in respect of the gold braid rings worn on the shoulder epaulettes. Equivalent to an army Captain (CAPT) and an airforce Flight Lieutenant (FLTLT).
PD	Periscope depth.
RADM	Rear Admiral. Two-star naval officer, one rank above Commodore.
RAN	Royal Australian Navy.
RN	Royal Navy.
SONAR	Sound navigation and ranging. A technique using sound propagation to navigate, measure distances, and communicate with or detect on or under the surface of the water.
Snort mast	Snorkel mast raised when at periscope depth to import fresh air into a diesel electric submarine and allow engines to be run to recharge batteries, and to improve habitability by expelling foul air.

SSBN	Nuclear-powered ballistic missile submarine.
SSGN	Nuclear-powered cruise missile submarine.
SSK	Diesel-electric powered submarine.
SSN	Nuclear-powered attack submarine.
VADM	Vice Admiral. A 3-star senior officer below the rank of Admiral (4-star).
GC	George Cross The George Cross (GC) is the highest award bestowed by the British government for non-operational gallantry or gallantry not in the presence of an enemy. In the British honours system, the George Cross, since its introduction in 1940, it has been equal in stature to the Victoria Cross, the highest military award for valour.
VC	Victoria Cross. The VC is highest and most prestigious decoration of the British honours system, awarded for valour in the presence of the enemy.

Australian Navy submarine AE2, between 1914 and 1915 (Wikipedia Commons)

1

Early Development and World War One

"I don't think it is even faintly realised, the immense impending revolution which the submarines will effect as offensive weapons on war. They are the battleships of the future." (Admiral of the Fleet Jacky Fisher RN).

The Historical Background to the Introduction of Submarines – World War I

In about 1910, the great powers jockeyed for dominance, if only by bluffing others. Some historians thought that while no one wanted war, together the forces acted together to coalesce alliances into a war that would go on to kill nine million people. Avoidable conflict rapidly escalated into an expected world war. The momentum became unstoppable. The possibility of war became a self-fulfilling prophecy. The new nation of Germany wanted its own navy to rival the immense battleships of the Royal Navy. Victorian torpor in Britain was ending, as it feared German domination in Europe, and it formed alliances with France and Japan. By 1910, with First Sea Lord Jacky Fisher driving the strategy, Britain was expanding its fleet and by 1914 it ruled the waves.

Adding to fierce debate over women's right to vote and the role of women in society, Britain in the summer of 1914 Britain was torn by social economic division domestically, with conflict over home rule for Ireland, and huge inequality of wealth. It became as volatile as the turbulent nations in Europe. It regarded Imperial Germany as an intolerable threat as it aligned with Austria and Hungary, possibly to become dominant in Europe, and so Britain began to align with France. In all the eventual protagonists, Defence spending generally ballooned.

In 1914, the stage was set for war, awaiting a crisis to light the fuse. War was seen by some as inevitable. The trigger was provided on 28th June 1914 by the assassination of the heir to the Hapsburg throne, Archduke Franz Ferdinand, and his wife, by a Habsburg citizen Bosnian Serb terrorist in Sarajevo. The Archduke's uncle was the Emperor of Austria, who promptly declared war on Serbia on 28 July. Russia mobilised three days later. The war sucked in one nation after another, each in pursuit of its own interests. The Russians backed the Serbians as a fellow Slavic nation, and the Germans backed Austria-Hungary, and on 31 July also declared war on Serbia. The French said they would back the Russians, and the British then backed the French. In the previous half century, Prussia had been victorious against Denmark, Austria and France, and the Kaiser's government was seen within as dysfunctional. Germany then invaded Belgium as a prelude to attacking France and it planned to invade Russia. On 4 August, Britain honoured an old treaty to defend the neutral Belgium. France swallowed its ideological opposition and allied with Russia to balance the power of the emerging Germany, which then felt surrounded.

Germany, Austria, Hungary and Italy faced off against France and Russia, which surprised the rest of Europe by mobilizing quicker than expected, with a large army and rail network that could move troops to a front with Germany. France and Britain underestimated German intentions and capability. Reports of atrocities soon emerged. Later research confirmed that Germany murdered 6,400 innocent Belgian and French civilians in the first months of the war. British attitudes hardened. The war changed the balance of power, the position of borders, and the way civilians and women were treated. It also changed the way people thought about each other in ethnic nationalism and an acceptance of violence as a means of settling disputes. Technology became decisive in warfare, as it had in history, with the demise of the horse and the mounted knight in favour of motorized transport and tanks. The highly significant development in history of the technology demonstrated in the submarine and submarine warfare is the focus of this book, particularly in relation to Australia.

Introduction

The prophetic statement at the head of this chapter was made by Admiral of the Fleet Sir John ("Jacky") Fisher in 1904. He became First Sea Lord and was a keen and clear-sighted advocate of the submarine as a weapon.
 Fisher was the architect of British naval policy before the "Great War". It became known as World War I only during World War II. Fisher was the second most important figure in British naval history after Lord Nelson. He was famously brash, enthusiastic and energetic.

Never one to undersell his opinions, within five years Fisher had reformed the stifling and moribund RN. "Fisher's opponents viewed war as a controlled, decent process in which civilians could be spared, private property respected and rules obeyed. They loathed Fisher with that special contempt well-bred fools reserve for men of ability."

Fisher's opponents complacently assumed Britain could afford to wait and respond to enemy challenges. By contrast, Fisher preferred pre-emption: he would kill off the competition before it got too serious. However, in spite of his reputation as an authority in naval warfare, there remained others who doubted the significance of the submarine. It is fair to argue that the thousands of ships sunk by submarines in two world wars and since are ample justification of his prediction.

Yet, opposition by some to a nation's investment in submarines is still apparent. Submarines became the weapon that twice brought Britain to the verge of defeat. Their greatest defensive and offensive weapon is their stealth, but paradoxically remaining undetected means they are out of sight and out of mind for many politicians and populations until it is too late. Australia needs to learn from the history of submarine warfare and the submarine's strategic and tactical role in deterrence. This review of history supports this.

This chapter describes the early development and deployment of the submarine as an offensive weapon in World War I. It introduces the long history of diverse opposition to submarines. This opposition came not just from a citizenry shocked at the loss of life this new lethal weapon was capable of causing, but also from contemptuous fellow officers in the navy's surface fleet, who felt both vulnerable and powerless. Neither source of antisubmarine prejudice has entirely dissipated.

Since the invention of the 125-ton Holland submersible in 1900, named after its creator, Irishman John Philip Holland, the submarine has endured a contentious history. Recognition of its likely impact on naval warfare was not immediate, but some of the apparent lack of interest from the Royal Navy in the Holland submarine is attributable to the British Admiralty's desire to maintain secrecy and not encourage other navies to build competitor vessels. Few glimpsed the potential of the submarine. As noted, one who did was Admiral of the Fleet Sir John Fisher. The Admiralty had ordered five submarines from Vickers in 1901, well before the Great War, in which unexpectedly, Germany would go on to sink 4,837 British ships.

The first submarine delivered to the Royal Navy in 1901 was built in Barrow-in-Furness in north-west England, under license to the Electric Boat Company USA, which held the patent to Holland's boat. In naval warfare it was then the battleship, and not the submarine, that was foremost in people's minds.

Remarkably, so early after Australia's Federation, in 1907 the Prime Minister Alfred Deakin proposed a fleet of nine submarines and six destroyers. This initiative was met with strong opposition from Australia's senior naval officer, Captain William Rooke Creswell (later Vice Admiral Sir William Creswell KCMG, KBE). Creswell argued that submarines "would be useless for Australia under present conditions or against any attacks possible to occur, and they are "expensive to maintain and difficult to crew". In 1909, the purchase of three small C-class submarines with petrol engines to charge their batteries, was proposed. This power supply was generally found to be dangerous and was abandoned before delivery. The C-class were low speed and had limited endurance. Submarines then were both primitive and ineffective. It was at least the beginning of a new era in technology, seafaring, and warfare.

Resistance to submarines endured, from other senior naval officers, as well as from some politicians. Cabinet overruled them, and in 1910, the Australian Government ordered two E-class submarines: *AE1* and *AE2*, to be built at Barrow-in-Furness in northwest England. They each displaced 111 tons, and had a length of 178 feet. With two 900 hp Vickers diesel engines, they could manage 15 kts on the surface at 9 kts submerged, with an endurance of only hours. In the long delivery voyage from England, they experienced numerous malfunctions. They were under tow by other naval vessels for about a third of the 13,000-mile passage, setting an endurance record. Conditions for the crew of 32 were arduous, cramped, and very hot. The new Australian boats arrived in Sydney to public acclaim on 24th May 1914. Within days, both boats and crews were called up for deployment and into conflict.

Regardless of the need, praise for the new platform in general was not universal, even within the Navy. Admiral Lord Charles Beresford, RN became known for his anti-submarine prejudice: "The submarine can operate only by day and in clear weather, and it is practically useless in misty weather". History records him as "a brave and charismatic leader, but one better suited to an earlier, simpler age".

A similar lack of enthusiasm, and of insight, was shown in 1901 by the Controller of the Royal Navy, Admiral Sir Arthur Wilson VC RN, often quoted for his dismissive criticism of submarine warfare as "underhand, unfair, and damned un-English. they'll never be any use in war. We intend to treat all submarines as pirate vessels in wartime and we'll hang all the crews". This misguided prejudice was hardly helpful in recruiting men to the new arm of the naval service in the defence of the nation. Fortunately, other views prevailed. Even Sir Arthur Wilson had changed his mind by 1914, and he later became an advocate for submarines. His celebrated contemporary, Admiral of the

Fleet Jacky Fisher RN, had earlier unleashed in 1899 a more pragmatic if unpalatable view: "The essence of war is violence! Moderation in war is imbecility."

So the war of words raged. Like them or not, submarines proliferated. While there was little affection for submarines in the senior ranks of the navy, there was the beginning of grudging respect for their unarguable capability and the threat they posed. The question was, and always is, how were they to be used?

Submarines are offensive by design and intent - they have no peacetime role such as constabulary or diplomacy in the same way that surface ships can be used. They exist to achieve the three primary elements of sea power: sea control, sea denial and power projection. Their reputation is that of the silent killer. Even their intelligence collection activities are related to the preparation for and conduct of hostilities. They contribute to deterrence by their presence, stealth, lethality, and general unpredictability."

Indeed, as weapons of offence and defence, for the projection of power, and deterrence of enemy aggression, submarines have no equal. Typically, along with intercontinental ballistic missiles, they represent the highpoint of a nation's technology, and they stretch their crews and equipment beyond almost any other form of military service. The submarine represents the projection of a nation's technology and naval power as a force to protect its people, its culture, and its territory. They are dangerous, and it appears historically, they are necessary in defence.

Strategy and Submarine Operations

For centuries, people have thought about vessels that could travel beneath the surface of the ocean. However, only in the recent past have the obvious challenges of constructing hulls strong enough to withstand the pressure of the water on them at effective depths been addressed, along with the requirements for propulsion, control, and habitability – air for the crew, along with their payload of offensive and defensive weapons and information systems.

Whether for exploration or military application, submarines have become sophisticated far beyond the early "submersibles" of previous eras. With hundreds of submarines now operating around the world, they are increasingly accepted routinely as vessels in the fleets of many navies. The size and type of any submarine and the weapons it carries depend on the individual nation's defence strategy, and the operating environment for which it is designed Operational and tactical options, safety, and cost, are significant matters to be addressed by decision makers in each case. A complex balance of these variables is required.

Introduction to Submarine Systems: Propulsion

Historically, submarines are propelled either by diesel engines that charge batteries to power electric motors, or by nuclear reactors that supply the heat to create steam to drive the turbines for electric power to the vessel's motors and other systems. The diesel-electric submarines are sometimes referred to as "conventionally-powered", with the designation SSK. They are often said to be quieter than nuclear-powered boats (with the designation SSN), except when running their diesels, and they are much less expensive than the nuclear-powered boats, which are capable of higher speeds, and have much longer endurance submerged.

To charge the batteries that drive the conventionally-powered submarine when submerged, its diesel engines need air to operate. The diesel-electric boat must either run its diesels only while the boat is on the surface, or if it has "air independent" propulsion that allows the engine to be run using stored liquid oxygen and hydrogen and its own exhaust gases. The Swedish *Gotland* class were the first submarines to use this air independent propulsion (AIP) system. Because it cannot run its diesel engines when submerged, the diesel-electric submarine can run submerged for only as long as its batteries permit. This may be for only several days, or much less depending on its speed, after which it must again surface and run its engines to recharge its batteries.

A third alternative for diesel-powered submarines is to run their engines when at periscope depth, with air available to its engines via the "snorkel". Originally this was a 20-foot long mast raised next to the periscope that sucks air into the boat, to ventilate the pressure hull with fresh air for the crew and to run the diesels to recharge its batteries. It has a valve at the top to exclude water when a wave washes over it. A submarine at periscope depth running its diesels in this way is referred to as "snorting". The danger is that when snorting the boat is exposed to detection by aircraft or surface ships' lookouts or radar, either ship borne or by an aircraft or satellite. Initially patented by a Scottish shipbuilding and engineering company in 1916, the air induction idea was initially disregarded by the Admiralty, then developed by the Dutch, and eventually picked up by the Germans, who retrofitted it into their Type VII and Type IX submarines in 1944. The *schnorkel* was to become standard in submarine design for diesel electric boats, and has remained so ever since 1944.

The most common type of batteries used are the classic lead acid batteries. More recent technology in some countries uses lithium-ion batteries, which have advantages of faster discharge rates and recharge times, and higher energy density resulting in enhanced silent running, better speeds and sprints, longer underwater endurance, and better overall performance. However, their use in submarines remains limited by the inherent danger posed by hydrogen gas and intense heat that can be released in the event of fire.

By contrast, the nuclear-powered submarine (SSN) can stay submerged for months without refuelling or surfacing. Its endurance is limited only by the food for its crew on board, and their resilience. SSNs make their own air and water by hydrolysing sea water, using their abundant electricity produced. Patrols lasting 70 days are not uncommon for SSNs, and for nuclear-powered ballistic submarines (SSBNs) much longer, even up to several months submerged.

The implications of a vessel that can operate underwater, undetected by an enemy, and can deliver offensive weapons such as torpedos or missiles, striking an adversary's warships or other assets on land, are immediately obvious. Even the threat of a submarine in an area may be sufficient to deter or coerce an enemy to stay in port. Roles additional to anti-shipping roles have come to include covert surveillance, protection of surface fleets, and support of special forces in clandestine operations, such as inserting small groups of special forces into hostile territory.

Introduction to C3 in Submarines: Command Control and Communication

Any Naval or military force relies on reliable and effective communication systems to undertake its mission. Because radio transmission from submarines is often limited by sea state and inherent limitations of radio signal reception and transmission when submerged, and the use of flags and signal lamps as with surface ships, early submarines faced and still confront particular challenges in C3. Range and reliability of the technology in communicating with each other and with shore-based command centres were significant factors in submariners' decision making. The ability of enemy forces to intercept radio transmissions was a major factor leading to the use of encrypted messages, Ultra was the project codename for Allied intelligence obtained by decrypting secret high level encrypted communications used by the German High Command during World War II. The term encompassed the intelligence from *Enigma* machines, a family of electro-mechanical cipher machines used for encrypting and decrypting radio transmissions in the navy and the military. German U-boats carried *Enigma* machines to decrypt and encrypt messages. C3 still presents its challenges to submarine operations. Satellites and other technology provide new and powerful systems.

Introduction to Sensors in Submarines

Critical to the use of submarines as weapons of war are the sensors that they carry, and the weapons they have available. These determine their capability, and thus the threat they pose to potential adversaries. The ubiquitous periscope allows a submarine to have visual observation of its surroundings without itself having to be exposed on the surface, although obviously the submarine must be close to the surface at "periscope depth" (PD), to allow the periscope to be raised. Then too, even the best optical periscope, or an optronics periscope with a high-resolution camera, and radar scanner, can be used only for short periods, lest it be detected by an adversary. In summary, being at PD with the periscope or snort mast raised calls for focussed attention by the commander, in view of the risk the exposure poses in allowing enemy detection of the boat's position.

Equally important as a sensor is SONAR (Sound Navigation and Ranging), originally in World War II called ASDIC by the British, using hydrophones built into the sides of the submarine, or as a towed array behind it, to listen for the sounds made by other ships. Banks of computers interpret the sounds in the water, from biologic sources such as whales to the unique electronic acoustic "signatures" of other vessels – fishing boats, surface warships, and other submarines.

In passive mode, the submarine quietly listens, without giving away its presence. In active mode the submarine sends out an electronic pulse (the distinctive "ping" made famous in submarine movies), and interprets the time taken for the pulse to bounce back from an external object, such as from another ship or submarine. This interpretation gives the range and bearing of a target. However, using active sonar has the disadvantage of disclosing to an enemy vessel the submarine's presence along with the range and bearing of the submarine. Remaining undetected has always been a desirable goal for submarines, for obvious reasons. Stealth is the submarine's major advantage. Thus, active sonar is not always advisable in operations.

Low frequency analysis of these signals allowed the approximate positioning of submarines by using arrays of sensors on the seabed to pick up the distinctive signatures of particular vessels. The network of these was called

SOSUS (Sound Surveillance System). Its meaning was secret until about 1973. It became the basis of the American and British detection techniques in Antisubmarine warfare. Information from this system can be fed to specifically equipped antisubmarine warfare (ASW) aircraft and other vessels. These sensors could be positioned at various choke points around the world, to monitor submarine activity.

Introduction to Submarine Weapons: From Torpedoes to Missiles

The weapons carried by submarines vary, depending on their mission. The best known are torpedos, which deliver an explosive charge at a distance away from the submarine, aimed to cause destruction of a target vessel, either by hitting it and exploding against its hull, or exploding under it such that the pressure wave thus created disrupts the hull integrity of the targeted ship. Submarines may also carry missiles, launched from their torpedo tubes or directly from within their hull in vertical launch system (VLS) tubes. These missiles can be anti-ship, anti-aircraft, or cruise missiles with long range effectiveness for attacking land-based targets. These missiles can be homing, multiple warheaded, with nuclear or non-nuclear warheads, and with ranges exceeding 1,000 kms. Current ballistic missile submarines (SSBNs) are very large, and may carry up to 24 missiles in VLS tubes. Four of the American *Ohio* class SSBNs, designated SSGNs, have been converted, each to carry seven Tomahawk land attack cruise missiles.

During the World Wars, torpedoes were unreliable and thus torpedo attacks often missed their quarry, or simply failed to detonate. More recent decades have seen the development of homing torpedos that search out their target or are guided to it by a trailing optic fibre transmitting data to and from the attacking submarine. Also, during World War I and World War II, many submarines were also equipped with deck guns, typically mounted aft of the fin, for use on the surface against enemy ships. In World War II, German U-boats had 105mm guns to fire on surface ships, and 40 mm antiaircraft guns to repel increasingly common (and effective) aerial attack, but these guns are now seen as obsolete, and are rarely if ever fitted to submarines. An American *Gato* class submarine was the first to embark rockets for its own defence, in World War II. However, missiles did not become commonly carried by submarines until much later, in the Cold War.

The Submarine War 1914-18

In the 1890s, submarines were regarded as neither proven nor trusted. Within a decade, attitudes began to change. At the beginning of World War I, submarine technology was still primitive, and many people in the navy then saw submarines only as short-range defensive weapons for coastal defence, with crews of grubby engineers, fighting their very limited war in a less than honourable way. Despite this, adversaries built many submarines in a short time, and they began to be active in conflict. Very publicly, the German High Seas fleet remained in port for most of World War I, ostensibly to avoid the British Grand Fleet in the Orkneys. The only time these fleets faced each other was for 20 minutes in the Battle of Jutland on 31 May 1916, when the Germans inflicted twice as much damage to the British as they suffered. By contrast, submarines operated alone and undetected until they struck, with increasingly deadly effect. Clearly the nature of naval warfare was changing.

The submarine was still yet to be recognised as a significant weapon. Numbers of submarines on both sides increased rapidly. At the beginning of the war, Germany had only 27 U-boats. By 1917 it had over 100. In 1917 it began unrestricted submarine warfare, sinking any vessels without warning that were bound to or from Britain. Half the world's merchant ships sailed under the British flag, and the island nation was heavily reliant on shipborne imports. A strategy for U-boats to blockade Britain was a significant threat. It should have been foreseen and a response developed.

In April 1915, German U-boats sank 900,000 tons of British shipping, leaving Britain with only six weeks of supplies. Though British antisubmarine warfare capability was still nascent, the years leading up to World War I had seen submarine development not only by Britain, but also by the US, France, and Germany. By 1914, some 400 submarines had been acquired by 14 nations. Britain had nearly 80, the largest submarine fleet in the world. Concepts of operations varied from coastal defence of harbours to proposed attacks on enemy ships in their home waters. Demonstrating deterrence, the RN had virtually closed the Baltic Sea to German iron ore traffic in those years.

However, international law still required that fair warning be given by a submarine before a merchant ship was attacked, to allow the crew to abandon ship. This required the submarine to surface, thus exposing it to enemy action and depriving it of the advantage of stealth, so the policy was abandoned. Even in 1916, German *Unterzeeboots* (U-boats) had four torpedo tubes and a 105mm deck gun, used for the more common surface attacks. Preferred over expensive torpedoes. Large numbers of ships and cargoes went to the bottom. The British had to take the U-boat threat seriously, and in 1917 began sailing in convoys across from the US, with up to a dozen merchant ships protected by accompanying armed escorts.

Sometimes "Q-ships" were used as decoys. These were converted merchant ships or tramp steamers with concealed deck guns to lure U-boats to within range, when the Q-ship would lower its covers, raise its flag, and fire on the U-boat. The Q-ships often flew the flags of neutral nations, instead of their own flag, to pass themselves off as neutral vessels and avoid German attack. The British regarded this tactic as a "perfectly legitimate *ruse de guerre* provided the national colours are hoisted before opening fire". Civilian funnel bands would be painted and different coloured bands repainted days later at sea. Instead of naval uniforms, crews wore seamen's rough clothing, and some even disguised themselves as women obvious on deck, to allay enemy caution. This was not as strange as it might appear. It was not uncommon for captains of such vessels to take their wives on board. Secrecy in fitting out the Q-ships was vital, with bogus untidy deck cargo concealing 12-pounders and Maxim guns. Overall attention to detail was a priority. Dummy funnels provided elevation for lookouts, and Plimsoll lines were painted over, as many neutral ships did not have them. Lack of naval discipline and ship handling were obvious to any observer, by their absence.

When approached by an enemy U-boat, the Q-ship's crew would perform elaborate theatre for the U-boats' lookouts, to the point of deck hands' taking to lifeboats while leaving all guns secretly manned and out of sight until the U-boat had come within range. Covers would then be dropped and the U-boat fired upon. The disguised Q-ships claimed eleven U-boats sunk. After 1 February 1917, the Germans responded with unrestricted warfare, sinking any ship thought to be bound for Britain. By that time, the convoy system had largely replaced the use of Q-ships as decoys. In 1915-17, some 30 of these "mystery ships" were commanded by ADM Sir Lewis Bayly

KCB KCMG CVO, and VADM Gordon Campbell VC, DSO and Two Bars RN. They had offered at least the opportunity for offensive action against the U-boats.

The Speed of World War I Submarines

In those early years of World War I, German U-boats could make 12.4 knots surfaced and 5.2 knots submerged. Their surface speed allowed them to keep up with slower British convoys. They needed to dive only to make an attack with torpedoes, or to evade attack by surface ships. However, submarine propulsion remained contentious. Within a few years of their advent, diesel engines were used to replace the dangerous petrol engines, which had a significant risk of fire and explosions because of fuel vapour. The first US submarine with diesel propulsion was commanded by Lieutenant Chester Nimitz (later to become famous as Admiral and Commander in Chief, US Pacific Fleet, in WWII). The 400 tonne USS *Seal* was laid down in 1909 and launched in 1911, with a crew of 24, and capable of 14 kts surfaced, and 10 kts submerged. She could loiter submerged at 2 kts for 48 hours. She carried four 18-inch bow torpedo tubes, and set a depth record of 256 feet. By the outbreak of war in 1914, Britain was exploring the potential offensive capability of submarines, but inexplicably, less attention was being given to defending its surface ships against submarine attack by an enemy.

In September 1914, the submarine was still perceived by naval strategists as constituting only a minor threat. That misperception would change quickly, but it was the awesome power of battleships that commanded naval and civilian attention. Their vulnerability to submarine attack was initially discounted, until after the U-boat showed its capability. Rather, the overwhelming visual impact of a battleship made it seen as the potent weapon of war. The very large ships were an undeniable ego boost to nations' leaders and their admirals, but their vulnerability to submarine attack was not fully understood. Typically, losing a battleship meant thousands of crew perished. Such unpalatable possibilities and defensive deficiencies were ignored, overshadowed by these towering edifices with big naval guns. They were unquestionably emotively imposing. An incisive simile from the time is critical of the priority given them: "The battleship is to an admiral what a cathedral is to a bishop."

The primacy of the battleship was an article of faith for many besotted senior officers, blinding them to the threat from other classes of vessels. Even British First Lord of the Admiralty Winston Churchill said in 1914 that he did not believe a submarine attack on Britain's critical seaborne trade "would ever be attempted by a civilised nation". One admiral huffed that the Germans would not use submarines in this way: "It would just not be cricket". A brave junior officer reminded him that the Germans did not play cricket. There was, as not uncommon in warfare, a serious British underestimation of the enemy threat. Along with his direct statement quoted at the beginning of this chapter, the brutal truth spoken by Jacky Fisher was that war is about violence and there is no benefit in moderation. Fisher was about to be vindicated in his statement of a self-evident though unpalatable truth.

At the outbreak of World War I, the British Royal Navy had 74 submarines, with 31 more being built. Germany began its war with 57 submarines. The British D-Class were early ocean-going submarines, and were the first submarines to operate successfully more than 500 miles from base. They could undertake reconnaissance missions and used wireless transmission to coordinate with surface ships. However, conditions for the crews continued to be cramped and arduous. Ventilation was inadequate for comfort, and equipment to facilitate personal hygiene was scarce. Sleeping accommodation was spartan and hot bunking was the norm. Condensation from expired air made for electrical malfunctions as well as foul conditions. Habitability was of secondary importance. Life in early submarines was unarguably squalid.

The Emerging Threat

The E-class submarines were the main element in the Royal Navy's attack submarine force during World War I. The British Admiralty was aware of the strategic possibilities of the ocean-going submarine, and of Britain's lack of such vessels.' Six weeks into the war, the submarine penetrated the Royal Navy's and the public consciousness when the small *U-9*, displacing only 543 tons, and commanded by the German Navy *Kriegsmarine* Lieutenant Otto Eduard Weddigen sank three RN armoured cruisers within 90 minutes (HM Ships *Aboukir, Cressy, and Hogue*), off the coast of Holland, with the loss of 1,459 British sailors. This unprecedented loss of ships and lives caused national shock in Britain.

The submarine threat became a front-of-mind concern for the public, as well as for alarmed politicians. There were clear reasons for submarine operations to be taken more seriously than before, strategically and tactically. With masterful understatement, future British First Sea Lord Admiral Dudley Pound wrote presciently at the time: "Much as one regrets the loss of life, one cannot help thinking that it is a useful warning to us. We had begun to consider the German submarines as no good and our awakening had to come sooner or later."

As has proven fatally frequent in conflicts through the ages, the threat posed by an enemy was underestimated, and only belatedly if ever acted upon, until its presence could no longer be ignored. Incalculable numbers of seafarers died, while insight developed and painful lessons were learned. Anti-submarine prejudice was being slowly and painfully overcome.

By 1915, Germany had 125 U-boats and had sunk an astonishing eight million tonnes of British shipping. It had a clear strategy of blockading and starving the island nation, thereby almost changing the course of history by bringing Britain to its economic knees. The evidence of the U-boat threat could no longer be ignored. Attitudes about submarines began to change. Only the convoy system of grouping merchant vessels together, protected by ASW escorts, saved Great Britain from being defeated at sea by the German U-boats.

In retrospect so logical, it is puzzling why it took until 1917 for the convoy system to be used routinely in World War I. This was because escort ships with depth charges and torpedoes that could defend against U-boats were in short supply. The British were resolutely unprepared to deal with the threat. Over 5,000 ships with their vital cargoes would be sunk by U-boats, and 15,500 sailors' lives lost. Britain built 56 of its 700 tonne E-Class submarines. These had crews of 30, with five torpedo tubes and a 12-pounder deck gun. Britain began the war in 1914 with 74 boats, and the submarine began to provide significant warfighting capability. Other nations also used submarines in World War I. France began the war with 62 submarines, which it operated mostly in the Mediterranean and Adriatic Seas. Russia began the war with 50 boats. Judging by these numbers, the submarine was being taken more seriously and not dismissed as a disreputable or inconsequential novelty.

British submarines made an auspicious entry into World War

I. In the Dardanelles campaign of 1915, two battleships, one destroyer, five gunboats, nine transports, and 30 smaller craft, seven ammunition and supply ships were sunk, for the cost of five British submarines. Three VCs were won by submarine commanders, the first being awarded in 1915 to Lieutenant Commander Norman Holbrook, RN, (1888-1976), commanding *B11*. Holbrook received the first VC of the war in 1915, and the first VC awarded for a naval action. He sank the Ottoman battleship *Mesudiye*.

On 13 December 1914, Holbrook had kept his boat quietly submerged for five hours, scraping slowly through the minefield guarding the entrance to the Dardanelles. After releasing his weapon at the moored enemy warship, he escaped with his crew through barrages of Turkish gunfire, remaining submerged for nine hours as he traversed the main channel back to the Sea of Marmara. He and his 12 crewmen returned home unscathed, to a hero's welcome. His crew were awarded either the DSC or DSM. Patriotic sentiment in Australia at the time recognised his courage, as expressed by the small NSW country town of Germanton that changed its name to Holbrook. The Australian town remains today a monument to his action, and maintains a popular museum to submarines. Norman Holbrook himself made celebrated visits to the town several times after the war. The action by Holbrook in *B11* in sinking the *Mesidiye* was observed by Cornelius Eggert, the American consul in Çannakale at the time, who quoted in his report even the German Vice Admiral Johannes Merten's assessment that the sinking was "a daring and mighty clever piece of work".

The Australian Submarine Service (1914-18)

Though a very young country, Australia had purchased its first two E-class submarines from Britain, *AE1* and *AE2*, in 1913.

AE1 was lost with all hands in 1914, presumably in a diving accident, in the south-west Pacific. Commanding *AE1* was Liverpool-born LCDR Thomas Desant RN, on loan to the RAN, described by his friend and colleague as "skilful, cautious and experienced." The *AE1* was involved in an operation to seize German colonies in New Guinea. A ventilation valve was left partially open, which it was reckoned would have flooded the engine room. An implosion would have killed all aboard instantly. Her exact whereabouts defied 14 search missions over the years, until December 2017, when her rusting hull was located in 300 metres of water off the Duke of York Island, near Rabaul, New Ireland, northeast of New Guinea.

A second notable Australian submarine in World War I was *AE2* with her 32-man crew. It deserves the books describing its actions. The *AE2* was the first submarine to penetrate the minefields and surface defences of the Dardanelles. The daring mission on the eve of the 25 April 1915 ANZAC landings in the Dardanelles by CO LCDR Henry Dacre Stoker DSO RN (on loan to the RAN) was a significant event in the history of the submarine.

AE2 distracted the attention of the Turkish navy from bombarding the invasion by the Allied forces at Gallipoli, on the western coast of the peninsula. The story of *AE2* at Gallipoli is given in detail by White. Stoker harassed his Ottoman enemies and attacked a Turkish battleship at Canakale. At length, AE2 was hit by enemy fire. Sustaining severe damage to the pressure hull from a Turkish gunboat and unable to dive in evasive action, with little alternative Stoker blew his boat's main ballast tanks to surface the submarine. The crew of three officers and 29 sailors surrendered as *AE2* was scuttled. Stoker and his crew spent the remaining three and a half years of the war under harsh conditions in a Turkish POW camp, during which three died. Some historians see the action by *AE2* as the greatest achievement in submarine history. What kind of leader was this Irish-born Australian submarine captain? At the very least, Stoker was both clever and courageous, and a great seaman. The submarine, still in its infancy, played a highly significant though often under-appreciated role in World War I.

It is of interest that after the war Henry Stoker became a successful stage actor in London, and was known as a writer and continuing supporter of his crew members who survived the war and the Turkish prison camp.[15] In World War II he served again, and was in Dover Castle planning for the D-Day invasion. He died on 2 February 1966, and the age of 81, remembered as a notable figure in Australian submarine history.

Significant U-boat Sinkings in the Early Years of World War I

In World War I, the German *Unterseeboot U-139* was commanded by *Kapitanlieutenant* Lothar von Arnauld de la Perriere. He became the most successful submarine commander in history, responsible for sinking 224 ships totalling 454,000 tonnes, mostly on the surface with his deck gun, rather than by torpedo. On his fifth patrol in 1916 in U-35, he sank an incredible 54 ships in just four weeks. He fought according to his rules of engagement. By convention, he stopped enemy vessels by threatening to fire his deck gun, waited for their crews to take to lifeboats, then boarded the vessel, inspected documents, told the crews how they could reach the next port, and then sank the stopped prize.

A century later, such behaviour amounts to chivalry, and may seem quaint. Never a Nazi himself, Von Arnauld de la Perriere was killed in 1941, in an air accident in France, having been promoted to Rear Admiral. We might spare a moment to think

---

[15] Carlton, M. (2024). *Dive!* Random House Penguin, Sydney, p. 169.

about how differently submarine warfare is now conducted. That early era of complying with the rules passed quickly. Industrial strength warfare required destroying the enemy's capacity to produce the resources to wage war. By 1917, attacks by U-boats had become unrestricted, with a blockade strategy intended to starve Britain into surrender. U-boats were authorised to sink any ship on course to Britain.

The Sinking of the Lusitania

One famous casualty of early World War I German U-boat action was the luxury 32,000 ton Cunard passenger liner *Lusitania*. Returning to Britain on a routine passage from America on 7 May 1915, the *Lusitania* sank with massive loss of life (mostly women and children) off the Irish coast. Within 18 minutes after a single torpedo was fired by *U-20*, the ship sank. Of the 1,266 passengers and 696 crew, only 761 survived. Significantly, 123 American passengers were lost. This sinking and the loss of these American lives was influential in changing American isolationist attitude about what had previously been seen as only a European war. Arguments raged over whether this was a legitimate military target. After the war it was revealed that the ship was carrying some four million rounds of machine gun ammunition, and 3,240 brass percussion artillery fuses—although the U-boat commander was not to know this at the time.

During the war, a painting of the *Lusitania*'s sinking was used extensively in Allied propaganda to encourage recruiting, contributing to the public perception of submarines as an unethical and improper weapon for waging war. The German U-boat captain Walter Schwieger did not give the customary warning to his target, and did not rescue survivors, as convention required. Such naivete about rules of engagement was eroded in the public mind. Allegations of war crimes persisted. Gradually, but slowly, the Admiralty and the public realised the danger posed by submarine attacks.

Three years after the *Lusitania* was sunk, on 27 June 1918, the U-boat *U-86* sank the Canadian hospital ship *Llandovery Castle* on its way back to Britain having delivered recovering soldiers to Halifax, Nova Scotia. *U-86* launched a torpedo attack, ignoring his right under the Hague Convention to stop and search the ship. After the ship sank in minutes, the U-boat rammed all but one of the lifeboats and machine gunned the survivors. Only 28 out of the 258 aboard the ship survived. *U-86*'s captain Helmut Brümmer-Patzig claimed his target was carrying troops and ammunition. He swore his crew to secrecy and faked the logbook, so *U-86* could not be connected to the ship they had sunk.

Predictably, there was international outrage, but to little effect. From 1917, unrestricted submarine warfare was shown to be devastating. After the war, three German officers from *U-86* were found guilty of war crimes, but their convictions were overturned on the grounds that they were only following orders. Canadians were appalled. The episode added to the reputation that U-boats and submariners behaved unprofessionally. The German captain fled the country but returned to serve again in World War II. He avoided trial, and was never prosecuted. He died in 1984.

Meanwhile, the horrific death rates on land in the conflict in France and Belgium had stunned the Western world. In different ways, the war at sea touched everyone, and submarines had become effective killing machines. The U-boat threat was increasingly taken more seriously. Nations gradually increased their acquisitions of submarines as weapons of war, and used them as such. In 1914-18 Germany launched a submarine campaign that almost brought Britain to its knees and caused it to lose the war. In April 1917, a total of 900,000 tons of British shipping was lost to U-boats. Britain was losing 17 ships a day, all loaded with essential supplies. Starvation in Britain was an imminent prospect. Such losses were overwhelming British expectations.

Submarines in World War I

In 1914, Germany had only 27 U-boats. By 1917 it had over 100. By the end of World War I, 360 German submarines and minelayers were officially accounted with sinking 4,837 merchant ships totalling 11,135,000 gross tons, taking the lives of 15,500 merchant seamen. It us believed that in 1917, there was only 10 days' supply of food left in Britain.[16] The submarine had proven its lethality in war, and its strategic and tactical significance as a threat to the very survival of the nation had become all too obvious.

By any estimate, the German submarine force subjected Great Britain to great danger, and near disaster. However, Germany underestimated the resilience of Britain and her allies. Germany lost 178 of its U-boats. In spite of the U-boats' blockade, by 1918, the flow of military supplies into Britain had actually increased. American aid sustained the island nation. The U-boat had posed a major threat, but could not save Germany from defeat. The German deployment of its U-boats against the Allies came at a fearful cost. Some 5,000 German submariners were lost. However, they had brought Britain close to defeat.

Attitudes in the Royal Navy and the population inevitably changed, towards seeing the submarine as a devastating

---

[16] Longstaff, R. (1984). *Submarine Command: A Pictorial History*. Book Club Associates, London, p. 9.

weapon of war.¹⁷ There was still a priority given to building very large and heavily armoured battleships with 15-inch and larger calibre guns, and there were the historic early signs of development of aircraft carriers that would become ubiquitous and decisive in World War II, along with a growing awareness of the threat posed even to mighty battleships by small submarines. Belatedly, navies began developing antisubmarine warfare (ASW) capability, largely with depth charges and sonar detection. These were to become greatly refined and destructive in World War II. With the push of massive losses and the pull of progress in technology, ASW belatedly received deserved priority.

In World War I, even the very primitive submarines were surprisingly effective in attack and deterrence. Their captains were professionals, individualistic leaders and skilled risk takers. They inspired loyalty and unique camaraderie in their crews. The lesson is that in spite of arduous conditions in dangerous submarines, they recorded astonishing achievements. The early submariners showed even so long ago, the personal characteristics that are often attributed to great leaders – commitment, daring, technical competence, and the ability to bring followers with them in pursuit of mission objectives. These characteristics of World War I submarine commanding officers are significant for an understanding of the culture of even present-day submarine services.

In 1917, the Royal Navy commenced its famous Periscope Course (later known as the "Perisher" Course) to train its submarine captains.¹⁸ It produced about 12 new submarine commanding officers each year between 1919 and 1939. The reduction of naval armament in 1930 and the London Submarine

---

[17] Marder, A. (1970). *From the Dreadnought to Scapa Flow: The Royal Navy in the Fisher Era 1904-1919*. Oxford University Press, London.

[18] See Chapter Eight.

Agreement between Britain and Germany in 1935 left Britain teaching its commanding officers to attack warships rather than merchant ships.[19] Introducing this submarine doctrine in World War I would change operations in the war that followed two decades later.

The End of World War I

Understanding the beginning of World War II requires understanding how the Great War ended. On land, the mindless slaughter of the Battle of the Somme in France led by British and Commonwealth forces had cost the Germans 600,000 soldiers. It distracted them from the 350,000 German soldiers lost in the battle of Verdun, which ended in December 1916. The catastrophic German failure at Verdun against the French Marshal Pétain led Kaiser Wilhelm to turn to Generals Carl Von Hindenburg and Erich Ludendorff to command the 8th Army in the quest for a quick victory over the Allies. The end of the war was still two years away.

Thousands of French and Belgian labourers were ruthlessly forced to build the heavily fortified Hindenburg line of barricades and defences. This was the background to Ludendorff's January 1917 ordering his 105 U-boats into the Atlantic in unrestricted warfare. They sank three merchant ships per day, totalling some five hundred in three months. The effect was to bring America into the war in April 1917. President Woodrow Wilson publicised 14 well-intentioned points for post-war world, including a body to be set up to mediate future international conflicts. This League of Nations proved unacceptable to European leaders and failed to achieve its potential in building a lasting peace.

---

[19] Franklin, G. (2015). *Britain's Anti-submarine Capability 1919-1939*, Routledge, London, p. 143.

In 1917, Russia disintegrated into a revolution and under the Marxist Lenin, and four centuries of czarist rule were ended. Of the 12 million Russians conscripted, by 1917 some two million were dead. On the 3 March 1917, Russia signed a treaty with the central powers, at Brest Litovsk, giving up vast territory in exchange for peace. Its population had had enough of war and its cost in Russian lives. Finland declared independence from Russia. Rumania, thus without Russian support, signed an armistice with Germany. This allowed Germany to deploy half a million troops from the eastern front to the Western front, in which over a million lives had already been lost. It was the beginning of the end. Many French troops were in open revolt. The Germans had advanced to within 60 miles of Paris.

The British naval blockade had been effective and Germany faced shortages of food and other essential supplies, such that its defeat appeared inevitable. In desperation, General Ludendorff planned a last major offensive in the spring of 1918 which pushed the British Fifth Army into full retreat. British Field Marshal Douglas Haig (1861-1928) was under pressure from Prime Minister David Lloyd George to secure victory. Eventually, French General Foch was appointed as supreme Allied Commander to bring French and British forces together. British and Australian forces stopped the German advance outside Amiens.

On 21 April 1918, near Amiens, Baron Manfred von Richthofen, Germany's most famous air ace, was shot down. He was credited as the war's most successful fighter pilot with 80 victories. Displaying respect and chivalry, he was buried by the Allies with full military honours. His loss was a huge blow to the young Luftwaffe. In May 1918, American forces won victory in the Battles of Cantigny and Belleau Wood. By then over a million US forces were in France. The Western alliance began to gain ground against the German offensive. Behind the lines, Ludendorff failed to see the disaster around him. The battles of the Marne had cost the German offensive 600,000 casualties.

On 8 August 1918, 16,000 demoralised Germans laid down their arms in one battle. Ludendorff called it "the black day of the German army". Desertion had become common. Ludendorff justified his ineptitude by claiming the German army was undefeated but had been undermined by the political left agitators. He demanded the civilian government surrender to American President Woodrow Wilson rather than face the ignominy of the army's having to do so. Preserving face, half a million soldiers died in the five weeks, waiting for a signature on the armistice document. Incredibly, Foch had tried to delay the armistice so the French rather than the British or the Americans could retake the Alsace Lorraine. The egocentric motivation exhibited by the leaders needlessly cost thousands of lives.

Woodrow Wilson demanded surrender, and Ludendorff advocated the Kaiser to abdicate. Instead, World War I lasted longer than necessary because the German military dictator Ludendorff refused to accept that his country's forces were beaten, although in private he admitted it. His attempts to retain autocratic control failed, and he blamed the German people for losing their nerve. After the failure of the misconceived spring offensive in 1918, the German army had effectively disintegrated. Ultra-patriots on the political right falsely blamed a disheartened population for undermining the army's morale. This was the *dolchstoss* legend ("stabbed in the back"). In October, Bulgaria, the Ottoman Empire and then on 3 November Austria-Hungary each signed armistice treaties. The Kaiser abdicated and a German Weimar Republic was announced.

However, the killing continued up to the eleventh hour. On 4 November 1918, Germany ordered its navy at Kiel to make a suicidal attack on the British fleet, and go down fighting, but they mutinied instead of sacrificing lives needlessly. On 11 November, a German delegation signed an armistice with the Allies to begin at 1100. Tragically, another 2,738 men lost their lives on that last day of the war. US Private Henry Gunter was the last soldier to fall, killed at 1059, a minute before the guns were to fall silent, when charging a German machine gun. Armistice Day on 11th November 1918 signalled the agreement to stop fighting, but it was not a peace treaty. Many Germans believed Ludendorff's propaganda and simply could not accept that Germany had lost the war. They claimed they never surrendered on their own territory.

On 16 November 1918, German troops were greeted by their politicians with the words: "You are returning unvanquished and undefeated". Thus, the war continued into the "peace". Genuine peace did not break out, but only a ceasefire. In reality, thousands of German soldiers had deserted the battlefield, looting and stealing as they made their way back home. Contrary to their leaders' self-centred claims, it was not the civilian population that was unheroic. Contributing to what would emerge as fanatical antisemitism, Jewish war profiteers were falsely blamed for obstructing supplies to the army.[20] These beliefs were important as the fertile ground for post-war developments and the resurrection of a belligerent military. The Kaiser's regime was criticised for lacking the will to survive. Along with Ludendorff, there was one German soldier in particular, who was in hospital who with many others refused to accept defeat, and would later demand national revenge. His name was Corporal Adolf Hitler, who famously in 1933 became

---

[20] Evans, R. J. (2020). *The Hitler Conspiracies: The Third Reich and the Paranoid Imagination*. Allen Lane, London. p. 72.

the Führer of Germany.

Europe became a continent in chaos. A peace treaty was not signed until 28 June 1919 at Versailles, marking the official end to the war. Eight million people had died. Germany had to hand over 5,000 guns, 30,000 machine guns, 2,000 aircraft, 5,000 locomotives, and all their U-boats. Huge reparations were demanded, to pay for the damage done. The harsh terms supposedly deprived Germany of any capacity to wage future war. Germany was not allowed submarines at all, or an army over 100,000, or an airforce. These limits were to prove in vain. Its navy had to be limited, and territory it had taken in Alsace-Lorraine had to be returned (although Germany had taken it earlier, in 1871). It lost its territories. in China, handed to Japan, despite China's protests. National boundaries were redrawn. Austria and Hungary had been there for a thousand years, had suddenly disappeared. Poland regained its sovereignty after a hundred years of foreign rule, only to lose it again later, in World War II. Yugoslavia and Romania emerged. Britain wanted to go back to being the world hegemon. It was concerned that the US was out-producing Britain, and pushing into its traditional markets. It acquired new territories in Africa and the south Pacific and in the vast territory in the Middle east. It effectively took over Palestine, Jordan, and Iraq, only to find it difficult to govern. Germany had reparations to pay to the Allies, but these restrictions on Germany were largely not enforced by a war-weary West. The French were bitter that Germany had invaded France and much of the war was fought in France, destroying its infrastructure, and in Belgium, which was similarly impacted. France argued that as it had not started the war, it should not have to pay to reconstruct the bridges and mines that Germany had destroyed. The French wanted security against a future resurgent Germany.

It was thought that Germany deliberately devalued its currency so it could repay its debt in cheaper German marks. Germany was not occupied by the victors, but was left claiming it had been humiliated by the victors in the Treaty of Versailles, and "stabbed in the back" by traitorous politicians. Ludendorff continually blamed socialists rather than his failed strategies for the military defeat, arguing the country had lost its will to survive. It was a myth on which Hitler capitalised in his rise to power. Germany consistently violated treaty restrictions as it reasserted its nationalistic pride. International tensions grew. Ironically, Marshal Foch said at the Versailles Paris Peace Conference in 1919: "This is not a peace. It is an armistice for twenty years." It sowed the seeds for future conflict.[21] Having talked their way into World War I, they were about to embark on a self-fulfilling prophesy,to retrieve what they saw as their honour. War was to break out again, all too soon.

In retrospect, the victorious Allies were traumatised by the losses they had suffered in what was called the Great War. France had lost 27,000 in one day in just one battle. Britain had suffered 65,000 casualties on the first day of the battle of the Somme. The British population was stunned. The war had claimed the lives of nine and a half million soldiers, and seven million civilians. In total, some 16 million people died in the 1914-18 war. Referred to as the Great War, it was not referred to as World War I until well into World War II. Paradoxically, France was technologically superior to Germany. It had produced over 5,000 tanks (Germany built only six), but after the war it lost its self-confidence. The trench warfare of (1915-17) in the Great War had taken an unimaginable toll on all participants. Britain and France had each lost over a million killed. Neither was willing to contemplate another land war on the continent.

---

[21] Epic History TV (2022). *World War One.*

The Legacy of World War I as Precursor for World War II

France knew it could not stand alone, and was worried it could not rely on its allies. By 1929, it was adopting a policy of appeasement with Germany. Though it had more and better tanks and guns than Germany, it lost the will to win or demand reparations from Germany. Verdun was no longer taught in France as a French victory.[22] Britain remembered the 1914-18 war as a strategic catastrophe. It was determined to never again become involved in another battle like the Somme. Thus, the legacy of World War I was not peace but rather the conditions for another world war that would break out only two decades later. The armistice in 1918 was not the end of "the war to end all wars", but rather was only a temporary cease fire. Germany used the interwar years to rebuild. By comparison, the Allies did not. Perversely, an exhausted Britain remained in denial, and refused to prepare for another war the Germans knew was coming. World War I failed to bring the hoped-for peace and stability, fundamentally because Germany refused to accept defeat, and deeply resented the treaty at Versailles in 1919, which they saw as illegitimate. The Armistice was only a pause in German operations in spite of the terms to which it was forced to agree and the reparations it was forced to pay. Understanding the actions of the German U-boats in World War II requires an understanding of the *kriegsmarine* in World War I. This was the background to the forces that drove nations into another devastating conflict. This time, submarine warfare would become even more significant.

---

[22] Hanson, V. D. (2001). *Carnage and Culture: Landmark Battles in the Rise of Western Power*. Anchor Books, New York.

2

Between the Two World Wars

History shows that wars are easy for nations to begin but difficult to end. The end of World War I failed to bring the hoped-for peace and stability. Germany simply refused to accept defeat. "When Germans spoke of "peacetime" they did not mean the years after the war, but the time before it".[23] By contrast with Britain, Germany had lost the war, but nursed a determination to quietly rearm and build its forces. Appealing to his people's history and sense of destiny, the populist Adolf Hitler came to power in 1933 as Chancellor. He mobilised his country for war, to avenge their loss in what was then known as the Great War. For him, the Great War was unfinished business, a running sore in German politics, which Hitler was committed to remedy. His personal vilification of Jews is now part of history, but it is significant that antisemitism was not rampant in Germany until after the Nazi seizure of power. Jews numbered less than half a percent of the German population. Hitler broadened the racist

---

[23] Evans, R. J. (2020). *The Hitler Conspiracies: The Third Reich and the Paranoid Imagination.* Allen Lane, London. p. 48.

"stabbed in the back" conspiracy theory to Jews worldwide for what he claimed were racially determined subversive instincts. Hitler was careful not to criticise the old imperial elites of Germany from before 1914, whose support he still needed, or to dwell on defeat in the Great War. Instead, he chose to lead Germany into another war on the basis of economics, historical prestige, and the ambitious and ruthless drive to acquire more territory. A megalomaniac obsessed with power, his personal egocentrism and demand to be seen as the saviour of Germany led him to make many strategic mistakes.

Hitler formed the view that he could overwhelm his former enemies, and began to prepare his military and his navy for another war, with rapid air-supported advances into neighbouring countries. Such a lightning strike strategy would later be labelled as *blitzkrieg* ("lightning war") in the next war. His hubris had fatal consequences for millions of non-combatants.

Technology Development in Submarines

After World War I, war weariness in protagonist nations and populations' perception of squandered national treasure contributed to an era of public lethargy and much reduced development in armaments. Reflecting its national economic contraction, a downturn in export manufacturing, and a public demand for defence budget cuts, the Royal Navy slashed its fleet during the 1920s and 30s. these became known as "the years of decay".[24]

---

[24] Kennedy, P. M. (1983). *The Rise and Fall of British Naval Mastery*, MacMillan, Basingstoke, p. 268.

Attempts to Limit Submarine Warfare

To comply with the Washington Disarmament Treaty of 1920, which stipulated that no submarine could have a gun bigger than 8-inch bore, the Royal Navy removed the deck guns from its submarines. Britain in the 1920s returned to a naval policy of a century before, with its comfortable *Pax Britannica*. Other than the Japanese, all maritime powers were reducing their submarine fleets. Seeing a diminishing threat to its naval superiority, Britain scrapped many of its C-class and D-class submarines. The ship-building emphasis stayed with the battleship lobby, and a preference for smaller and lighter cruisers. Perhaps oddly, in retrospect, at conferences in Versailles in 1919, at Washington in 1920, and at London in 1931, Britain tried to have submarines universally banned.

The Cruiser Rules

Efforts were made to outlaw unrestricted submarine warfare. Article 22 of the Treaty of London 1930 declared that the so-called "cruiser rules" applied to submarines as well as to surface vessels. These rules held that an unarmed vessel (as distinct from an armed warship) should not be attacked without warning. It could be fired on only if it repeatedly failed to stop when ordered to do so or resisted being boarded by the attacking ship. The armed ship could only intend to search for contraband (such as war materials) when stopping a merchantman. If so, the ship could be allowed on its way, after removal of any contraband. However, if it was intended to take the captured ship as a prize of war, or to destroy it, then adequate steps had to be taken to ensure the safety of the crew. This may mean taking the crew on board and transporting them to a safe port, as some argue it was not acceptable to leave the crew in lifeboats unless they could be expected to reach safety by themselves and have sufficient supplies and navigational equipment to do so. During diplomatic negotiations in World War I these rules were often softened to stopping a vessel with a warning shot, offering the crew time to embark into lifeboats, before sinking the vessel. It is also suggested that ships in convoy with armed escort were not covered by this protection.[25] Some 35 nations signed up to this, including the US, Britain, Germany and Japan. This restriction on operations was followed for several months after the international outrage over the 1915 sinking of the *Lusitania*, but because it caused submarines to be detected and exposed to attack on the surface, Germany adopted a policy of unrestricted submarine warfare in February 1917. A second London Naval Treaty in 1936 sought to limit submarines to less than 2,000 tons and deck guns to less than 5.1 inches. These treaties would be ended when war was declared in 1939. In the period between the wars, German U-boat successes in World War I against merchant shipping were largely forgotten by the British – along with the lessons that should have been learned and remembered. The Royal Navy reduced its submarine fleet from 184 boats to an interwar nadir of 54 boats in 1936.[26] In 1919, with the end of the war, Australia was gifted six J-class boats by Britain. The J-class boats were large and fast, capable of 19 kts on the surface. However, preparedness for their arrival in Sydney was inadequate, and their significant maintenance challenges along with budgetary considerations threatened the viability of the submarine service as a whole. Four of the J-class boats were placed in reserve. By 1921, a severe shortage of experienced crew further limited operations. By 1922, the Australian Naval

---

[25] Treaty for the Limitation and Reduction of Naval Armaments, (Part IV, Art. 22, relating to submarine warfare). London, 22 April 1930.see also Mallison, S. V.& Mallison W.T. (1991). Naval Targeting: Lawful objects of attack. *International Law Studies*, p. 64,

[26] Ranft, B. (ed). (1977). *Technical Change and British Naval Policy 1816-1939*, Hodder & Stanton, London.

Board had decided to scrap all the J-class boats.

The British Admiralty ordered O-class designs in 1924 (Oberon and Odin class 1927-45). They were single-hulled with saddle tanks that held both fuel and seawater ballast. These were long-range patrol submarines, which included two boats for the Royal Australian Navy (HMAS *Oxley* and *Otway*), but these arrived in Australia in 1929 in poor condition. They were seen as too expensive to maintain. With defence spending cuts and a naval treaty that limited tonnages, these were subsequently paid off from the RAN in 1931, and they were returned to the Royal Navy. They each displaced 2,038 tons, were and their engines produced 3,000 bhp to give them a surface speed of 15 knots. Perhaps fortunately, the RAN experience with the *O*-class forestalled any desire to acquire the *K* class that the British planned as the larger successor. The Australian Submarine service was in for years of historical recess. ADM Jacky Fisher opposed these boats from the start, predicting too accurately: "The most fatal error imaginable would be to put steam engines in submarines".[27] Regardless, the RN did exactly that, and introduced 18 of the steam-propelled *K*-class submarines. Six sank with significant loss of life.

British Submarine Development (1918-1945)

In the period 1931-45, Britain built 62 of the small S-class submarines beginning with HMS *Swordfish*, for coastal operations. These displaced 727 tons and had crews of 30. Armament was seven 21inch torpedo tubes and a 76 mm deck gun, but not for antiaircraft. They were slow (15 kts surfaced and 10 kts dived), and although had a range of 6.000

---

[27] Fisher, J. Cited in Porter, D, (2023). History's Doomed Inventions *Military History*. July 11.

nm, they were confined mostly to the North Sea and English Channel. like the American boats built then, air search radar was fitted. Their mortality rate in World War II was to be particularly high. Very few of this *S*-class would survive the war that came too quickly for the Royal Navy to be ready. The subsequent T-class (1934-44) was another large class (53 boats) followed by the U-class training boats (670 tons) and the V-class (1941-58) (6,700 tons, and 15 kts speed). In spite of this incremental development of one class building on the lessons of its predecessor class, the interwar years leading up to 1939 saw Britain's submarine capability at a historic low. By contrast, Germany had been secretly building an effective submarine force in the Netherlands. By 1933 it had established a submarine training school in Kiel. Within three years it was to cause Britain to regret its decision to reduce its fleet.

American Submarine Development before World War II (1920-39)

America had built *S*-class boats between 1920-25, but these too were intended only for coastal defence. They were cramped, slow and had limited range and payload. Two competing doctrines emerged. One saw submarines as forward scouts in support of the fleet. The other saw submarines as intended to operate as independent weapons platforms. Still, naval thinking was that submarines would attack only other naval vessels. Under international guidelines, they would not attack merchant ships without first providing warning. This was in spite of the German use of unrestricted U-boat warfare in World War I. Tactical planning and training was hampered by this, and there was little role for commerce raiding. The Allies were naively confident that Germany would play by the rules of warfare, though World War I had demonstrated otherwise, and such behaviour would likely recur.

The famous American naval strategist CAPT Alfred Thayer Mahan USN had expected that naval warfare, were it to be conducted, would take the form of a climactic battle between battleships.[28] However, the submarine was still seen to be valuable only in a secondary role, scouting ahead for the fleet. The American *Plan Orange* was a series of United States joint Army and Navy war plans for dealing with a possible war with Japan during the years between the first and second World Wars. It had included a priority on the destruction of the enemy's economy, but it failed to foresee the significance of technological changes in naval warfare, including in naval aviation and the potential of aircraft carriers. The submarine was marginalised, to participate only as a commerce raider. It had little place in strategic planning. Only late in the war would its contribution to operations be appropriately recognised.

American designers focussed on a boat that could exceed 20 kts to match fleet warships. The years 1921-34 saw America build V-boats of 2,119 ton displacement, powered by 2,250hp direct drive diesels and 1,000hp auxiliary diesels to charge the batteries. They were capable of 20 kts surfaced and 9 kts submerged, with six 21-inch tubes and a crew of 87.

These were the *Barracuda, Argonaut* and *Narwhal*[29] classes in the 1930s, and the *Salmon* class (1936-38), but still did not satisfy speed or range requirements. Their engines were unreliable. Only when diesel engines developed for railway locomotives were used to power electric motors did *P*-class submarines arrive, with speeds of 19 knots and a range of 12,000 miles. These fleet submarines offered the higher speed

---

[28] Mahan, A. T. (1890). *The Influence of Sea Power upon History 1660-1783*, Little Brown and Co, Boston.

[29] Named after the Arctic whale.

and a greater number of torpedoes and six forward and four stern tubes, along with a 5-inch deck gun. Habitability was improved with air-conditioning for tropical operations and to minimise condensation which affected electrical systems, and with freshwater distillation units.

Design and Strategy

Submarine design adapted rapidly to changes in strategic planning for how the boats were to be used. Design and form began to follow intended function. The 12 *Tambor* class boats met the requirements formulated in a USN submarine officers' conference in 1938. This 300-foot long 1,500-ton class had a speed of 21 knots and 10 knots submerged – respectable speeds even by today's standards. They could dive to periscope depth in under a minute to evade attack. These were followed by the *Gato* and *Balao* classes later in World War II, with 77 *Gato* class built by Electric Boat in Groton (1941-45) and 127 *Balao* class built (1943-45).[30] These became the most numerous classes of submarines built for use by the USN against Japanese shipping in World War II. Warfare strategy changed as surface fleets increased speeds that submarines could not match, so American submarines became hunter killers for attacking Japanese merchant ships, and with a 5-in deck gun for destroying trawlers and sampans. Older boats received SD series air search radar in 1941, and towards the end of the war the much more effective SV series was fitted. The final American class of the war was the ten *Tench* class built, similar to the *Balao* class, and which went on to serve with modifications for another 30 years.

For all the building of new submarines by both Britain and

---

[30] Martindale, E. V. (2024). *Submarines of World War II 1939-1945*, Amber Books, London, p.109.

Germany, the effectiveness of the submarines' weapons between the wars still left much to be desired. The American Mk 14 torpedo was notoriously unreliable until its defects were remedied by mid-1943. It frustrated crews who put their lives in danger to close on the enemy, only to hear their weapon strike the target hull but not detonate, or to run harmlessly beneath the enemy hull. Incredibly, official intransigence meant that more than one American submarine commander was reprimanded for complaining (even with evidence) about the torpedoes' performance, on which depended mission success and crew survival. Officialdom simply refused to accept criticism.

The reasons appeared to be that those officers who had earlier designed the detonator fuses were by then in senior positions, and resisted any challenge to their previous work. Despite the unarguable reality of torpedoes' failing to detonate or running uselessly deep, improvements came only slowly. However, there were gains made with other technology in submarines. Until 1940, estimation of a target ship's range and speed was done by periscope, or error-prone human observation. In determining when to fire a torpedo, The angle between the waterline and the target's masthead allowed calculation of range by simple trigonometry. Speed was estimated from the sound of the target's propellers. Changes in course and speed meant the firing solution had to be continually recalculated, using the bearing of the target to the submarine and angle on the bow (an estimate of the difference between the target's heading and the observer's line of sight. In the 1930s, the US Navy had begun installing the torpedo data computer (TDC) in its submarines. This analogue device, though primitive by today's standards, gave the captain much improved situational awareness, a solution to the equations of motion in real time, by inputting the submarine's and the target's course and speeds to provide firing solutions to release weapons. It was also able to automatically track the target instead of simply providing an instantaneous firing solution. The TDC remained highly classified for decades after World War II. A remarkably reliable and successful instrument, it would become the standard for American submarine torpedo fire control during World War II.

The years between the world wars were marked by recovery from World War I and belated preparation for what would later be known as World War II. Britain appeared to be stuck in denial until the mid-1930s, and only slowly realised the emerging threat posed by German U-boats. Also in the 1930s, Polish cyber experts had made progress in cracking the German communication code later used with the *Enigma* machines to send secret messages and orders to and from U-boats, with devasting effects. When Poland was occupied, this Polish work was given to the British code-breakers at Bletchley Park. It would later prove a critical foundation for their secret efforts in cracking the Enigma code.

German U-Boats

By 1935, Hitler proposed to build a significant U-boat force. However, by 1939, it still had only 57 U-boats. It had quietly continued to build U-boats for Sweden and Finland, so Germany's submarine skills were not lost, and production of U-boats could be and was scaled up quickly. The Germans created a dummy corporation in the Netherlands, *NV Ingenieurskantoor voor Scheepsbouw* (IvS), to secretly continue development of submarines. This was in violation of Article 191 of the 1921 Treaty of Versailles, which prohibited Germany from possessing or building submarines for any purpose. IvS built several submarines for foreign navies. Germany had used the inter-war years to rebuild its fleet, but not its numbers of U-boats up to the 300 that the U-boat leader Admiral Karl Dönitz wanted for the *kriegsmarine*. Both Britain and Germany were guilty of giving priority to their battleship construction and strategy for operations, rather than to the threat posed by the emerging technology and capability of the submarine and the torpedo. For the money spent on the two *Bismark* class battleships, Germany could have built another 100 *Type VIIc* U-boats, with considerable negative consequences for the British. After 1939, Germany built hundreds of Type VII U-boats, and continued to build up to the *Type IX*, until 1945, at a high rate (up to one boat per week). The ocean-going Type IX would not arrive until the end of the war, but would remain influential for later submarine design.

Japanese Submarines (1930-41)

The 2,174 ton C-1 submarine was built by Japan (1937-42) to carry cradles for the 47 ton midget submarines which it used to attack Pearl Harbour in 1941 and later Sydney Harbour. The C-1 had eight torpedo tubes and carried 20 torpedoes. Japan had developed a highly effective submarine weapon in its type 93 Long Lance torpedo, which gave small ships and destroyers and submarines the capability to sink or damage battleships. These weapons had gyroscopes to help maintain course, and detonators that were reliable, and superior to the American torpedos. The Imperial Japanese Navy had Japan built midget submarines (which later attacked Sydney in 1942) and several large submarines, but in relatively low numbers, and thus were not prepared in 1941 to undertake any major submarine offensives. The line of KD (*Kaidai*) submarines began in 1925 with KD1, and developed through to the KD7 (1940-43).[31] The

---

[31] Martindale, E. V. (2024). *Submarines of World War II 1939-1945*. Amber, London.

Japanese attack boat had a surface speed of 23 kts, very high by contemporary standards.

Overall, the interwar years of "peace" after World War I (1918-1939) were anything but quiet and peaceful. The governments of both Britain and the United States were in sluggish denial. They were slow to respond to the emerging threat posed by Germany and Japan, both in building their forces and with some exceptions in development of new technology that would contribute to the different kind of warfare they would be required to conduct.

In summary, all three protagonist nations committed disproportionate resources to building very large battleships of 70,000 tons with 18-inch guns offering a range of over 20 miles. Ships like *Bismark* and *Tirpitz* and *Yamato* were undeniably impressive and threatening, but the major innovations would appear in aircraft carriers and submarines. Britain and Germany both entered the war in 1939 with about 60 submarines each. In the course of the war, each nation would build hundreds more. Only when hostilities were declared did German and Allied governments belatedly embark on the massive production campaigns necessary to sustain the war effort on land, air and sea – and below the surface of the sea. In response to the attack on Pearl Harbour in 1941, the US carried out unrestricted submarine warfare from its entry into the war. Germany and Japan also undertook unrestricted submarine warfare. Earlier limitations on submarine weapons and operations were ignored.

The war had come a few years too early for all the protagonists. Rapid design and huge increases in production were required. Submarines would figure prominently in defence planning. Had Germany produced the 300 boats the *kriegsmarine* requested of Hitler, the outcome of the battle of the Atlantic, and of the war, might well have been very different.

3

World War II

Submarine warfare cannot be fully understood historically without an understanding of the German U-boat campaign, and by association, the context and causes of World War II. In this, it is impossible to avoid the need to know something of the person of Adolf Hitler, and the general history of World War II.

Hitler (1889-1945) and World War II

More than any other individual, Adolf Hitler was generally held responsible for WWII, the most deadly conflict in human history. Who was this megalomaniac who caused so much death and destruction? Adolf Hitler was born in Austria to an abusive father, a minor customs official, but with a warm and gentle mother who cared for him obsessively. His father changed the family name from Schicklgruber to Hitler. Adolf Hitler hated Austria, and drew inspiration from the fantasy world in the music of Wagner. He had a brutality and ruthlessness that surprised and confounded even his friends. He later led German initiatives and continued years of the most destructive war in history, leaving 65 million people dead, and the worst horrors the world had seen.

Hitler bought into the view that there were many races competing with each other, but the purest was the German Aryan, and Jews were the worst. Earlier, he applied to join the art academy in Vienna but was turned down. The fact was that he had little talent as an artist. This rejection appears to have left a psychological scar that he attempted to overcome with grandiosity and an intensity that might be characterized as extremely antisocial at best and homicidally as well as suicidally psychopathic at worst.[32] It may also have been significant that he was monorchid.[33] He suffered problems with digestion and Parkinsons Disease, but a former Dean of Medicine at Yale Medical School examined his behaviour in detail and was of the opinion that none of his ailments were likely to have impaired his decision making. The many publications looking (mostly posthumously) at Hitler's psychopathology appear to conclude that he was not mentally ill, and that "he knew what he was doing, and he did it with pride and enthusiasm."[34]

In Just before World War I, in spring 1913, at the age of 24 years, Hitler left Austria for Germany to avoid compulsory military service. He had a deep conviction that somehow, he would make good. Hitler wanted to be part of the excitement, and though he was neither German nor Bavarian he refused to join the multinational Austrian army and instead joined the Bavarian army. His war service gave his miserable life a purpose. It appears he was a brave soldier, and he was awarded the Iron Cross. What the World War I soldiers did not realise was that technology had made war even more dangerous. Tanks, machine guns and aircraft that dropped bombs on people had been introduced. Germany lost the war in 1918, the Kaiser

---

[32] Evans, R. J. (2020). *The Hitler Conspiracies: The Third Reich and the Paranoid Imagination*. Allen Lane, London.

[33] Langer, W. (1973). *The Mind of Adolf Hitler*. Secker & Warburg, London.

[34] Redlich, F. (1998). *Diagnosis of a Destructive Prophet*. Oxford University Press, Oxford.

abdicated, and the army surrendered at Compiegne. Germany ceased to be an empire, to become a liberal democracy known as the Weimar Republic, led by leftist Social Democrat Party. The war lasted four years and the industrial scale trench warfare claimed the lives of some 40 million people. The Armistice was signed in November 1918, sealed by the treaty of Versailles and took 13 percent of its prewar territory. Reparations were demanded from the defeated Germany. However, the military leadership promoted a conspiracy theory that in fact Germany had not lost the war, but rather that Jews and socialists had undermined the Army, stabbed it in the back by spreading dissent. The defeat was felt by many Germans to be bitter and humiliating, and the ensuing period of "peace" was illusory. Right wing army leaders opposed the left-wing bolshevists. Hitler, like his father, was quick to anger, but his passionate speech-making impressed colleagues, and he became a speaker for the German Workers Party in Munich. He appealed to resentful extremist right wing army veterans who also believed they had been sold down the river by the populace.

Jews were less than one percent of the population, but Hitler painted them as conspirators against Germany. He adopted the Nazi party symbol. The group changed the name into the Nationalist Socialist German Workers Party – the Nazi Party. Nazism was born out of World War I. The brutal brownshirts attacked the Weimar republic in gang warfare. The year 1923 was violent. Hyperinflation took a toll. Civil strife offered Hitler a chance. In 1923, He tried to overthrow the government, speaking at a beer hall in Munich to foment a people's revolution, but instead was imprisoned for nine months, where he wrote his book *Mein Kampf.* In 1926 Joseph Goebbels became Berlin and later the nationwide propaganda chief. The message was anticommunist. Hitler crafted his image as saviour of Germany. In 1929, the stock market crash in the US also saw mass unemployment in Germany. Hitler gathered personal support by maintaining an anti-immigrant populist message. Unusually, women appeared to be fascinated by his power and paternalism. By 1932, the elderly Hindenburg's term as president had run out and he stood for re-election. Hitler sold himself as young and modern. President Hindenburg won with a 53 percent majority but refused to name Hitler as chancellor. In 1933, he grudgingly agreed to appoint him as chancellor with a minority Nazi party government, hoping to put limits on Hitler's unilateralism. The German Army objected to the SA or *Sturmabteilung* (brownshirts) as an uncontrolled threat. Hitler disposed of his political opponents by having them murdered.

The stormtroopers were violent in establishing nazi regime by force. The "night of the long knives" happened when Hitler had founder of the SA Ernst Röhm arrested and shot with other SA leaders shot. Convinced that therefore they would not be replaced, the army pledged allegiance to Hitler as the Fuhrer, by then clearly a dictator. In June 1933, the Nazis ordered a nationwide boycott of Jewish businesses. Antisemitism had been growing only slowly. Hitler's deep hatred of the Jews lead him to have some six million men, women and children murdered in concentration camps. Hitler was convinced of his own god-like qualities in his megalomanic mission to save Germany.

In 1938, the Austrian Anschluss had Hitler returning Austria into the German Reich. Hitler expelled the Jews by unleashing the SA and the SS on them. The *Kristallnacht* (the night of broken glass) saw them looting and killing Jews. Hitler openly aimed for the eradication of the Jewish people in Germany. He justified this as securing *lebensraum* (living space) for the Germans. He invaded the Sudetenland, saying it was to reunite Germans living there in Czechoslovakia with Germany. Britain and France conceded. This opened the road to Prague. Hitler gambled that the Western Allies would not stand up to him. The British and French warned that if Germany attacked Poland they would resist. Hitler formed a non-aggression treaty with Stalin (which he later broke, as he did all other treaties). This was the Germany that Hitler led into war.

1939 The beginning of WWII

In September 1939 Hitler began bombing Poland. Unprepared, it fought bravely but uselessly, with equipment from the 1920s and cavalry wielding lances against fast moving tanks. Soviet forces entered from the east on 17 September, to partition the country under a secret protocol in the non-aggression pact. The Germans took 700,000 prisoners, the Soviets rook 217,000, and the independent state of Poland ceased to exist. The cost to Germany was 45,000 casualties.[35] In May 1940 Hitler ordered attacks on the Netherlands and France. His troops swept south through Belgium and the Ardennes Forest. Field Marshal von Rundstedt used 1,500,00 men and 1,500 tanks to push British and French forces into a corner on the beaches of Dunkirk. in June 1940, with a fleet of small boats manned by civilian sailors and 41 RN destroyers, the British managed a famous escape of 300,000 of its expeditionary force back across the channel, to fight another day. Some 85,000 vehicles and tons of equipment were abandoned, but the British army had avoided a humiliating defeat. Within six weeks, France surrendered. The French formed a puppet government under the collaborationist World War I hero Marshal Philippe Pétain 1856-1951) at Vichy in France, and General Charles De Gaulle in Britain called all French citizens to follow him in support of the Free French Forces, who would ultimately participate in the liberation of

---

[35] Dudley, M. (2024). *Great Battles of World War II*, Arcturus, London.

France in 1944. The British could not risk the French navy under the control of the Vichy government falling into the hands of the Germans, so seized all French ships in ports under its control. But the French still had a fleet at its naval base at Mers-el-Kébir in Algeria. On 3 July 1940, given the opportunity to surrender to the RN or move it out of German reach to the West Indies, or face destruction, the French admiral refused, apparently thinking the British would not open fire. Reluctantly, the RN opened fire, sinking a battleship and killing 1,297 French sailors. The French saw this as a betrayal and Pétain severed diplomatic relations with Britain on 8 July.

1940: The Battle of Britain

In August 1940, Hitler prepared to invade Britain but needed air superiority to do so. Air Marshal Göring promised Hitler that his Luftwaffe, with 1,137 aircraft compared to the British with 620, could shoot the RAF out of the sky. D-day was set for 15 August. The British Hurricanes and Spitfires were a match for the Messerschmitt e109s and Heinkel 110s. Also, the British had the best air defence radar in the world, enabling early detection of German aircraft leaving the ground in France, so the RAF could be airborne ready to meet them when they crossed the channel. Britain, the sole remaining democracy in Europe faced the German onslaught alone. The dates of this epic battle, fought by RAF Hurricanes and Spitfires, and the RN Fleet Air Arm, are recognised as 10 July-31 October 1940. It was one of the few battles named before it happened. It came from the famous "this was their finest hour" speech by Winston Churchill to the House of Commons on 18 June 1940. He called on his population: "Let us brace ourselves to our duties".[36] The future of the world's civilisation "including all we have known and cared for", was daily under extreme threat. Churchill's impact in Britain's defence was extremely significant, politically and socially. Because the Battle of Britain was being waged in the summer skies over England, when a German fighter was shot down, the Luftwaffe lost both aircraft and pilot. On 15 August 1940, 70 German aircraft were brought down. Only 28 Spitfires and Hurricanes were lost, but more than half the pilots returned to their squadrons. By the end of October Germany had lost 1,733 aircraft to Britain's 1,379. With favorable weather and tides not predicted for another year, Hitler postponed the planned invasion indefinitely and turned his attention eastwards.

In June 1941, Germany invaded Russia in Operation Barbarossa, the largest invasion in human history. It was portrayed as a struggle between Nationalism and Marxism. The Wehrmacht was effectively defeated by the Russian winter. The main theatre became the eastern front. The order from Hitler was to exterminate the entire Jewish population. In 1942 alone, the *einsatzgruppe* (paramilitary death squads) executed 1.5 million civilians. A further million were killed in Auschwitz. Stalingrad was a major defeat, yet Hitler refused to surrender. Field Marshal Paulus, commanding German forces there, surrendered, but 150,000 Germans died. Hitler was furious but unmoved.

Hitler never accepted that his vaunted Third Reich would fail. He exhibited all the symptoms of toxic leadership: rigidity, fear of failure, and ruthless ambition. Impatience and hyperactivity also feature in this personality structure. He was deeply authoritarian: excessively subservient to senior officers, while

---

[36] Churchill, R. S. (1942). *Into Battle: Speeches by the Right Hon. Winston S Churchill CH., M.P.* Cassell and Company London, p.134.

demanding fawning acquiescence from juniors. To this must be added his ethnocentrism and obsession with notions of power and dominance. Emotionally he was cynical, and without compassion for the suffering of others. This rigidity resulted in is refusal to surrender any ground gained, and his insistence that his generals fight to the last man. Intolerant of critical intelligence reports, when battles went badly, like Haig in WWI, he was quick to absolve himself and find others to scapegoat. This trait made for his monumental military incompetence in decision making. His rigidity resulted in is refusal to surrender any ground gained, and his insistence that his generals fight to the last man. A coward to the end, he committed suicide hours before his Berlin bunker was overrun by Russian troops. His deranged psychopathology had led millions of his people to their deaths and caused the deaths of millions of others.

Submarine Development and World War II

Submarines are not developed or operated in isolation. To gain perspective, it is important to see the development and operation of submarines during the years 1939-45 in the context of the history of the war in general. What became known as World War II after 1941 began as a series of border wars between contiguous countries that became the spark that ignited Europe. Germany invaded first Austria then Czechoslovakia and subjected their citizens to brutal and murderous occupation. In September 1939, Germany invaded Poland, and in 1940 Denmark. It quickly occupied Norway, the Netherlands, Luxemburg, France and Belgium. In May 1941, Greece and Crete were occupied by German forces. This had significant consequences for the Mediterranean theatre.

It became a World War when Germany invaded Russia, a long-held ambition of Hitler, on 22 June 1941, and when Japan attacked the US at Pearl Harbour on 7 December 1941. Britain had gone to war on principle, because Poland was attacked. Russia and America joined the war only when they themselves were attacked. Hitler thought the conflict would last six weeks. It would take six years.

The Second World War would go on to kill 65 million people, more than in any other war in history. Of these, 80 percent were civilians. It was a war in which Germany and Japanese soldiers killed 45 million Russian and 17 million unarmed Chinese civilians. The German army killed about seven times the number of people it lost, and Japan killed about eight times their own losses. The world had never before seen such ferocity.[37] With higher technology and more lethal weapons and mechanised rather than widespread horse-drawn transport, it was a war unlike any other, on an industrial scale. Germany had felt itself humiliated by the Versailles Treaty after World War I and believed it had not been fairly beaten. It resolved to redress the injustice they saw that had been done to them. America was isolationist and had passed a series of Neutrality Acts in the 1930s, designed to prevent the US from becoming entangled in foreign conflicts. Hitler thought Britain and France would not fight and would soon sue for peace. The onset of World War II took everyone by surprise. This was the war involving great change. Horses were replaced by vehicles, and battleships by aircraft carriers. Along with air power, the submarine became the critical weapon, at least until 1945, when the atomic bomb was used.

Critics accused the US of effectively standing aside and watching as Britain was bombed, and while it headed in the direction of an appeasement strategy with Hitler. High-ranking

---

[37] Hanson, V. D. (2020). *The Second World Wars*. Basic Books, New York.

British aristocrats including the Duke of Windsor, later though briefly King Edward VIII, even drew up plans for Britain's appeasement with Hitler. From Germany's perspective, Britain had lost its deterrence capability. Along with air power, the submarine became the critical weapon, at least until 1945, when the atomic bomb was used.

The European Theatre and the German U-boats

The impact of the submarine was even greater in World War II than in World War I. Italy and Japan had large submarine fleets, but arguably the most disproportionately significant was the fleet operated by the Germans. In 1939, Germany had only 57 U-boats. These U-boats sank 138 merchant ships in their first year of operation. The phenomenon of the German submarine campaign deserves special attention. In retrospect it was not a strategically successful campaign, but it did capture the imagination of a fearful British population, and it entered popular mythology as ruthlessly efficient and frighteningly lethal. It was certainly extremely destructive.

Prevented by the Treaty of Versailles from rebuilding its submarine fleet after the 1914-18 war, the Germans had secretly developed and built their U-boats in the Netherlands. In the 1930s, under the guise of general ship building, it supplied submarines to Sweden, Finland, and the Soviet Union. The *Kriegsmarine* (German Navy) had not forgotten its earlier strategy from World War I, that of maintaining a blockade to starve their enemies into submission, and they planned to deploy their U-boat fleet against Britain to do exactly that. The campaign had significant effects in disrupting Allied shipping, with considerable economic impact as the U-boats sent increasing numbers of merchant ships and their cargoes to the bottom.

The most famous name associated with the German submarine campaign in World War II is that of Admiral Karl Dönitz. Born in 1891, he became a disciplined and obsessive Prussian naval officer. He had been a U-boat commander in World War I, when he was forced to scuttle his boat (*U-68*) in 1918, and he was captured by the British. He spent the remainder of the war as a prisoner of war of the Allies in Malta. During his imprisonment, Dönitz planned how to implement his conviction that Germany could win by blockading Britain with a powerful fleet of what he called "torpedo boats". He was repatriated to Germany in 1919 and avoided trial and probable execution as a war criminal by feigning madness to a US Army psychiatrist.

Back in the nascent *kriegsmarine*, Admiral Dönitz had used the years in the 1920s to establish his doctrines of U-boat attacks on convoys by night, for which during World War II, he was to become famous. In 1924 he attended a course led by Rear Admiral Erich Raeder, Chief of the German Naval High Command, who reported that Dönitz was "a clever, ambitious officer, a very good organiser, with clear judgement about naval war leadership".[38] Similar positive reports by others in the years following, noting his "verve and gift for getting along with his men" gained this lean, taciturn commander rapid promotion.

By 1934, Karl Dönitz was 43 years of age and in command of the cruiser *Emden*. In 1935, he became chief of the first U-boat flotilla. Admiral Dönitz was appointed commander in chief of the German U-boat service. He set about developing the U-boat arm, rapidly building capacity and numbers, convinced that his U-boats could win the war for Germany. In the years 1939-43, Allied leaders feared that Dönitz might succeed. He was later to clash with his then superior officer Admiral Raeder, who did not share his passion for U-boats and his strong advocacy

---

[38] Padfield, P. (1984). *Donitz: The Last Führer*, Panther, London, p. 132.

for them over battleships to win the war. Ironically, when Hitler later dismissed Raeder in 1943 because the battleships he asked for were not winning the war as he was promised, it was Dönitz whom Hitler selected to replace him. After the war, the conservative Nazi Erich Raeder was sentenced to life imprisonment for war crimes of planning and executing aggressive naval actions. Hitler had mobilised his army for a land war, but in 1939, his navy was simply not yet ready for a war at sea. Germany began the war with only 27 operational U-boats. The war had come 10 years too early for Hitler and for Admiral Dönitz.

In the interwar years, Britain had reduced its fleet in favour of fewer but larger battleships. This resulted in an acute shortage of escort vessels to protect the all-important transatlantic sea lines of communication. The essential 1.5 million tons of supplies per month that Britain needed to survive were being imported mostly from the US with vulnerable merchant marine ships. The *Kriegsmarine*'s U-boats in 1939 and those built in the immediate years following had a disproportionate impact on the British war effort, until mid-1943. In addition to disrupting Allied shipping and partially blockading Britain, the U-boat campaign diverted scarce Allied resources into otherwise unnecessary antisubmarine warfare.

The Sinking of the *Athenia* and the Battle of the Atlantic

On 3 September 1939, within hours of the declaration of war, The Type VIIA U-boat *U-30*, displacing 626 tons, and commanded by Fritz-Julius Lemp, fired two torpedoes at the blacked-out passenger liner *Athenia*, enroute in the Atlantic from Glasgow to New York. She sank at 1030 the next day, taking the lives of 93 civilian passengers, among them 85 women and children, and 19 crew. The 16 children killed were among these first casualties in World War II. The U-boat had given no warning. The U-boat commander, Fritz-Julius Lemp had been ordered to treat all British ships as hostile. To him, the *Athenia* was very probably a troopship, an armed merchantman with concealed cannon (a "Q-ship"), and possibly carrying munitions, or perhaps even a naval cruiser. He was not to know the *Athenia* was carrying 1,103 passengers, including hundreds of Jewish refugees, escaping the anticipated war in Europe by sailing to the USA. Within minutes, Lemp realised his disastrous error. On his arrival back at base, German Navy officers came on board to warn his crew not to speak to anyone of the event. Lemp, the youngest U-boat commander in the navy, was ordered to erase any record from his log and expunge any record of his action. Such sinkings and losses of civilian lives contributed to the public perception that submarine warfare was uncivilised treachery.

Officially, the *Athenia* sinking was a propaganda victory for the Nazis, who claimed the British had carried out the attack, in order to bring the USA into the war. For the British, it was a brutal outrage and a wakeup call. It demonstrated that Germany was fighting with unrestricted submarine warfare. The Royal Navy had until then been almost dismissive of the U-boat threat. The reality was tragic: some 4,000 Allied ships and 19,000 seamen would be lost in the Battle of the Atlantic.

German U-Boats

Type VIIc: One of the reasons for German success with its U-boats was the skill of their submariners and their manner of conducting attacks. Another was the compact but highly effective *Type VIIc* U-boat, produced in large numbers (more than any other class ever) and ideally suited to its purpose. These boats had a displacement of 770 tons and a range of 6,500 miles. They roamed far and wide across the world's oceans. The German *Type VIIc* had a displacement of 770 tons with five 21-inch torpedo tubes, with 14 torpedoes, and an 88mm deck gun. Surfaced, it had a 17.7-kt surface speed that could match that of most of their targets, and so could get ahead of a convoy.

Submerged, they could manage 7.6 knots submerged for an hour, or for about 80 miles at 4 kts. They could loiter submerged at 7.6 knots for 80 miles and had an endurance of 40 days on patrol. They could dive to about 600 feet, and they became the scourge of Allied convoys in the Atlantic. These U-boats spent most of their time on the surface, running on their diesel engines, and diving using battery power only to conduct a torpedo attack – or to evade an ASW attack from the sea or the air. Many surface attacks were carried out by U-boats using only their deck gun. It quickly became the most feared weapon confronting the British Prime Minister Winston Churchill, and reputedly the only adversary weapon that kept him awake at night. By contemporary standards, the *Type VIIc* was small, about the same length as *AE1* and *AE2* in World War I (220 feet). In the course of World War II, 568 boats of this *Type VIIc* were built between 1939 and 1945. They were the most numerous of any class of submarine built. Being relatively small, the *Type VIIc* submarines were difficult to detect, and were commanded by aggressive and well-trained captains. These U-boats carried four officers and 31 sailors, in cramped accommodation with only two toilets (in navy parlance known as "heads"). Before going on patrol, food would be stowed in every available space.

These boats could remain submerged for about 24 hours, after which they needed to surface to run their diesels to recharge their batteries, and to replace the stale air in the boat. Crews often went weeks or months without washing or shaving. It was said that the smell of diesel and unwashed bodies was overwhelming. Time ashore for the crew between deployments was highly valued, with high quality food and accommodation provided, to compensate. Typically, on return to base, their clothes worn during a patrol were so contaminated they had to burnt and replaced. Crew members took long hot baths for a few days, to rid themselves of the diesel fuel smell in particular. Non-submariners may find this difficult to imagine.

With the U-boats' poor sea-keeping properties on the surface, seasickness was common. Standing watch on the bridge meant days of cold wet clothes which might not be washed or dried for weeks or even months. In spite of the lack of habitability in the squalor and extremely demanding conditions in U-boats, morale in the elite German U-boat arm was high, and would remain so until 1943 and even beyond, when the Type *VIIc* U-boat was made effectively obsolete by developing technology and the improved Allied ASW capability.

Type IX: With similar submerged endurance to the Type *VIIc*, the later oceangoing *Type IX* was bigger at 1,600 tons, and faster, with longer range (24,000 km at 10 kts). It had a 105mm deck gun and twin 37mm anticraft guns on top of the fin. The *Type IX* had six torpedo tubes, with crews of 55. *Type IX* boats were used in patrols off the eastern coast of the USA. *U-505* was captured and is now preserved in Chicago, one of only four World War II U-boats remaining in existence. The Battle of the Atlantic was fought mainly by these two types of U-boats: the *Type VII* and the larger, faster and longer range *Type IX*. The *Type IX* could manage 48 hours of silent running while submerged. Fortunately for the Allies, the *Type IX* arrived for the now better accommodated German submariners only very late in the war. This longer endurance and lower hydrodynamic noise performance was significantly better than that of the smaller *Type VII*.

Type XXI: Later, the revolutionary streamlined *Type XXI* was developed and was much bigger (1,800 tons submerged) and faster (18 kts for 1.5 hours or 12-14 kts for 10 hours submerged).

The *Type XXI* was fitted with a snorkel from its introduction in 1944. Only 118 *Type XXI* boats were built and only two saw any combat service. The type was to have its impact later. After 1946, the design of the type XXI was to be very influential in the streamlined design not only of the USS *Nautilus* (in the 1950s), but also of the 236 conventionally powered *Whiskey* class boats built later by the Soviets.

On 17 September 1939, three torpedos from the *Kriegsmarine* type VIIA *U29*, commanded by Captain Lieutenant Otto Schuhart, sank Britain's oldest aircraft carrier, the 22,500-ton HMS *Courageous*, with the loss of 519 of her crew, including her captain. Though laid down in WWI as a light cruiser she was converted with a flight deck, and with her 41 Swordfish aircraft, she was one of the most important ships in the Royal Navy, and the first British warship to be lost to enemy action in World War II. The *Kriegsmarine* was jubilant, and Admiral Raeder recommended Schuhart for the Iron Cross First Class, and all others in the crew the Iron Cross Second Class. German submariners were hailed as heroes by their compatriots.

On 14 October 1939, only four weeks after the loss of the *Athenia*, U-boat captain Gunther Prien in a *Type VIIb* (*U-47*) carried out an extraordinarily brave attack against the British fleet in Scapa Flow, sending the anchored battleship HMS *Royal Oak* and 786 of her crew to the bottom in 10 minutes. It was another major propaganda success for Germany, sinking the flagship, and a battleship, in the Royal Navy's principal protected anchorage. Prien returned to an adoring German public.

These U-boat victories over warships in the first year of the war were impressive to Hitler and alarming to Churchill, but to Dönitz and his *kriegsmarine*, warships were not the principal target. They knew they could win the war only by blockading Britain from her supplies and forcing surrender, so sinking merchant ships became the priority. Seeking air superiority, Reich Marshal Herman Göring demanded resources for his Luftwaffe and battled with Dönitz who instead wanted German resources for the 300 U-boat fleet he tried to convince Raeder he needed to starve Britain. The ongoing rivalry between Göring and Dönitz, meant that there were never enough long-range German aircraft to provide reconnaissance patrols for the U-boats. Göring brushed off the battle of the Atlantic as a side show.

The Early Impact on Britain

The venerable Royal Navy, and the British people, were stunned by these acts of asymmetric warfare, where small but stealthy U-boats were inflicting crippling losses on them. Within a year, Gunther Prien was being hailed in Germany as a U-boat ace, after sinking seven ships in two weeks (three in one day). In that first year of World War II, the German losses amounted to 28 U-boats, but the increasingly effective German U-boat force had sunk a British aircraft carrier, one battleship, five cruisers, three destroyers, two submarines and 238 merchant vessels,[39] for the loss of only nine U-boats. The British had been largely unsuccessful in hunting their undersea foe. The outlook for the Allies was grim indeed. World War II had begun badly for the

---

[39] Werner, H. (1969), *Iron Coffins*, Arthur Barker, London, p. xii.

Royal Navy. It was a portent of things to come.

Sister ship to HMS *Courageous* was another converted aircraft carrier, HMS *Glorious* On 8 June 1940, off Norway, HMS *Glorious* was sunk by German battlecruisers *Scharnhorst* and *Gneisenau*, with the loss of 1,519 men. The circumstances were controversial and the impact severe. Unbelievably, the RN ship was sailing alone, with no combat air patrol (allegedly because her captain Doyley-Hughes was not on good terms with the aviators), and there were no lookouts posted who might have seen the German ships and initiated avoidance of them. The destroyer HMS *Ardent* gallantly attacked both German ships, but seriously outclassed, was also lost. The first two years of the war did not go well for the British.

British Convoys and German Wolf Packs

In 1939 and 1940, unescorted ships crossing the Atlantic with vital supplies for Britain were being picked off by vigilant U-boats. The British reverted to the obvious World War I tactic of grouping ships and sailing as escorted convoys, these often comprising about 40 ships. The convoy's speed was limited by the speed of the slowest ship, not infrequently about 8 kts. The much faster Cunard liners (*Queen Mary* and *Queen Elizabeth*) relied on their 28 kt speed for defence, so did not travel with convoys. Escorting these convoys required American destroyers and British corvettes in numbers, with their costly losses in ships and crews. Canada alone lost 4,700 sailors escorting convoys.

Early in the war, Germany's U-boats were largely confined to operating out of northern Germany ports such as Hamburg and Kiel. Hitler invaded both Denmark and Norway, opening the way for operations from Bergen in April 1940. Germany planned to build 250 U-boats to starve Britain of its seaborne supplies. She needed 60 million tons of imports annually. Dönitz calculated that his U-boats needed to sink three British vessels each per month to effectively blockade the nation, which needed to import 70 percent of its food. The strategy of the third Reich was to isolate and starve England by sinking the merchant ships critical to Britain's survival. At the close of 1939, German surface ships had sunk 15 merchantmen, and U-boats had accounted for 114 Allied vessels.

The U-boat Wolf Pack Strategy

German U-boat fleet commander Admiral Carl Dönitz encouraged what became known as the wolf pack concept, where the first U-boat to locate a convoy would radio its position to headquarters and other U-boats within range, using the *Enigma* encrypted system which was impervious to British coded breakers until 1941.

As ambush predators, the U-boats would then position themselves ahead of the slow-moving convoys and wait until night to avoid detection. When submerged, their speed was less than most convoys, so positioning relative to the convoy was critical. They would attack both with torpedoes and their 3.5-inch deck gun. Although they hunted in coordinated wolf packs of dozens of mostly *Type VIIc* U-boats, competition between U-boat commanders was fierce, and only the larger *Type IX* captains were authorised to range further (up to 9,600 kms) and alone.

The U-boats still needed to be resupplied at sea. This they accomplished with 10 specially built and dedicated 2,000 ton submarines known as *'milk-cows' (milchkuh)*, each carrying 232 tons of fuel, to replenish U-boats with fuel, food, and torpedos. They could even carry out basic repairs of other damaged U-boats in the open ocean. U-boats. The Allies gradually shifted their operations to tracking and attacking the milk-cow U-boats, understanding that sinking a resupply submarine effectively incapacitated approximately six operational U-boats.

The Strategic Situation for Britain in 1940

Western nations were in shock when Hitler launched his aggressive and successful lighting war (*blitzkrieg*), quickly taking Poland, Czechoslovakia and then France and Belgium. The large French army collapsed in six weeks (10 May-22 June 1940). Churchill was hastily appointed as British Prime Minister, as British forces were being pushed by German forces back to the coast at Dunkirk. They faced annihilation by the relentless German Panzers driving westwards in France. Air Marshall Herman Göring had convinced Hitler that his Luftwaffe should be given the honour of defeating the trapped Allies. Much to his generals' surprise and dismay, who wanted to push Allied soldiers physically out of Europe, Hitler ordered the exhausted Panzers to halt their advance, within a few miles of Dunkirk.

Theories abound as to why he did so, when the German army was so close to killing or capturing the entire Allied force. Perhaps it was to leave Britain with enough government to negotiate surrender. Perhaps he knew he did not have the forces to occupy Britain. Perhaps he wanted his troops to recover from the gruelling campaign they had been waging. Whatever the truth, Hitler's order gave the Allies a window of opportunity to escape and survive. Miraculously, on 4 June 1940, some 340,000 Allied troops of the British Expeditionary Force and over 100,000 French troops retreated from the port and the beaches of Dunkirk back to England, saved from annihilation or capture there, by a remarkable mass evacuation by sea. They were famously rescued from the French beaches by a flotilla of naval and civilian small craft called up from harbours on the English Channel. However, they lost most of their equipment. The encircled Allies in Dunkirk abandoned their 85,000 vehicles, mostly jeeps, trucks and tanks, in the chaos of the escape. The perimeter around Dunkirk was heroically defended by remaining British soldiers, sacrificed as the escaping troops were embarked on all manner of ships and boats to return to Britain. To profound national relief, the remarkable evacuation from Dunkirk became legendary, and is famous still for uniting the country with "the Dunkirk Spirit".

With a powerful speech to parliament, vowing Britain would never surrender, Churchill rallied the British population to fight on. Lord Halifax and other members of the British cabinet who had secretly been seeking peace talk with Germany, fell silent. Halifax was posted as British Ambassador in Washington DC. Churchill remarked "there is no place for him in Britain". Joseph Kennedy, the father of President John F. Kennedy and advocate of British surrender, returned to the US, his political career was effectively ended. One wonders what the isolationist US President Roosevelt made of this.

1940 Allied Losses at Sea

The year 1940 was not kind to the British. Britain had begun the war with 21 million tons of shipping, made up of 3,000 deep sea vessels, and 1,000 coastal vessels. Some 58 ships were sunk in June alone. The liner *Empress of Britain* was lost to a combined U-boat and Luftwaffe action. In just seven months of

1940, some 1,200 allied ships were sunk by U-boats, reducing vital imports to Britain by a fifth. Allied losses climbed from 160,000 tons per month in 1939 to 350,000 tons per month in 1940. It was a war of tonnages. In May 1940, Germany cracked the British merchant navy code and could learn the positions and course of Allied convoys. In five months, U-boats sank 274 merchant ships, for the loss of only six U-boats. This was asymmetric naval warfare on a grand scale.

1940 ASW Development

The British were desperate to develop ASW capability. Old merchant ships had superstructure removed and decks built on top to enable up to 30 Swordfish or Albacore aircraft to take off and land, providing close in air support, defending convoys. These were known as MACS (merchant aircraft carriers), and they proved successful in bombing surfaced U-boats. Other merchant ships had catapults fitted with a Hurricane fighter that could be launched to shoot down enemy Condor aircraft that bombed the convoy. This required the unfortunate Hurricane pilot to ditch near his ship and hope to be rescued at the end of his short mission - bearing in mind that human survival after three minutes in the cold Atlantic was doubtful.

A partial solution was found with ASW *Flower* class Corvettes, their design developed from British fishing trawlers, which were cheap and easy to build. They were capable of 16 kts, with good ASDIC sets, and carrying 70 depth charges. Their speed could not match ships they were protecting, such as the *Castle* class which could make 31 kts. In the mid-Atlantic conditions, these small ASW ships were very uncomfortable for their exhausted crews, with decks awash much of the time, but they were effective in sinking U-boats. Their sea-keeping properties left much to be desired. The class was made famous by the mythical *Compass Rose* in Nicholas Monsarrat's book and iconic 1953 war film "The Cruel Sea".

The convoys were being decimated by U-boats. Between July and October 1940, Germany sank 217 Allied ships. On 16 October 1940, convoy SC7 from Halifax Nova Scotia to Liverpool was attacked by seven U-boats. Only 17 of its 35 ships survived, despite air cover by the escorting Sunderland flying boats, which could reach as far as 15degW, to protect convoys for the final two days of their transit into the Western Approaches. Convoy HX79 lost 14 ships. Within one week, the Allies had lost 38 ships. By the end of 1940, the disastrous British losses were 1,059 ships sunk in the north Atlantic. This amounted to 220,000 tons of shipping.[40] Supplies had been cut to 50 percent of the former 22 million tons needed per year. U-boats were sinking more than three Allied merchant ships every day. With dark humour, the German U-boat commanders referred to the summer of 1940 as "the happy time". They would shadow a convoy by day on the surface and submerge to attack at night. Allied ASW was slow to develop.

Britain could not sustain such a haemorrhaging attrition for very long. The situation for Churchill was desperate. The only consolation was the RAF fighters' victory over the Luftwaffe in September 1940, in the Battle of Britain. This lack of air control convinced Hitler to abandon his Operation Sealion plan to invade the island nation. Though critical as this was for outcome of the war, it did not change Britain's dependence on seaborne support from the US. The battle of Britain may have ended, but the Battle of the Atlantic raged on.

Britain still had inadequate numbers of escort vessels, on

---

[40] Wikipedia (2024). Losses during the Battle of the Atlantic. *Wikipedia*. Accessed 19 April 2024.

average providing only two per convoy. German long-range Condor aircraft with a range of 500 miles were able to locate and report the positions of Allied ships well out in the Atlantic, in addition to bombing them. It was the beginning of the longest battle in WWII: the Battle of the Atlantic, which was to last until May 1945. Altogether, it cost the Allies 3,500 ships and the lives of 72,200 sailors.

1940 the U-boats in France

By June 1940, the north of France and its seaports were occupied by the Germans. Italian dictator Benito Mussolini joined the Axis powers threw his Italian navy in with the Germans, contributing 15 capital ships, 37 cruisers, nearly 200 destroyers and 200 submarines, and virtually closing off virtually the entire Mediterranean. France had fallen within weeks of invasion. The German occupation of that country allowed it to reposition its U-boats to operate from bomb-proof bunkers in French Biscay ports directly into the Atlantic, only a day's sailing to its operational areas. The U-boats could be on station around Britain quickly, spend more time at sea, and return to refuel and reload torpedoes and be back in action in the mid-Atlantic. U-boat Admiral Dönitz established his headquarters at Kerneval near Lorient, in France, to coordinate his fleet's operations.

In 1940, ship building was in overdrive. Germany was launching 13 new U-boats every month. With excellent radio direction finding equipment, and an efficient network of intelligence-gathering spies, the Germans knew the positions of Allied convoys and directed their U-boats to intercept them accordingly. They used radio transmissions of coded signals for this tactical command and control. which worked well until the Allies broke the code in 1941. Conversely, Germany was continually decrypting the insecure British communications and was able to read 80 percent of British cyber transmissions.

The result of the growing threat of the U-boat was that in June 1940 alone, 64 British merchant ships were sunk. On one momentous day, 15 October 1940, six U-boats sank 16 British ships. In just one disastrous week, 38 ships were lost. In November 1940, the British aircraft carrier HMS *Ark Royal* was sunk off Malta. It was a major blow to the British. This so-called "happy time" for the Germans persisted until November 1940, when a series of heavy storms in the Atlantic limited U-boat operations. Britain was exhausted but remained resilient.

In 1940, the British moved their naval assets north and west to Liverpool and Scotland, away from their vulnerable traditional home ports of Portsmouth and Chatham. Admiral Sir Percy Noble GBE KCB CVO replaced Admiral Sir Martin Dunbar-Nasmith VC, a World War I submarine commander, as Commander-in-Chief Western Approaches (February 1941- November 1942). His crucial contribution was organising convoys from the US. In turn, he was replaced by Vice Admiral Sir Max Horton, GCB, DSO and Two Bars, formerly Flag Officer Submarines, who was the first submariner to sink an enemy ship in World War I. He signified his victory then by flying the skull and crossbones pirate flag on return to port – a tradition after a successful mission, still followed by the Royal Navy.

1941 Allied Intelligence: The Enigma Breakthrough

Information and communication are critical in war. The Germans had a sophisticated encryption system known as

Enigma.[41] It referred to a family of cypher machines adopted by the German military after World War I.[42] They allowed encryption and decryption of messages about troop movements and other information vital to Allied operations. The British were desperate to crack the German code, so they could prepare for German attacks, and in particular to learn the High Command's U-boat positions and plans. In 1938, the Secret Service bought a rambling mansion in the countryside 50 miles north of London called Bletchley Park and installed a radio receiver to monitor German transmissions. Bletchley Park's own call sign was *Station X*. It was to become famous as the home for a unit tasked with breaking the code. Personnel from a mixture of disciplines genders and ages, and the nation's best mathematicians, were employed, all with a common esoteric gift for pattern recognition and crossword puzzles. What they did was to prove crucial for an Allied victory. It bears close examination.

A German operator pressed a key on an Enigma machine, which was a keyboard attached to three mechanical wheels with letters on, that could be rotated by hand. Depending on the rotors' position, a different letter was printed. Each press of a key produced a different letter. The number of different combinations to produce the letters that were transmitted ran into millions of millions. Without the codes, the result was unintelligible. It was transmitted in morse code to receiving operators in the field with similar machines which when their rotors were moved to the same positions as the sending machine, allowed the encrypted messages to be interpreted.

The codes for the rotors were changed every day and transmitted to the operators. With so many possible combinations possible,

---

[41] Enigma Code.
[42] https://en.wikipedia.org/wiki/en:Museo_Nazionale_Scienza_e_Tecnologia_Leonardo_da_Vinci accessed 19 April 2024.

the German High Command was supremely confident that their code was unbreakable. The code-breaking task was as complex as it was both difficult and urgent. Much depended on it. The 130 devoted staff in 1939 grew to 10,000 by 1945, working in great secrecy. The effect of their work was spectacular. It allowed critical top secret radio intercepts in morse code to be decrypted back into German language and understood by the British. The designation *Ultra* was given to this decrypted German information. Based on captured and reconstructed machines, pioneering work by the Polish Cyber Bureau in the 1930s had laid the foundation for breaking the German cypher code. This intelligence was transferred to the British only two weeks before Poland was occupied in 1939. The Polish cryptographers were captured and executed. Breaking the code was quickly seen as a priority for Britain, who needed to monitor German secure communications. *Station X* cryptographers were completely baffled. Breaking the naval enigma code was their greatest challenge.

In 1940, U-boat commanders used Enigma machines to secretly report their positions and sightings of convoys to Dönitz at U-boat headquarters, and they were directed to intercept Allied ships. All the while, unknown to the British, the Germans had cracked British signals and were also reading the British communications at the same time the British were receiving them. The British were frustrated and under extreme pressure in their attempts to crack the elaborate German Enigma system. Initially, the code breakers in *Station X* at Bletchley Park were able to break the code for the airforce and army, but not for the *Kriegsmarine*. In February 1940, a commando raid on a German trawler *Krebs* by the British destroyer *Somali* captured the Enigma codes for that month. The information was vital to the code breakers at Bletchley Park.

A further advantage was gained on 7 May 1941 with the capture by the RN of two weather reporting ships the Germans maintained near Iceland and Greenland - the *Munchen* and the *Lowenberg* - with their Enigma machines and the code books for them. Gradually the code breakers were finding ways to interpret the intercepted German transmissions. Allied losses remained high. In 1941, U-boats sank 61 ships in June and a further 23 in July. *U-37* alone sank 11 ships in two weeks. In mid-1941, Britain stood alone against Hitler. The war was going badly for the British. In 1941, U-boats sank 61 ships in June and a further 23 in July. *U-37* alone sank 11 ships in two weeks. The Germans had used three rotors in the Enigma machines. After 1 February 1942 a fourth rotor wheel was installed, vastly increasing the number of combinations for each letter in a coded message. This put a 10-month stop to Allied interception of the German communications, and hundreds of thousands of tons of British shipping were sunk each month. The Allies were desperate to regain access to this source of its critical information.

9 May 1941: The Capture of U-110

The events involving the British capture of *U-110* and *U-559* inspired the fictional movie *U-571*, made in 2000, in which American sailors were credited with capturing material relevant to breaking the Enigma code. Regardless of this triumph of entertainment over historical accuracy, the outcome of the various efforts and sacrifice by so many people to successfully intercept enemy communications was that breaking the Enigma code at Bletchley Park was to prove essential for the eventual Allied victory in the Battle of the Atlantic.

Ironically, U-boat commander Fritz-Julius Lemp, who in *U-30* had sunk the passenger liner *Athenia* in 1939 on the first day of the war, was to come to Allied attention again on 9 May 1941, when in command of the type IXB *U-110*, he came across a 38-ship convoy. He attacked and sank two merchantmen. Two British destroyers accompanying the convoy counterattacked with depth charges, which brought the U-boat to the surface. Commander Joe Baker-Cresswell, captain of the destroyer, HMS *Bulldog*, fired on *U-110*. In his boat, thinking he was about to be rammed by HMS *Bulldog*, Lemp ordered his crew to abandon ship, apparently with the intent of saving their lives. He ordered everyone to get out of the stricken U-boat, and set charges to sink the boat, but he did not have time to destroy the highly sensitive equipment he had on board. The explosives set to scuttle the boat failed. It appears that Lemp wrongly assumed the *Bulldog* would sink his disabled U-boat.

The *Bulldog* crew saw U-boat crew emerge onto the U-boat external casing and expected them to be preparing to use their deck gun against them. They opened with small arms fire on the U-boat. When the Germans showed they were not about to use their deck gun but instead were surrendering, HMS *Bulldog* ceased fire and stopped, Unfortunately, 15 of the U-boat crew were killed in the action. The remaining 32 men, but without Lemp, were captured. The *Bulldog* lowered a boat with a boarding party under Sublieutenant David Balme that boarded *U110* and climbed down into the deserted U-boat. What they discovered changed the Battle of the Atlantic, and the course of history. King George VI called it the most important event in the war at sea thus far. By capturing *U-110*, damaged but afloat and effectively intact, HMS *Bulldog* had inadvertently made one of the most significant intelligence breakthroughs of the war. Lemp had effectively surrendered his submarine to a small British warship, whose crew rescued the U-boat's 32 German sailors from the water. That was not all they recovered. Crucially, the British boarding party also captured the highly secret Enigma code machine and code books. This gave the Allies an enormous intelligence gain. Lemp died in the action, possibly by suicide. He was last seen by his loyal crew to be swimming back to the stricken submarine, presumably to open its sea cocks and send it to the bottom. It was too late. He was never seen again, after abandoning his submarine. He was aged just 28 years.

The captain of the British destroyer received the DSO and was promoted to captain. The *Bulldog*'s boarding officer, Sublieutenant David Balme, was later quietly awarded the DSC in recognition of the bravery and significance of his action.[43] Radio operator William Stuart Pollock was on the second boat to board U-110 and retrieved the Enigma machine and code books. The *Bulldog* boarding party spent several hours in *U110*, stripping it of any possibly valuable documents and returning these to *Bulldog*. The captured German crew were quickly imprisoned separately in Canada to preserve the secrecy of the capture of the machine and code books. It was vital not to alert the German authorities to this breach in their communication security. The capture of the Enigma machine on which all coordinated attacks by wolf packs depended was kept secret by Britain until 1974. The British deliberately let the Germans believe that *U-110* had sunk with all hands, conveniently taking its Enigma machine and its secrets to the bottom. Were the codes or rotors to have been changed, the precious intelligence secrets would be rendered useless to the British.

By late 1941, the brilliant 28-year-old British mathematician Alan Turing built a code-breaking machine, which tested various combinations far more quickly than humans could.[44] Leading the code breakers at Bletchley Park, *Station X* was

---

[43] LCDR Balme DSC died in 2016 at the age of 95.

[44] Hodges, A. P. (2014). *Alan Turing: The Enigma*. Princeton University Press, Princeton, NJ.

able to crack the reputedly unbreakable Ultra code from the Enigma machine, and could listen to U-boats as they reported their positions to the centralised German command in Berlin. The British were able to divert convoys away from the German submarines, but without the Germans' realising they were doing so. This was obviously a major tactical achievement, and saved thousands of Allied seamen's lives, and thousands of tons of supplies needed by Britain.

British losses were reduced from 325,000 tons in May 1941 to 90,000 tons by July. Despite this sudden reversal for the *Kriegsmarine*, the Germans refused to believe that their communications could have been compromised. They instituted brutal investigations of their own staff, and civilian contractors, to find the source of the leak they suspected. Erroneously, French and British spies in the ports were blamed. The challenge for Allied intelligence was to use the secret information they acquired from what became known as Ultra to save their convoys, but not in any way that could alert the Germans, who would then change their codes and neutralise the code breakers' efforts. Secrecy was a day-to-day obsession.

In the event, so convinced were they that their code was unbreakable, the Germans did not change their operations. They believed their addition of a fourth rotor to their Enigma machine in 1942 made the odds against its being compromised overwhelming in their favour. In this, they were wrong, and they deceived themselves with a false sense of security. Like any delusion, it was a fixed, false belief. Churchill's instruction was that any action taken on the basis of the Ultra intelligence that the Enigma code facilitated had to have a cover story that it was obtained from another source such as a spotter aircraft. It was critical that the Germans never knew the code was broken and would not change the codes or rotors in the encryption machines.

The code-breaking technology that Alan Turing had developed remained secret for 30 years and was used by British intelligence to spy on the Russians for decades through into the Cold War. *Station X* found the Germans had produced a new secret encryption code on a 12-rotor machine called the Lorenz, using the teleprinter to generate random letters as an obscuring code added to each message. *Station X* called this new code *Fish* and broke it within three months. Hitler never suspected the Lorenz had been broken. In 1943, a telephone engineer called Tommy Flowers joined *Station X*, and he built a 1,500-valve machine that was the world's first programmable computer, called *Colossus*. It was able to read paper tape optically at the astonishing rate of 30mph, processing vast amounts of information. It contributed to Operation Overlord in June 1944. *Station X* continued to decipher German code until the end of the war. It is credited with shortening the war by two years. Later regarded as an information technology genius, Alan Turing was nevertheless persecuted as a security risk because he had been arrested as a homosexual. He took his own life in 1954. The existence of *Station X* was not admitted by Britain until 1976.

1940   The RN in the Mediterranean

In 1939, Britain had been able to exercise virtual control over the Mediterranean, allowing its oil supplies to pass through the Suez undisturbed. Italy's entry into the war changed that. The large Italian navy directed its forces against the British island of Malta, which had become the base for Royal Navy attacks against German shipping carrying supplies to North Africa. In May 1940, Italy bombed Malta and began a two-year campaign against the island, subjecting its citizens to great suffering. Britain was later to award the George Cross to the whole island of Malta, to recognise its civilian courage in resistance. In the Mediterranean, on 11 November 1940, the Royal Navy's Swordfish torpedo bombers launched a surprise attack from aircraft carriers against the Italian fleet at Taranto, crippling its six battleships. It was a turning point for the Italians in the Mediterranean. Germany realised its supply lines to Africa were at risk. For months in 1941, it continued its attacks on Malta and on British supply convoys to North Africa. In the Mediterranean in 1940, as in the Atlantic, Britain stood alone as a fighting force. On the land, Italy controlled Abyssinia and Libya. Britain knew that if it lost Egypt and the Suez Canal it would lose access to oil and the war would be lost. It was to draw some million soldiers from its old empire, the dominions of Australia, Canada, South Africa and India. Hitler decided he had to help his Italian ally, and Germany took Crete with parachute troops in February 1941.

1941   British Political Intrigues

In May 1941, in a baffling act that defies logic, German Deputy Führer to Hitler Rudolph Hess flew himself from Augsburg to Britain in a Heinkell 110. Bailing out over Scotland, his purpose in undertaking this unilateral initiative remains an enduring mystery. The question arose whether Hess was on a solo peace mission to meet the Duke of Kent to discuss peace with Germany, or if the flight was sanctioned by Hitler and others in the British establishment. The British royal family's House of Windsor had diplomatically changed its name from Saxe Coburg Gotha only in 1917. Several members of the royal family still had relatives in German aristocracy, and incredibly Edward, the Prince of Wales, was sympathetic to Hitler, whom he visited for two weeks in October 1937. Deceptively, the Nazi propaganda portrayed Germany as the natural allies of the British. However, there is no evidence that Prince Edward was critical of Hitler's *Anschluss* to occupy Austria for his "Greater Germany" expansionism.

British Foreign Secretary Lord Halifax and other members of the war cabinet, including Edward, Prince of Wales (later King Edward VIII) and after his abdication in 1936 known as the Duke of Windsor, were surreptitiously seeking peace talks with Germany. Hitler expected Britain to sue for peace. A theory emerged that the royal family wanted Churchill removed. The brother of King George VI was Prince George (later Duke of Kent), who was also implicated in these secret negotiations. He was killed as a passenger in the controversial crash of a Short Sunderland in Scotland, inexplicably enroute to Iceland, in August 1942. A long-lasting cover-up by the authorities was alleged. The mystery of his unlikely death continues to the present day.

The Duke of Windsor gave up the British throne to marry American multiple divorcee socialite Mrs Wallis Simpson, and the by-then unpopular couple moved to France. In May 1940, they escaped German occupation of Paris and moved to Portugal. Churchill sidelined Edward by appointing him as ambassador to the Bahamas until 1945, and they lived out most of their remaining years in France until his death in 1972, shunned by the British. Prince Edward appears to have believed Germany could defeat Britain, by "bombing it into peace" (which he thought preferable to a land invasion) and would re-establish him as King of England. Wallis continued to live in Paris, until she died in 1986, supported by an allowance from Queen Elizabeth. King Edward VIII was the shortest reigning British monarch in five centuries. His subversive and unforgiven sympathies for the Nazis had destabilised British politics prior to and during WWII. He was an ongoing embarrassment to the Royal family, and a puzzled and divided population. The intrigue and failed reign were a distraction to Prime Minister Winston Churchill with his focus on winning the war.

1941 The Atlantic Surface War: The *Hood* and the *Bismark* are sunk

In surface warfare, 1941 saw the German capital ships *Admiral Scheer*, *Scharnhorst*, *Gneisenau*, *Bismark*, and *Prinz Eugen* conducted successful raiding missions. In May, *Bismark* sank the British battlecruiser cruiser HMS *Hood* (taking with her all but three of her 1,319 crew), *Bismark* was herself sunk by RN battleships *King George V*, *Rodney* and aircraft three days later.

The British were confronted with the probability that the German battleship *Bismark* and *Prinz Eugen* could break out into the Atlantic and savage its convoys on which survival depended. Virtually the entire Royal Navy was ordered to "Hunt the *Bismark*". Five days into its first patrol, heading west into the Atlantic, the giant warship was spotted by the crew of a Catalina flying boat from coastal Command, and all available ships, totalling almost 90, began what would become a widely reported nine-day pursuit of a deadly enemy.

In an engagement with HMS *Hood*, this pride of the RN was destroyed by a salvo from the *Bismark*. and the *Hood* sank within minutes. But for three survivors, her ship's company of 1,483 were all killed. It was a massive blow to the RN and to Britain. Fourteen obsolescent Swordfish torpedo bombers from HMS *Victorious* and *Ark Royal* changed the history of naval aviation by being successful in disabling *Bismark*'s steering gear, jamming her rudder 15deg to port. This forced her to sail only in wide circles as she tried to escape to the French port of Brest, 300 miles away. Two powerful battleships, the *King George V* and the older but still dangerous *Rodney* pursued the doomed *Bismark*, along with smaller destroyers which pumped shells fire into the pride of the German Navy as she struggled to reach the protection of land-based Luftwaffe aircraft. Of her 2,200 crew, only 114 survived. The number of ships crossing the Atlantic stepped up after 11 March 1941, when Churchill and Roosevelt negotiated the Lend Lease agreement in which for the price of access to certain British assets in the Caribbean, America, not yet in the war, would provide food, arms and oil to Britain.

The Lend Lease Act allowed the US to lend or lease war supplies "to any nation deemed vital to the defence of the United States". Russia, China, and France were also recipients of the products of American industry. It was the end of America's isolationism. The aid, worth $49bn, was to be paid for later, but it did not come cheaply. It took Britain until 2006 to pay off the debt. Though Britain was alone and threatened in 1940 during the battle of the Atlantic, isolationist America waited until it was attacked by the Japanese in December 1941 before committing its massive industrial capacity to the Allied cause. ADM Ernest King USN allocated most of its submarines built to the Pacific rather than to the Atlantic and European theatre.

1941 Hitler invaded Russia in Operation Barbarossa

On 22 June 1941, Hitler began his attempt to defeat Russia, sending three million troops east to take Moscow. It was the largest land offensive in human history. His Operation Barbarossa bought widespread destruction to Russian cities. In November his forces were defeated by heavy rains' turning roads to mud, and the freezing Russian winter. It reduced divisions to regiments and regiments to battalions. The German military and German production capacity were stretched beyond capability. With German units only five miles from the Kremlin, the offensive was abandoned on 5 December 1941, two days before the Japanese attack on Pearl Harbour brought the US into the war. The RN and the US battled treacherous Arctic weather in convoys to Murmansk and Archangel to supply Russia in its war in what was Germany's second front. The losses were crippling. Of convoy PQ17, with 35 ships, 24 merchant ships are lost. Arctic convoys were suspended.

As in in the sinking of the Italian fleet in Taranto, and in the December 1941 Japanese attack on Pearl Harbour, battleships were shown to be vulnerable to air and torpedo attack. The *Bismark* with its eight 15-inch guns, though representing a quarter of German battleship power, was sunk. Its sinking was a significant victory and morale boost for Britain. However, on 14 November 1941, the British lost the iconic aircraft carrier HMS *Ark Royal* to a single torpedo from *U-81*.

1941: The Western Desert and Tobruk

The 16,000-strong *Afrika Korps* arrived in 1941, led by the brilliant and charismatic tank commander General Erwin Rommel. The Axis powers were victorious and began pushing British forces east out of Libya back to Egypt. If Germany took Egypt, it would have won the war. Thousands of soldiers become POWs. The deepwater port of Tobruk in Libya was crucial to holding the vital Suez Canal, essential for ship movements to and from the Indian Ocean and British interests in Asia. It was defended by the 14,000 Australian 8th and 9th Divisions of infantry, dug in under constant German bombardment, and led by Australian General Sir Leslie Morshead in a defiant and ultimately successful siege of 246 days, beginning in April 1941. The troops were supplied nightly along the coast from

Alexandria by the Royal Australian Navy "Scrap Iron Flotilla": Destroyers HMA Ships *Vendetta, Waterhen, Voyager,* and *Stuart.* Some 30 ships were lost. The Australian infantry and British artillery took the fight to the enemy to save Egypt. For the first time in World War II, the *Wehrmacht* had been stopped.

After eight months under siege and bitter hand-to-hand fighting with artillery action, the Australians were withdrawn each night over three months by the RN and RAN destroyers. The Allies had lost 5,989 soldiers. Rommel had referred to Tobruk defenders as "rats", a name which these resilient soldiers took on themselves as a proud appellation. They became famous as the "Rats of Tobruk" who would not be caught, and who blocked German progress eastwards. It is a name still revered in Australian military history. Their stubborn refusal to concede or retreat laid the foundation for the later battle of El Alamein in July 1942, signalling defeat for the Germans in North Africa. General Bernard Montgomery's 8th Army replaced an exhausted General Claude Auchinleck. If Auchinleck had not held the Germans at Alamein, Britain would have lost the Middle East oil supplies and therefore likely the entire war.[45]

1942: North Africa and The End of the Beginning – Operation Torch

Churchill convinced Stalin and Roosevelt to invade North Africa in November 1942, in an operation code named Torch, losing 16 ships, mostly to 25 U-boats. American Lieutenant General Lloyd Fredendall's inexperienced soldiers were ambushed in Tunisia by the Afrika Korps. Defeated at the battle of Kasserine Pass in February 1943, He was relieved of command after losing 3,000 troops and another 3,000 into captivity, in the space of 48

---

[45] Dixon, N. F. (1976). *On the Psychology of Military Incompetence*, Cape, Aldershot.

hours. Hundreds of tanks were lost. He was replaced by George Patton who drove into Tunisia and outflanked the Germans. Italian dictator Mussolini had seized the opportunity in June 1940 to join Hitler, and to invade Libya and Egypt in an attempt to gain a foothold in North Africa and restore the Roman empire under his rule. The British 8th Army confronted the Italian army and regained control. Some 230,000 German and Italian troops became prisoners. Eventually the Allies operation was a success. Churchill claimed: "This is not the end. It is not even the beginning of the end. But it is perhaps the end of the beginning." In retrospect, Churchill and Roosevelt made out that this was the hinge on which victory turned. Operation Torch had American and British forces invading further west and gradually pushed east in a pincer move with Montgomery coming up from the south and east, to trap German General Erwin Rommel in February 1943, resulting in the humiliating surrender of 250,000 German troops. It was more than double the number who had surrendered at Stalingrad in 1942, four months earlier. This was yet another disaster for Germany. In retrospect, operation Torch may have been unnecessary, as the supply line from Sicily to Axis forces in Tunisia could have been blockaded and the Germans and Italians in Tunisia forced to surrender. It had cost 76,000 Allied lives. The Allied forces that landed in Morocco could have landed directly in Sicily in 1942. The strategic focus became that of the attacking the Royal Navy surface and submarine fleet,[46] and the RAF that were keeping safe the British supply convoys from the US. Mussolini had invaded Albania and Greece in 1939 and was later in April 1941 supported by half a million German troops sweeping south into Yugoslavia and Greece. Some 15,000 soldiers in the British forces were evacuated to the British controlled island of Crete and 18,000 were taken prisoner in May 1941, when German

---

[46] Dornan, P. (2010). *Diving Stations*, Pen & Sword Books Ltd, Barnsley.

Para troops invaded and overran the island. The British and Dominion garrison was ineptly commanded by the obstinate and muddled New Zealand MAJGEN Bernard Freyberg VC, who in spite of contradictory intelligence reports, stubbornly planned for a seaborne invasion.[47]

1941 Allied Advantage

In April 1941 America had become more involved, with President Roosevelt extending the safety zone off the US coast from 60degW to 25degW, stretching it to 2,300 nm across the Atlantic, thus including the Azores. He offered to repair and refit British ships in American dockyards. The destroyer USS *Reuben James* was sunk by *U-552* on 31 October, with heavy loss of American lives - 100 of its 144 crew. The US regarded itself as being unofficially at war. As late as November 1941, and only after U-boats had sunk three American destroyers, did Roosevelt reluctantly agree to allow US navy ships to join with RN warships to escort convoys across the Atlantic. His motive appeared to be to keep Hitler away from America, while Britain and her dominions confronted Germany. The convoys from the US kept Britain alive. The RN increased its efforts in escort duties. Significantly, no convoys were lost to U-boats in the second half of 1941. Legendary U-boat killer CMDR Johnny Walker CB DSO and Three Bars RN led a team of 500 men out of Liverpool in a fleet of specialised ASW ships in escort groups with advanced Sonar, that sailed ahead of the convoys and attacked U-boats with depth charges. Gradually the Allies became more effective in warding off the U-boat threat.

By 1942, better ASW capability in the Allies and use of joint intelligence in combined operations resulted in fewer losses. Sinkings of U-boats increased. U-boat ace Gunther Prien was

---
[47] David, S. (1997). *Military Blunders*, Constable, London, p. 337.

lost when attacking convoy OB293 in March 1942. Another ace was Otto Kretschmer, responsible for sinking 46 ships, representing 200,000 tons of shipping. Awarded the Knight's Cross with oak leaves and swords by Hitler, he became a POW after being forced to scuttle his *U99*. A third, Joachim Schepke, was killed when his boat was rammed and sank. Thus, five significant U-boats and three well-known U-boat aces were lost in three weeks. Dönitz moved his nine available deep-sea submarines to establish a control line at 30degW. The convoy SC26 lost 11 ships for the loss of just one U-boat. The British moved Sunderland flying boats and Hudson bombers to bases in Iceland to provide more protection to the convoys crossing through the dangerous "Mid-Atlantic gap". On 7 December 1941, the declaration of war by America became official, after Japan attacked Pearl Harbour.

January 1942:   U-boats cross the Atlantic

On 11 December 1941, four days after Japan had attacked Pearl Harbour and brought the US into the war, Germany was forced to declare war on America. German U-boats could then attack shipping from America in unrestricted warfare. In January 1942, Dönitz sent six U-boats across the Atlantic to attack American ships that were transporting fuel and munitions to Britain. The result was a catastrophe for the Allies. On 15 January 1942, British Intelligence warned the US that U-boats were patrolling the coast off New York. The Americans were totally unprepared for these attacks, with many of the escort ships that could have been available were already sent to Britain.[48] In first six months of 1942, the German "Operation Drumbeat" (*Paukemschlag*) sank 25 American ships, at that time relatively unprotected in American waters. The small number of U-boats ranged freely

---

[48] How did the Allies wage war against Germany's U-boats. *Battlefield War Stories*.

from the Caribbean to the Canadian border. The German U-boat crews could not believe their good fortune, sailing so close to the shore they could see car headlights on the coastal roads.[49]

German commander Reinhart Hardigan in the *Type IXB U-123* actually entered New York Harbour and torpedoed ships at anchor, easy prey with the lights of the city behind them. Ignoring British advice, the Americans refused to turn off the city lights. He fired all his torpedoes and sank 50,000 tons of cargo. Exemplifying the impact of submarines, this one U-boat sank 45 ships during the war, totalling over 200,000 tons. In some cases, the U-boats operated with impunity so close to shore that burning tankers were within sight of the sunbathers on southern beaches near New York. American merchantmen were still sailing with full lights. They were easy targets for the waiting U-boats. Sinkings outran construction of merchant ships in his "unparalleled massacre of American shipping".[50]

The U-boats sank 600 American vessels in five months, estimated at three million tons, at the cost of 5,000 American seamen. This was very confronting for the US, who appeared to be in denial of the situation in which the Atlantic Ocean was no longer their traditional buffer against a European war affecting them. In just one month, U-boats sank 40 ships off the American coast. It was a second "happy time" for U-boats (after the first such period in mid-1940). In the first quarter of 1942, U-boats sank 216 vessels in the North Atlantic, representing 1.25 million tons of shipping. American ASW was embarrassed and humiliated. At great cost, America stubbornly continued to refuse British appeals to darken ships and coastal lighting in coastal cities, and to institute convoys for the ships on which Britain depended.

---

[49] Werner, H. (1969), *Iron Coffins*, Arthur Barker, London.

[50] Cohen E. & Gooch J. (1960). *Military Misfortunes: The Anatomy of Failure in War*, The Free Press, New York, p. 59.

The Americans were puzzlingly stubborn in their slowness to learn, refusing to benefit from British experience of fighting U-boats, and not until April 1942 were blackout conditions ordered on the east coast of the USA. Close examination of the situation reveals failure on a massive scale: "The United States Navy was woefully unprepared, materially and mentally, for the U-boat blitz on the Atlantic coast that began in January 1942".[51] In January 1942 alone, 40 ships were sunk by U-boats off the American coast.

In the year 1942, the U-boats sank 400 merchant ships off the American seaboard, totalling two million tons, with the loss of 5,000 seamen. Again, these figures are staggering. The losses were both economically and psychologically crippling. Particularly galling was what Churchill called the "slaughter" of hundreds of tankers in the Caribbean and Gulf of Mexico with their precious cargoes bound for a fuel-starved Britain. He wrote to American authorities: "The situation is so serious that drastic action is necessary".[52] For a time in early 1942, U-boats sank half the shipping that was keeping Britain alive. The losses were unsustainable. The British were desperate to defeat the U-boats. At last, in April 1942, the Americans complied with frustrated British pleading. They turned their coastal city lights off and instituted daylight sailing only and in convoys, with escort corvettes and destroyers.

Quite why there was such a wilful failure on the part of the USN to learn from the British Royal Navy in Antisubmarine Warfare in 1942 continues to baffle naval historians. One reason might be that the demanding and ruthless and famously ill-tempered Admiral Ernest King USN, commander of America's Atlantic

---

[51] Cohen E. & Gooch J. (1960). *Military Misfortunes: The Anatomy of Failure in War*, The Free Press, New York, p. 66.

[52] Holmes, W. J. (1979). *Double Edged Secrets: U.S. Naval Intelligence Operations in the Pacific during World War II*. Naval Institute Press, Annapolis, Md., p. 41.

Fleet, regarded the Pacific as the prime theatre of operations. He was well-known to be strangely antagonistic to the British, who found him to be an abrasive ally "combining a powerful intellect and superb organisational skills with a thoroughly unpleasant character and vitriolic hatred of the Royal Navy."[53] The Lend Lease agreement with the US offered materiel to Britain (but still only one percent of Britain's needs) in return for access to Britain's colonial ports and lifting of protective trade barriers. This meant that Roosevelt could be seen as opposing Hitler by authorising arms shipments to Britain, incidentally, bringing the US out of a depression at virtually no cost to the USA.

ADM King strongly opposed convoys as being defensive, rather than offensive, and at every opportunity actively denigrated the Royal Navy's performance. He refused to send ships in convoys since he did not have the escorts to protect them. The desperate British loaned the US 10 ASW corvettes to protect the convoys on which they depended. Even the exasperated American Secretary of War Henry Stimson was scathing in criticising his own country's conservatism and lack of common sense in failing to recognise the threat posed by submarines as "Admirals' refusal to look at the experience of others or even common sense... Hidebound Admirals who frequently seemed to retire from the realm of logic into a dim religious world in which Neptune was God, Mahan his prophet, and the United States Navy the only true church".[54]

1942: The Information War

In another less-publicised event, on 30 October 1942, *U-559* was seized by HMS *Petard* 70 miles north of the Nile Delta,

---

[53] Lambert, A. (2008). *Admirals*, Faber and Faber, London, p. 409.
[54] Stimson, H. L.& Bundy, G. (1947). *On Active Service in Peace and War*. Harper, New York, p. 516.

and her codebooks retrieved by three sailors from *Petard*. Lieutenant Anthony Fasson RN and Able Seaman Colin Grazier were drowned, trapped on board when *U-559* suddenly sank before they could return to their destroyer. They were posthumously awarded the George Cross. The third sailor, Seaman Tommy Brown, received the George Medal. This new intelligence allowed the Bletchley Park codebreakers to solve the ever-changing Enigma mystery again.[55] Thousands of Allied sailors' lives were saved. The recovery of material from *U-559* in October 1942 would prove of great importance for British interception of German communications, through to the end of the war.

The contest was in information warfare: an intellectual exercise demanding the collection, organisation, interpretation and dissemination of many different kinds of data – fixes, sightings, direction finding and decrypts, along with less urgent intelligence on enemy procedures and tactics, even down to the habits of individual commanders. The British ASW effort was highly successful with an Operational Intelligence Centre coordinating advice to convoys and Royal Navy vessels. By contrast, internecine organisational dysfunction and decentralisation in the US Navy and Army Air Force led to a failure to develop needed similar doctrine and cooperation.[56]

There seemed to be an incredible organisational denial by the US Navy to avoid any requirement to respond to the extent of the losses being suffered by the Allies. It took the USN ASW organisation ("disastrously ineffective in early 1942") until mid-1943 to structure itself (with coordinated use of intelligence inputs as practiced by the British) to match the problem confronting it. Clearly, "a centralised planning and operational

---

[55] Sebag-Montefiore, H. (2004). *Enigma: The Battle for the Code*. Wiley, London.
[56] Morison, E. E, (1960). *Turmoil and Tradition: A Study of the Life and Times of Henry L. Stimson*. Boston, Houghton Mifflin. p. 567-68.

authority was needed".⁵⁷ Organisational inertia and failure to adapt cost many ships, and lives. Doctrine and standardisation were lacking – learning by doing was an unrealistic expectation as aircrew might experience only one U-boat attack in the whole of their career, and most sailors fruitlessly patrolled shipping lanes for U-boats that were not there. They might have only one opportunity to apply their knowledge.

1942 The Convoy Carnage

British Prime Minister Winston Churchill was desperate to secure support beyond American President Roosevelt's rhetoric. Churchill pleaded but Roosevelt had prevaricated, citing a divided Congress and isolationist public opinion who still thought their war was only with Japan. Churchill felt he had failed in his hope to bring America into the war. In hindsight, he did correctly foresee the danger of Russian expansionism. Roosevelt took an opposing view and offered to send American materiel to Russia to support its confrontation with Hitler.

In the event, the US supplied Russia with thousands of trucks. These were delivered by convoys undertaking treacherous weather conditions from Britain north to the ports of Murmansk and Archangel in the Arctic. They were often under attack from U-boats and the Luftwaffe based in occupied Norway. The Arctic convoys were incredibly dangerous for the brave civilian crews. Losses of merchant ships and civilian lives continued to be disastrously large. To be torpedoed in Arctic waters meant almost certain death. Immersion was fatal in only four minutes, so survival was infrequent. In 1942, Germany had 88 U-boats

---

[57] National Defense Research Committee (1946). *Survey of Subsurface Warfare*. Washington DC, pp. 9-94. Cited in American Antisubmarine Warfare in 1942, in Cohen E. & Gooch J. (1960). *Military Misfortunes: The Anatomy of Failure in War*, The Free Press, New York, pp. 59-94.

at sea, and Britain was again desperate to develop effective ASW capability.

In March 1942 alone, 37 U-boats attacked two convoys, sinking 21 ships. Merchant ship sailors and escort crews knew the odds were against their safe crossing to Britain. Admiral Ernest King could not dispute the losses. Intensely Anglophobic, in the face of overwhelming evidence, he did eventually but belatedly change his views, to become a supporter of convoys, although not until May 1942. Allied loss rates dropped immediately.

Nevertheless, by July 1942, U-boats had claimed 505 merchant ships in the north and west Atlantic. Convoy ON113 lost three merchant ships SC94 lost a third of its ships. The British changed tactics and formed the Escort Support Group, a specialised squadron of ASW ships under the command of legendary ASW officer CMDR Johnny Walker RN that could go to the aid of threatened convoys. These combined with more long-range aircraft with radar to score several successes against U-boats transiting out of the Bay of Biscay bases. By late 1942, while 85 U-boats had been sunk, more than a hundred U-boats at sea in the Atlantic were still wreaking havoc with catastrophic losses to Allied shipping.

September 1942: The Sinking the *Laconia*

On 19 September 1942, Korvettenkapitan Werner Hartenstein (*U-156*) fired two torpedoes at the British liner *Laconia*, 700 miles off the coast of West Africa. She was carrying 463 officers and crew, 80 civilians, including the wife of the British governor of Malta, 286 British soldiers, and 1,793 Italian prisoners of war. An hour after being torpedoed, the *Laconia* sank. Hartenstein ordered his crew to save as many survivors as they could. Hartenstein began a large humanitarian rescue operation of 200 survivors into four lifeboats towed by his U-boat and crammed 200 into the surfaced submarine. With two other U-boats they headed for West Africa. He sent out a general uncoded radio message in plain English appealing for assistance, and the French Vichy government dispatched two ships. Four days after the sinking, *U-156* was overflown by an American *B-24* Liberator dispatched by radio operators on the secret base on Ascension Island. The aircraft circled the U-Boat with its crowded casing and a large red cross draped on the gun deck and the pilot radioed his base for instructions. He received an unambiguous "sink the sub". His bombs did minor damage to the U-boat but killed hundreds of survivors in the lifeboats. Observing the *B-24* lining up for a second pass, *U-156* dived to avoid further damage. The pilot claimed a kill and was subsequently decorated for his action. The following day, the Vichy-French ships sent by Dönitz arrived and rescued 1,113 of the *Laconia*'s complement of 2,732. Most of those lost (88 percent) were Italian prisoners. Hartenstein radioed Dönitz for instructions.

The attack on a submarine that was engaged in a mission of mercy while flying the flag of the Red Cross angered the Germans generally and Karl Dönitz in particular. In response to this attack, the Admiral reluctantly issued a sweeping order to the entire U-boat fleet that became known as the Laconia Order: "All attempts to save survivors of sunken ships, also the picking up of floating men and putting them on board lifeboats, the setting upright of overturned lifeboats, and the handing over of food and water are to be discontinued. These rescues contradict the primitive demands of warfare to destroy just enemy ships and their crews."[58] This order changed the very definition of submarine warfare. Up to this point, German

---

[58] Laconia incident 12-17Sept 1942.ww2db.com/battle_spec.php?battle_id=325 accessed 1 Apr 2023.

U-boats operated more or less under the prevailing maritime doctrine known as the Cruiser Rules, which called for ships to engage in the kinds of actions Hartenstein had done in this case. The "Laconia Order" unleashed the new and brutal doctrine of Unrestricted Submarine Warfare that remained in place for the rest of the war with dire consequences for many merchant seamen.

On 8 March 1943, Hartenstein and *U-156* were lost with all hands to an aerial depth charge attack on their next patrol, east of Barbados. During the post-war Nuremberg trial of Karl Dönitz for various war crimes, the *Laconia Order* was displayed prominently in the case against him, a decision that squarely backfired on the prosecution. The German side of the *Laconia* sinking came out for the first time and US Fleet Admiral Chester Nimitz provided unapologetic written testimony on behalf of Dönitz, admitting the US Navy in the Pacific had engaged in very similar unrestricted submarine warfare since the very first day the US had entered the war. The American officer who ordered the *B-24* aircraft to sink the U-Boat was not charged. Admittedly, he was acting on instructions from his superiors, though it is difficult to see how the fog of war could have clouded his momentous decision. It is said that war brings out the best but also the worst in people.

There are records of German U-boat commanders altering their logbooks to conceal their similar misdeeds.[59] However, it must be noted that Germany was not alone in this kind of unethical behaviour. Accusations were laid against the Royal Navy too.[60] Lieutenant Commander Anthony Miers (later Rear Admiral Sir Anthony Miers VC KBE CB DSO) was then CO of T-class submarine HMS *Torbay* in 1941, near Crete. He was accused

---

[59] CO of U123 Horst von Schoeter. https://en.wikipedia.org/wiki.Horst_von_ Schoeter, accessed 26 Sep 2023.
[60] Ballantyne, I. (2013). *Hunter Killers*, Orion, London.

of war crimes, for using submarine's Lewis machine gun to fire on enemy sailors in the water after sinking their ship. He threatened to shoot one of his crew who objected and refused his CO's order to kill the survivors. Miers received a "strongly-worded reprimand" instructing him not to repeat the practice.[61]

1942: The Hunters Become the Hunted

What had started as the submariners' battle, with huge losses of up to half of a convoy, gradually began to turn on technology and strategy, to the hunters' becoming the hunted. At the end of the First World War, *Asdic* had been invented and made available to Allied warships. It was an early form of Sonar, giving range and bearing by sending two beams of electric pulses down from the hull and waiting for the return "ping" (made famous in so many war movies) bouncing back from the submarine to be picked up by the ship's sensors. This was a significant advantage for the hunter, but Asdic still didn't determine the depth of the submarine. The ping of the beam became known as the dreaded sound heard in a U-boat, as the ASW corvette or destroyer used sonar and made its adjustments just before it launched depth charges.

Radar was minimally effective against a dived submarine, because objects as small as a periscope on the surface were difficult to discern and the wavelength was too high. Eventually it got better, and combined with Asdic, Allied successes improved, giving the ASW captain information on the position of the U-boat. High frequency direction finding (HFDF) became refined, with a range of 25 kms, giving the ASW captain a bearing on the submarine. All he had to do was sail down the

---

[61] Padfield, P. (1995). *War Beneath the Sea: Submarine conflict 1939-1945*, Random House, London,

bearing and launch depth charges. Against the preference of Admiral Dönitz for priority on sinking the Atlantic convoys, Hitler ordered U-boats into the Mediterranean in 1942. It cost his *Kriegsmarine* the loss of 65 of its U-boats.

Meanwhile, the battle of U-boats against Atlantic convoys continued. In December 1942, Convoy ONS154 sailed unto a force of 20 U-boats. The convoy lost 14 ships, for the loss of one U-boat. Convoy TM1 from Trinidad bound for Gibraltar lost 77 percent of its ships without sinking any U-boats. In February1943, Convoy SC118 lost 13 ships, at the cost of three U-boats sunk and four badly damaged. That month, convoy ON166 was attacked by 21 U-boats and lost 14 ships, with two U-boats sunk. Convoy SC121 was attacked by 24 U-boats. The escorts were unsuccessful, and 13 ships were lost. MX228 suffered heavy losses. SC122 and Convoy MX229 lost 22 ships for the cost of only one U-boat. The German navy was optimistic, and the Allies were desperate.

1942: Wrens and Wargames at WATU

The Allies' ship losses in Atlantic convoys from the US meant hunger and food rationing for the British population and severe disruptions to supplies of munitions. In 1942, Churchill appointed retired Commander Gilbert Roberts RN to the Western Approaches Tactical Unit (WATU) in Liverpool to analyse German attacks and to develop tactics as countermeasures. Convoys of about 30 ships arrived there each week. These tactics were tested in wargaming with models spread on a floor marked out with gridlines used to direct ASW and ships escorting convoys. Roberts and two other retired naval officers staffed the unit with four Women's Royal Naval Service (Wrens) officers and four ratings all aged (17-21 years) but with strong mathematical skills. Their contribution in teaching

Royal Navy officers to outmanoeuvre experienced U-boat captains was crucial. Notably, only one Wren had ever been to sea herself, and none had ever seen a submarine. The recruiting posters of the time denoted the organisational culture at the time: "Join the Wrens - Free a Man for the Fleet". Attitudes changed gradually, as within months the value of their work began to be recognised.

Working from battle reports, they created scenarios that taught and tested seagoing officers about patterns observed in U-boat tactics, and how they could respond to variables including speed, turn parameters, torpedo ranges and visibility at night. Typically, U-boats used their superior speed on the surface to penetrate a convoy and sink merchant vessels before submerging and escaping to astern of the convoy. Various tactical procedures with deliberately comical names like *Raspberry*, *Banana*, *Gooseberry* and *Pineapple* proved remarkably successful in combating the U-boats. For example, *Raspberry* had escorts falling back to form defensive lines to locate the retreating U-boats and drop depth charges.

The impact of WATU was tested in May 1943. The German U-boats were under the command of Admiral Karl Dönitz, and they had, up to this point, enjoyed considerable success in the North Atlantic. Convoy ONS 5 consisted of 43 ships sailing from Liverpool to Nova Scotia and was targeted by U-boat packs. The battle lasted just over a week as the wolf packs tried to get in among the ships but were constantly frustrated by the escort ships. The escorts, using WATU tactics, accurately depth charged the submarines. However, by the end of the engagement, though 13 ships of the convoy had been lost, the Germans had lost 14 U-boats. In total that month, 34 German submarines were lost. That rate of loss, as Hitler pointed out to Dönitz, was unsustainable. In late May 1943, the Germans withdrew U-boats from the Atlantic. It signalled the end of the U-boat war. Convoy ONS 5 was a decisive turning point in the Battle of the Atlantic and was a complete vindication of the WATU tactics. Strangely, this important battle does not feature in British naval history. However the Germans did give it a name: *Die Katastrophe von ONS 5*.[62]

During the war, 5,000 officers undertook the WATU 6-day training course. Between 1942 and 1945 when the unit was disbanded, 66 Wrens had served in WATU. Top secret at the time, it was a highly successful though historically a largely underappreciated initiative.[63]

After the attack on Pearl Harbour in 1941, Roosevelt could no longer prevaricate on his promises. America had mobilised quickly and effectively in its war with Japan. It started building freighters, reaching an unprecedented rate of one Liberty ship each week. Eventually it was building one B-24 Liberator bomber every hour. Neither Japan nor Germany ever produced an effective four-engine bomber beyond a few prototypes, so the continental US was not subjected to bombing. America rapidly fielded an army of 12.2 million, more quickly than any army in history. Over a million American soldiers were on British soil in preparation for the eventual invasion of France from across the English Channel on D-Day on 6th June 1944. Despite these inherent weaknesses in the Axis powers by comparison with American productivity, they still believed in 1942 that they could win the war against the Allies. In February 1943, the Australian 9th Division was withdrawn to return home to defend Australia from the Japanese. The New Zealand Division fought

---

[62] Wrens, Wargames and the Battle of the Atlantic - Historic UK (historic-uk.com) Accessed 16 May 2024.
[63] Sloan, G. (2019). The Royal Navy and Organizational Learning – The Western Approaches Tactical Unit and the Battle of the Atlantic. *Naval War College Review*, vol. 72, no. 4, Article 9.

on in Tunisia, and eventually with the British 8th Army north along the east coast of Italy towards Padua and Trieste, still under MAJGEN Bernard Freyberg VC.

1943: Sicily and Italy

In January 1943 at Casablanca, a conference of Churchill and the US decided to invade Sicily, preliminary to invading Italy. With 3,000 ships and 160,000 men, Montgomery's 8th Army landed in South-east Sicily and Patton's Seventh Army landed further west. By July 1943, the British and Americans had forced Germany out of Sicily, although 40,000 German troops escaped to Italy and would be confronted there by Allied troops who invaded Italy on 25th July. The Italian population overthrew Mussolini, and after a gruelling stalemate, battles followed at Anzio in January 1944 and in February 1944 Montecasino, tragically destroyed by bombing in a mistaken belief it was occupied by German troops, who had not occupied the abbey because of its cultural and religious significance. The Vatican was furious. What Churchill optimistically but unrealistically predicted and argued would be a rapid defeat of the "soft underbelly of Europe"[64] became a slow and bloody grind, with American Lieutenant General Mark Clark defying Eisenhower's and General Alexander's orders to move east from Anzio to trap the retreating German army, and instead racing north to take Rome, although it was strategically irrelevant, and the Germans had already withdrawn. The bombing killed 70,000 civilians. Clark's egoistic personal triumph lasted only a day before news of his victory was displaced by the greatest invasion in military history the next day. With naval and air

---

[64] This was the term used by Churchill to convince Roosevelt to commit forces to an Italian campaign to gain access to Germany from the south, rather than by a more dangerous invasion of France. It was a strategic failure for which Churchill continues to be criticised.

superiority, a better commander would have landed troops in northern Italy. Eventually, after D-Day on 6 June 1944, Hitler, by then pathologically paranoid, forced Rommel to commit suicide. The war in the European theatre was coming to a slow and painful conclusion. The Italian campaign proved to be expensive in lives lost and materiel destroyed along with villages and towns as the Germans staged a fighting retreat. It was also strategically unjustified, with thousands of Allied lives lost in small pointless operations. Allied generals continued to fight to gain ground in Italy for over a year, when they could have bypassed it and landed in southern France, saving thousands of lives. Churchill's and Eisenhower's reasoning remains obscure. The campaign cost 313,000 casualties, with 119,000 American and 90,000 British and 8,000 aircraft lost. It was an Allied disaster.

1943: The Tide at Sea Began to turn

In the spring of 1943, the Allies were still losing ships sunk at the rate of 145 per month, which was more than the replacements they could build. Effectively, they were still losing the U-boat war. Though the tide was turning against Hitler, The Allies' convoys in mid-Atlantic were beyond the protection of most land-based aircraft, with a range of only 400 miles, out from Britain to 15degW. Only the American Consolidated B-24 Liberator bombers and Catalina seaplanes operating from Newfoundland, Iceland and Northern Ireland had the range to provide air cover for the 180,000 sq km "black gap" in the middle of the Atlantic where U-boats roamed. The Short Sunderland flying boat was particularly effective in bombing U-boats on the surface. However, most long-range bombers had been allocated to Air Vice Marshall Arthur Harris RAF to bomb Germany. Until virtually the German surrender in 1945,

The Battle of the Atlantic would continue to claim ships, men and women, and precious cargoes.

1943: The End of the Wolf Packs in 1943 and the Battle of the Atlantic

With the arrival of the *B-24* Liberator aircraft, and ASW destroyers' and corvettes' superior sonar and radar, the days of the U-boats were numbered. Numbers of escort carriers, smaller than the few fleet carriers available, helped, as did "evasive routing" of convoys closer to Iceland, where they could be protected by aircraft operating out of Reykjavik. The escort carriers were often old freighters with a deck built on its superstructure and embarking half a dozen Swordfish, the famed and suicidally obsolete though successful biplane torpedo bomber, nicknamed the "Stringbag". They were enough to keep the U-boats' heads down, and to disrupt their operations.

The balance of the battle began to turn in the spring of 1943, when the Allies produced large numbers of frigates, bigger than the *Flower* class corvettes, based on a design for whale catchers. These small ships were rudimentary and cheap to build. Though their sea-keeping properties made them very uncomfortable for crews, as specialist ASW platforms and equipped with radar and Asdic, they had the offensive capacity of a destroyer. Corvettes could make 17 knots (later 21 knots), faster than U-boats, and could carry 70 (later 150) depth charges. The corvettes proved very effective in ASW duties.

Allied ships with high frequency direction finding equipment called "huff duff" could establish a U-boat's exact position up to 25 kms away from the convoy. The air gap in the mid-Atlantic that had until then allowed U-boats to prowl unmolested, was closing. Hitler's beloved *Bismark* had been sunk by the RN, and unarguably Admiral Erich Raeder's battleships had been ineffective. Hitler removed him from his position in charge of the *Kriegsmarine*. He was replaced by Admiral Dönitz, and the production of U-boats was increased, though belatedly.

The combination of ASW forces against the U-boat was overwhelming: Frigates with radar, and long-range aircraft with radar and depth charges, meant that for example, convoy SC130 triumphantly arrived safely to England without loss and had sunk three U-boats on their Atlantic crossing. However, convoys were still losing two thirds of their ships. The Allies learned from these convoys that they needed to provide more escorts and air cover. During March 1943, 123 ships were sunk by U-boats. It was the closest the Germans came to fatally disrupting communications between Britain and the US.

However, between 1941 and mid-1943, when increasingly they were gradually defeated largely from the air with newly developed S-band radar, the U-boats had posed an enormous risk to the Allies. In the month of May 1943 alone, while Britain lost 34 merchant ships, Germany lost 41 U-boats, which was nearly double the number they had built during the same period. In just a few weeks, some 40 percent of the German U-boat force was lost to overwhelming Allied attacks.[65] This was one third of the German fleet. The Germans called this "Black May", during which over 40 U-boats were lost. Such losses were unsustainable. Germany was losing one U-boat per day, for every Allied ship sunk.

In 1943, 248 U-boats were sunk. In one wolf pack of 35 submarines on 5th May, 28 U-boats were lost; 40 were lost in four weeks. It became known by the *kriegsmarine* as "Black May". In June, 17 U-boats were sunk. Confronted with such

---

[65] Gannon, M. (2010) *Black May: The Epic Story of the Allies' Defeat of the German U-Boats in May 1943*, Naval Institute Press, Annapolis.

losses, Karl Dönitz had to withdraw from the North Atlantic. Even his son Peter's U-boat (*U-954*) was among those lost with all hands. On one day, 35 U-boats were sent out, and only five returned. Such losses effectively crippled the *Kriegsmarine* U-boat arm. Within a month, by May 1943, the hunter had become the hunted. Dönitz had lost the U-boat war, although single U-boats continued to sink Allied ships until the end of the war. In September 1943, Churchill proudly announced to Parliament that in the previous three months, no ships had been lost to enemy action.

22 September 1943 Operation Source

Australian LEUT Kenneth Hudspeth RANVR commanded a midget submarine X-10 in a mission to attack the battleship *Tirpitz* in a Norwegian fjord.[66] These were only 16 metre length, displacing 27 tons, with crews of four. Towed by a conventional T or S class mother submarine to their operational area, a 52hp electric motor drove them at 4 kph to beneath an enemy ship, where they would drop their two-ton explosive charges carried on opposite sides of their hull. These would be detonated by timed fuses and the x-craft returned to their mother submarine to escape. Of the six x-craft participating, three were commanded by Australians. Two VCs were awarded to two surviving COs of the X-craft (LEUTs Cameron and Place) for their bravery in disabling the *Tirpitz*. For his cool courage, Hudspeth was awarded the DSC.

In November and December 1943, no British convoys suffered U-boat attacks. A delighted Churchill proudly addressed a relieved British parliament. Simply, America and Britain out-produced Germany. Allied ASW had also become more

---

[66] Kemp, P. (2003). *Midget Submarines of the Second World War*. Caxton Editions, London.

effective. An important factor was the loss of many experienced submariners as so many U-boats were sunk.

Too late, ADM Dönitz reassured Hitler that his U-boats could recover from these losses by using the invention known as the "Schnorkel". Now common in diesel-powered submarines as snorting masts, the schnorkel mast did not come into general use until 1944. It allowed U-boats to run their diesel engines while the boat was running at 6 knots at periscope depth, recharging their batteries, rather than requiring the U-boat to stay surfaced for several hours, and thus exposed to both aircraft and ASW surface vessels. By 1944, its incorporation into submarine design and the *Type XXI* U-boat was too late with what was by then obsolete technology. Even the deployment of schnorkels with radar absorbent coatings which reduced its radar signature by two thirds over a surfaced U-boat offered only a temporary and limited reprieve. With triple the battery power of a *Type VIIc*, and an advanced hull design, they could make 16 kts submerged. Only two were ever deployed, but they did not see combat.

1944: Australians in Operation Neptune D-Day 6th June

On D-Day, Lieutenant Kenneth Hudspeth DSC and Two Bars, RANVR had commanded a midget submarine in September 1943. On 6 June 1944 he was one of some 500 Royal Australian Navy personnel serving in the British fleet on D-Day. More than 400 of these were officers in the RANVR. Some commanded destroyers and frigates, corvettes, minesweepers and torpedo boats. Several Australian officers endured the cramped and dangerous conditions of midget submarines. Hudspeth was commanding X-20, codenamed *Exemplar*, a 15-metre-long midget submarine displacing 30 tons. LEUT George Honour RANVR was in command of *X-23*. Both were tasked with dropping off special forces' divers onto Normandy beaches and then serving as navigation beacons to guide landing craft to the beaches. Over the next three weeks, 850,000 men and 148,000 vehicles would be landed on these beaches, in the largest amphibious invasion in history. Hudspeth's courage was recognised in a second bar to the DSC. He served the rest of the war as First Lieutenant of the destroyer HMS *Orwell*.

Demobbed in 1946, he returned to life as a schoolteacher in Tasmania. LEUT Max Shean received the DSO for his actions in X-24, and later in the Pacific theatre in July 1944, a bar to his DSO for commanding a midget submarine and cutting the cable between Singapore and Saigon. His Australian diver SBLT Kenneth Briggs RANVR received the DSC. The midget submarines made an impact in submarine warfare out of all proportion to their size. Australians in X-craft had won two DSOs and four DSCs. The Australian Submarine Service did not operate conventional submarines during World War II, but continued its distinguished history at least in embryonic size, with the X-craft.

1945: The Final Demise of the U-boats

The U-boats' war was coming to an end. Their main defence of underwater invisibility had been compromised. The ratio of merchant vessels sunk to the number of U-boats sunk had gone from 60:7 in 1940 to 18:9 in April 1943. Eventually, The Germans were losing a U-boat for every merchant ship sunk. By this time, the average life for a U-boat at sea was two months.[67] Germany was losing 18 U-boats per month. In the last five weeks of the war, 83 U-boats were sunk. The U-boat's fate was sealed.

---

[67] Sternhell, C. M. & Thorndike, A. M. (1946). *Antisubmarine Warfare in World War II. Operations Evaluation Group Report no. 51*, Navy Department, Washington DC.

On 4 May 1945, Dönitz gave the fateful order to his U-boat captains to surface and surrender to the Allies. Even so, some 221 German boats were scuttled by their understandably despairing defeated commanders, unwilling to hand them over to their enemies. Only 156 out of the 776 U-boats were found. At least two Type XXIII U-boats would be recovered after 1945 and returned to service in the new German Navy after World War II. In 1945, Dönitz and other senior German commanders escaped Berlin to the relative security of Schleswig-Holstein near the Danish border, not wanting to be captured by the advancing Russians. Hitler opted to stay in Berlin and avoided capture only by ending his own life on 30 April. Joseph Goebbels was appointed Führer and followed Hitler's example of suicide the next day. Hitler had planned for Dönitz to be his successor as President of the Reich. Within a day, Dönitz became the last Führer of Germany, on 24 May 1945. It was a role he was able to fill for only 20 days, until he signed the instrument of German surrender, and became a prisoner of war again.

In spite of the harsh operating conditions in the North Atlantic, and the cramped confines of U-boats with their demanding lack of sanitation and other elements of habitability, submariner morale remained high in the face of extremely dangerous missions. By the end of the war, the U-boats had destroyed an incredible 2,882 merchant vessels totalling 14.5 million tons, and 175 allied warships, but at a fearful cost. During World War II, 784 U-boats were sunk out of 1,162 commissioned. Some 32,000 German submariners lost their lives.

In the foreword to the personal account of the German U-boat battles of WWII by German U-boat captain Herbert Werner, a pragmatic anti-war book called *Iron Coffins,* British submarine commander Vice Admiral Sir Arthur Richard "Baldy" Hezlet KBE CB DSO and Bar DSC RN paid tribute to the courage and endurance of his opponents, but observed that as in the despairing title of Werner's book, "the U-boat could never have won".[68] While the German submarines were not notably far ahead of the British and American boats of the day, their numbers and the manner of operations had made them formidable adversaries.[69]

Airpower had made major contribution to Allied success in ASW. It accounted for many sinkings: whereas 246 U-boats were sunk by Allied surface craft, 288 were sunk by Allied aircraft (excluding bombing raids).[70] Some 111 U-boats under construction in Germany were destroyed by bombing. The Second World War had seen the submarine evolve through the German U-boats and the formidable German *Type VIIC* to the *Type IX* and hull design of the larger 1,600-ton *Type XXI* to become forerunners of the current diesel electric and the nuclear-powered boats now common throughout the world.

However, it should not be forgotten that even the feared U-boat was also subject to technological failure, with torpedo reliability variable and torpedo development still in its infancy, resulting in many missed opportunities as weapons failed to explode. Magnetic detonators were often faulty and the G7e torpedo often ran six feet below the set depth, compromising its effectiveness, even passing under and past the target's hull.

Finally, faced with insufficient aerial reconnaissance and delays in equipping his U-Boats with effective radar, Admiral Karl Dönitz had been forced to rely on reports from U-boats to locate enemy convoys. His command-and-control system sought efficiency by centralising communications through

---

[68] Werner, H. (1969), *Iron Coffins*, Arthur Barker, London.

[69] Hoffman, M.D. (1998). *The American and German Submarine Campaigns of the Second World War: A Comparative Analysis.* University of NSW, Canberra.

[70] Roskill, S. W. (1960). *The Navy at War 1939-1945*, London, p. 448.

Berlin and his later French HQ, and tasking submarines from there. Unfortunately for the Germans, the Allied cryptographers at Bletchley Park near London had broken the code used by the Enigma machines carried on U-boats, and the British were learning the German plans as quickly as the U-boat commanders. When U-boats surfaced, day or night, they found ASW aircraft waiting for them. With long range aircraft, radar and better ASW ships, and access to German communications with Ultra (the intelligence gained through the Enigma codes). By what the Germans called "Black May" 1943, the Allies had effectively beaten the Germans in the submarine-dominated Battle of the Atlantic. By 1943, life expectancy for German submariners was down to two months. In mid-1943, Germany was faced with mounting losses of boats and crews. With new and inexperienced commanders, many old hands in the U-boats understandably saw their orders to be for suicide missions. In the Battle of the Atlantic, only two percent of U-boat captains were responsible for 30 percent of sinkings. Some 850 U-boats never did any damage at all to an Allied ship during the entire war. The risks for a crew's survival or otherwise in the U-boat campaign were not evenly spread among their boats. From a force of 39,000 German submariners, only 7,000 survived. A fortunate 5,000 were captured, which effectively saved their lives. The cost of the German U-boat campaign was high. Four out of five German submariners never returned from sea. Frequently, when a new U-boat set out on its first patrol, it was likely to become its only patrol, when it failed to return. In 1944, only one in ten U-boats that left port ever returned.

The German U-boat fleet had been made obsolete by technology and overwhelming ASW forces. In 1941, the Type XXI U-boat was delivered, with its schnorkel mast and improved performance, a speed of 16 knots and 18 torpedo tubes, but it was too little, too late. Only a few actually saw service. Had

Hitler diverted resources to give Dönitz the 300 U-boats he requested in 1939, the outcome of the Battle of the Atlantic, and even the war, could have been very different.

By mid-1943, the Germans had been beaten by Allied technology. At last, American isolationism ended, and the might of American industry to build such numbers of merchantmen "Liberty Ships" so quickly, and to deploy its massive military, would be available to support Britain. A desperate struggle ensued as the longest battle of the war, the four year-long Battle of the Atlantic, was waged by aggressive U-boat commanders and grimly determined Allied navy and merchant navy seamen. Thousands of lives on both sides were lost. Convoys from the US and Canada, each of some 50 merchant ships, were tasked with keeping Britain supplied with the necessary 55 million tons of food and munitions it needed per year and preparing for the eventual D-Day landings in June 1944.

In retrospect, the U-boat had posed the greatest threat to an Allied victory in World War II. The figures were astonishing. Of the 1,162 boats Germany launched, 785 were sunk. Though ordered to surface and surrender, some 221 U-boats were scuttled to avoid handing over their boats. Of the 632 U-boats sunk at sea, Allied surface ships and shore-based aircraft accounted for the great majority (246 and 245 respectively).[71] They had sunk 2,771 Allied ships, totalling 14.5 million tons, and killing thousands of sailors.

Some 39,000 men went to war in U-boats, and 32,000 died in them. They suffered the highest mortality of any fighting unit ever. Such figures almost defy comprehension. It was a casualty rate higher than any other service in any country. This history still looms large in submarine culture. Submariners are still seen as a courageous elite in their navies. Crews then tended

---

[71] Ray, M. (2023). U-Boat. www.britannica.com/technology/U-boat.

to be young working class with metal-working backgrounds, and their officers were professional and dedicated. One error by one person could cost the lives of all 50. Their courage was enormous, and by some accounts, their captains were inspired, professional, and dedicated. Crews tended to be well trained and competent at least until about 1943, when losses at the rate of 15 U-boats per month reduced their numbers of recruits and their compromised education and experience levels in preparation for service.[72]

Admiral Karl Dönitz, in charge of U-boats during the Battle of the Atlantic, became chief of the German navy, and followed Hitler as the last Führer, on the day of Hitler's suicide. He was still unable to accept that U-boats could not win the war for his country. At the Nuremberg crimes, Dönitz received a 10-year sentence of imprisonment in Spandau prison, lighter than those given to his colleagues. By some estimates because he was a military officer following orders, not making policy. However, there is evidence that he knew what was happening in the extermination camps in the holocaust, and he is on record supporting antisemitism. He was released in 1956 and wrote his memoirs. He died in 1980, without expressing remorse for what today might be seen as war crimes. He was denied a state funeral by his government. His modest grave is next to that of his wife, in a small cemetery outside Hamburg.

The German Reich had built 1,162 U-boats of which 830 took part in operations. Of these, 784 were lost. Of the 41,000 submariners who manned them, 26,000 were killed. In total, 2,828 Allied merchant ships were sunk, taking 30,000 merchant sailors with them. The Royal Navy lost 175 warships, trying to protect them. In the RAF, 5,880 airmen died in the brutal,

---

[72] Wiedersheim, W. A. (1947). *Officer Personnel selection in the German Navy, 1925-1945*, US Naval Institute Proceedings, Washington DC.

wasteful, but critically important Battle of the Atlantic. "If the Allies had not won the Battle of the Atlantic, they could not have won the war."[73] Without the Battle of the Atlantic, in which submarine warfare played such a decisive part, there could have been no D-day invasion in June 1944. The outcome of the war would have been very different.

Overviewing Atlantic Submarine Operations 1939-45

Overall, the years 1939-43 were expensive for the Allies in the Atlantic, and very successful for the German submarine force. Between July and November 1940 alone, U-boats sank some 1.5 million tons of allied shipping. In just 18 months, the Allies lost 700 ships to U-boats, totalling 3.4 million tons. The figures invite considerable reflection about the cost and the strategic and tactical impact. In 1940, the British response was to cluster the cargo ships coming for the US and Canada into convoys for the transit, protected by a few surface ships, typically destroyers and corvettes, built in their hundreds, and the ASW frigates tasked to keep the merchant ships safe across 77 million square kilometres of the Atlantic.

Even so, some 30,000 merchant seamen lost their lives to the U-boats. In just one night of its 17-day crossing, one convoy of 35 ships lost 21 vessels, their crews and their cargoes. The escorting armed warships were under orders not to stop to rescue survivors, lest they too fell victim to the attacking U-boats.

Remarkably, the German U-boat commander *Kriegsmarine* LCDR Otto Kretschmer in *U-99* sank 46 allied ships by positioning his boat on the surface *inside* the convoy rather than

---

[73] Cohen E. & Gooch J. (1960). *Military Misfortunes: The Anatomy of Failure in War*, The Free Press, New York, p. 89.

firing a spread of three torpedos from outside the convoy. It was the tactic of a brilliant young submarine CO, and a fearless leader. Otto Kretschmer became a national hero at 28 years of age, and Hitler decorated him with the Iron Cross.[74]

Successful U-boat commanders were treated as "submarine aces" and were afforded adulation and notoriety like that given to airforce fighter aces. They received excellent food, double pay, and the privileges of royalty when ashore. Leaving port to go on patrol, and returning, they were usually feted with brass bands and cheering crowds. Admiral Karl Dönitz himself liked to attend the waterfront on such occasions, to hand out medals to victorious crews. There was no doubt that U-boat crews knew themselves to be part of an elite force. Men such as Gunther Prien with the sinking of 33 ships to his credit, Otto Kretschmer (*U-99*), and Wolfgang Lüthe (*U-43*), were each credited with 46 ships sunk, the highest-scoring aces. They became personal legends in the U-boat culture.

However, the triumph did not endure. In 1941, the Battle of the Atlantic was becoming more difficult for the German U-boat commanders. The British were providing stronger escorts to their trans-Atlantic convoys. Within a few days in March 1941, of the three most famous German submarine aces, Commanding Officers Gunther Prien (*U-47*) and Joachim Schepke (*U-100*) were dead. Otto Kretschmer had his boat sunk, and he was taken prisoner of war. Churchill saw this as a turning point in the Battle of the Atlantic. Support Groups of ASW destroyers with radar, sonar, and radio direction finding equipment operated mid-ocean, and would speed to the aid of any convoy reporting U-boats. There were signs that the U-boat's domination of the Atlantic was beginning to wane, although they remained a

---

[74] Blair, C. (1997). *Hitler's U-Boat War: The Hunters 1939-1942*, Weidenfeld & Nicholson, London.

destructive force until 1943 and to a lesser extent beyond. Still, from 1940 till spring 1942, the *Kriegsmarine* U-boats enjoyed what they called "happy times", sinking two million tonnes of Allied shipping. They were operating 330 type VII U-boats. Incredibly, with increasing efficiency, German shipbuilders were launching a new submarine every two days. The German U-boat Admiral Karl Dönitz would send up to 15 submarines out in a wolf pack to attack a single convoy. Some 71 percent of sinkings were by U-boats operating in wolf packs.

The German U-boat Culture

Examining the history of the German U-boat force in World War II allows lessons to be derived about the "U-boat culture". German Submarine captains were young and fearless, sacrificed by their navy in hazardous and uncertain conditions, with little hope of survival. Were they pragmatic professionals or simply everyday heroes in a hopeless cause? The question still stirs debate. The German submariners evidenced a range of variable levels of commitment to Nazi political ideals and the values that Hitler espoused. What does appear clear is that they were intensely proud of their profession as submariners, and of their successes in carrying out their missions, in spite of the appalling conditions of service in their boats.

In the second half of the war, they knew their comrades in other U-boats were losing their lives in record numbers, yet their devotion to duty remained on the whole undiminished. Even when missions were unarguably suicide missions and life expectancy was down to a few weeks or months, young German men lined up for recruitment to a proud yet ill-fated submarine service. Some of this cultural feature can be attributed to nationalistic loyalty, to serve the Fatherland, but knowing their country's war was effectively lost, and that their chances of survival were slim. This did not appear to lessen their commitment to their duties as submariners. It can be assumed that the promise or experience of intense camaraderie offered some appeal. This cultural norm appears to remain in the submarine community worldwide, sometimes superseding even national identification. The loss of a boat by any navy almost invariably triggers sincere sadness and condolences in communications from other submariners in other navies.

One other feature of the submarine culture that is often mentioned is the degree of autonomy exercised by commanders. A measure of independence and risk tolerance is granted to a greater extent than in surface commands. Though within the boat the crew may function as a highly organised interdependent and efficient team, higher level decision making my offer the appeal of autonomy and authority consistent with desirable individuality rather than being subject to external orders at a tactical level. The history of the U-boats highlights the danger of excessive centralisation in decision making. Complex organisations need "just enough" centralisation to provide overall coordination and ensure guidance and resources, but not so much that individual autonomy and decision making by those closest to the action is compromised.

A final lesson is given in the history of the U-boat war and the Battle of the Atlantic in 1943. Tragically, the huge losses suffered by the proud and committed German submariners reflected what happens when leaders become obsessed with a strategy which while initially successful becomes obsolete because of changing environmental circumstances – which the leaders obstinately refuse to consider until too late, if ever. It is often accompanied by irrational escalation of commitment. Germany continued to wage its U-boat war in the face of changes that made its operations impossible. The brave German submariners followed their orders well, but the orders were wrong, and appropriate only for an earlier time. Their leaders had failed to adapt to unwelcome change. They were beaten by advances in technology, to which they could not quickly adapt, much less defeat.

All the while in 1942-43 the Battle of the Atlantic raged on. For British submarines and German U-boats, there was no relief. Clearly, for an Allied invasion of Europe, millions of tons of supplies would be needed to be ferried from the US to Britain and across the English Channel. Losses of ships due to U-boats were still high until mid-1943. Churchill and Roosevelt belatedly gave priority to the Atlantic theatre.

British Submarines in World War II

The British had begun in World War II with 14 submarines based in Hong Kong as a deterrent against the Japanese, until a British fleet could be sent out to defend the Empire's interests in the curiously labeled "period before relief".[75] The L, S and T class submarines bore the brunt of the war.[76] Some 34 *Unity* Class boats were built. The British had their share of successes at this time. Operating out of Malta, the *Unity*-class HMS *Upholder* was a 630 tonne 58 metre craft, with a speed of 11.5 knots, commanded by Lieutenant Commander Malcolm Wanklyn VC DSO RN. In 1941, he pressed home an attack on the 18,000 ton liner *Conte Rosso*, carrying troops for North Africa. In September 1941, he torpedoed two other liners (*Oceania and Neptunia*), each of 19,500 tons, loaded troopships going south

---

[75] Goldrick, J. (2014). Buying Time: British submarine Capability in the Far East 1919-1940, *Global War Studies,* p. 3.

[76] Longstaff, R. (1984). *Submarine Command: A Pictorial History*. Book Club Associates, London.

to North Africa, in a fearful loss, drowning some 5,000 enemy troops.[77] HMS *Upholder* sank an estimated 120,000 tons of enemy shipping including two U-boats, and an 18,800-ton destroyer, before being lost off Malta in 1943.

The most successful British submarine captain in World War II was Commander (later Commodore) George Hunt DSO and bar RN, CO of HMS *Ultor*, famous for his highly effective service in the Mediterranean, sinking enemy supply ships.[78] In addition to the Mediterranean, the RN operated submarines in the Atlantic, and the Far East, including basing some boats in Fremantle, Western Australia, and Manilla, in the Philippines. From there they undertook successful patrols against the Japanese in the Indian and Western Pacific Oceans. In total, the Royal Navy lost 74 submarines in World War II, mostly in the Battle of the Atlantic. By late 1943, the German Navy was almost powerless. It had lost its battleships, and its U-boats had been beaten by the British technology and its ASW capability. The Battle of the Atlantic, in which 2,775 merchant ships were lost for the loss of 781 U-boats, was all but over.[79] The Allied victory at sea allowed the buildup of men and machines in Britain that could be projected into Europe in the D-Day invasion of June 1944, for the eventual defeat of the Axis powers, beginning in France and Germany.

The Pacific Theatre 1941-45

Meanwhile, in the Pacific, Japan in 1940 had resolved that the

---

[77] Simpson, G. W. G. (1972). *Periscope View*, MacMillan London, p. 152.

[78] Dornan, P. (2010). *Diving Stations*, Pen & Sword Books Ltd, Barnsley. George Hunt was one of two submarine officers selected by the Admiralty to have their portraits painted for the Imperial War Museum.

[79] Carruthers, R. (ed.) (2012). *The U-Boat War in the Atlantic vol 1 1939-1941*. Pen and Sword, Barnsley. South Yorkshire.

US would not fight if Japan were to take the oil in present day Indonesia and the rubber in Malaya. France and the Dutch had virtually left South-east Asia. Japan had seen America isolate itself and not intervene while its British ally was desperately enduring German bombing, losing 50,000 citizens in just six months in 1940. Only the US Navy stood in the way of Japan's ambition to take the raw materials from Asia. Japan anticipated that its 11 aircraft carriers in the Pacific (against America's three) and more battleships, would give it competitive advantage. It expected the US to sue for peace rather than fight.

Though Prime Minister General Tojo and others counselled caution, Admiral Yamamoto demanded approval for a Japanese naval strike. In retrospect, Japan's mistake, at Yamamoto's urging, was to provoke the US by attacking the US fleet at Pearl Harbour at 0756 on Sunday 7 December 1941.[80] Most of the island's defenders were still asleep. The US fleet lost five battleships sunk, three cruisers sunk or damaged, and took 2,400 casualties with 2,200 wounded. Remarkably, the four submarines in Pearl Harbour at the time were not attacked, and the main oil storage tanks for the fleet were not hit. Japanese aircraft strafed the airfields, and 188 US aircraft were destroyed. However, unknown to the attacking Japanese, two of the American aircraft carriers were at sea and not in Pearl harbour at the time, and so survived. The capability they provided was to prove crucial.

Three days after the Japanese attempted demolition of the surface fleet in Pearl Harbour, Hitler declared war on the US. The surprise attack by Japan unleashed a massive American response. The next day, America declared war on Japan. No full-sized Japanese submarine was engaged in the Pearl Harbour attack, which was almost totally an aerial assault.

---

[80] Roosevelt called this "A date that shall live in infamy".

Japan expected a swift victory over a pleasure-loving culture with no resilience for casualties or a lengthy war. It assumed the US would quickly sue for peace. Japan had 10 battleships, 10 aircraft carriers, and the world's most advanced naval aircraft. America had eight World War I battleships and two aircraft carriers. While the sleeping giant of the US was still waking to its attack, Japan invaded Malaya and Thailand. The target was Singapore.

Japanese Submarines

The Japanese had 64 boats at the end of 1941, mostly armed with the very effective Long Lance torpedo. Their captains wanted to attack merchant shipping, but once again the official attitude from Admiral Yamamoto towards submarines constrained his submarines to attacking aircraft carriers and preferably, other warships. This was both surprising and ill-advised.

"The only explanation available to this day is the opinion of the Japanese admirals, who were every bit as obtuse as the generals, that the submarine was a weakling's weapon that could justify its existence only by attacking other warships."[81] The Japanese were able to deliver only occasional victories with their submarines. Their submarines were barely adequate to the task of operating in the broader Pacific Ocean. Their torpedoes were generally superior in speed and reliability to the American Type 14, but the Japanese concept of operations for their submarines was self-limiting. Reconnaissance and mine laying operations were given priority over sinking enemy warships and merchant ships. Commerce raiding with its different set of skills required, was neglected. Some types embarked a scout plane and catapult to radio the position of

---

[81] Van Der Vat, D. (1994). *Stealth At Sea: The History of the Submarine*. Weidenfeld & Nicholson, London, p. 255.

enemy ships back to the submarine or to its surface fleet. A total of 42 merchant ships were sunk by Japanese submarines in 1942. The aircraft carrier USS *Saratoga* was put out of action twice for several months in 1942, by *I-5* and *I-26*. In January 1942, three Australian ASW *Bathurst* class corvettes HMA Ships (*Deloraine, Lithgow*, and *Katoomba*) attacked and sank Japanese submarine minelayer *I-124* off Darwin. During the Battle of Midway, I-168 administered the *coup de grace* to the fleet aircraft carrier USS *Yorktown*, and sank the destroyer, USS *Hamman*. Finally, in 1945, only two weeks before the Japanese surrender, *I-68* torpedoed and sank the heavy cruiser USS *Indianapolis*, with heavy loss of life. By the end of the war, Japanese submarines had sunk a million tons of Allied shipping (184 ships). By contrast, its Axis partner Germany had sunk 14.3 million tons (2,840 Allied ships) in the Atlantic. The US sank 5.2 million tons (1,314 ships). Japanese submarines did not pose a threat to Australian or American sea lines of communication in the same way that German U-boats did in the Atlantic.

After 1941: The Submarine War in the Pacific

Historically, in 1941, the American population, and its President, had been gripped by the sentiment and policy of isolationism, regarding the conflict as a European war in which America neither had nor wanted any part. Britain's Prime Minister Churchill's entreaties to President Roosevelt had elicited only an evasive verbal agreement from Roosevelt that the US would supply Britain with materiel to fight its war, but would not ask Congress to declare war on Germany. In the years between the world wars (1918-1939), international arms limitations treaties had declared unrestricted attacks to be immoral. The "cruiser rules" specified that submarines should surface, stop suspect enemy ships, examine their papers and only disembark their crews to the safety of lifeboats, with directions to the nearest land. Stealth and unheralded attack were not allowed. USN thinking was that submarines would serve only in a fleet support role, scouting ahead of the major capital ships.

This doctrine demanded boats over 300 feet in length with 20 knot speed capability and long range, to keep up with the fleet. Big 5,000 hp diesel engines designed for railway locomotives were able to be used to drive generators to charge the banks of batteries needed for submerged propulsion. Operationally, one hour at high speed or up to 48 hours at slow speed depleted the batteries, requiring the submarine to surface for air to run its diesels and recharge its batteries. This could take eight hours, and so was usually done only at night. An example submarine of this era was the USS *Gato*. Plans for the USS *Gato* in 1939 included air conditioning to counter condensation in electrical equipment and provision for a large crew, better habitability, fresh water and good food. They had a patrol endurance of 75 days.

Displacing 2,400 tons, these 73 *Gato* class boats were 300 feet long, more than twice the size of German boats in the Atlantic and carried a crew of 80. They could dive to 300 feet, and make 19 knots on the surface, with a very long range of 10,000 miles at 10 kts.[82] However, submerged speeds were not much higher than their World War I predecessors. The biggest development was in endurance, weapon capacity, and diving depth. The 73 *Gato* class were the first of 221 American fleet submarines in a massive building program. They had six torpedo tubes forward, and four aft. A boat typical of this class was the USS *Bowfin* (US287), now preserved in Pearl Harbour in her wartime configuration and open to the public. She made nine war patrols

---

[82] Alden, J. D. (1979). *The Fleet Submarine in the US Navy: A Design and construction History*. Arms and Armour Press., London.

in World War II and sank 67,000 tons of enemy shipping.

In 1941, the USN had the second largest submarine force in the world, with 111 boats. Though much of the American surface fleet was destroyed in the Japanese strike on Pearl Harbour, the submarine base there was unscathed. Within hours of the attack, Admiral Harold Stark ordered unrestricted submarine warfare against Japan. This changed the American warfare doctrine away from primarily defending capital ships to taking an offensive role against merchant ships. Older American submarine career commanders were cautious in letting go the now obsolete Plan Orange restrictions. They had not been trained in offensive tactics, they carried out attacks submerged and using passive sonar to determine range and bearing, rather than coming to periscope depth and aggressively pursuing targets on the surface. American captains still used passive sonar in targeting. A total of 96 torpedos were fired by American submarines with only 12 sinkings in the first three weeks after the Pearl Harbour attack. Lack of offensive thinking and the unreliable Mark 14 torpedos until 1943 further hampered their success. Courageous crews were wrongly blamed for poor results. RADM Thomas Withers was Commander Submarine Force. He had worked on the torpedoes before the war and refused to believe his submariners' repeated reports that the torpedoes were running at least 12 feet deep, and failing to explode even when they hit their targets. Magnetic detonators were found to be at fault. Less than aggressive initiative by commanders, and the frequently defective torpedoes, often detonating in less than 50 percent of firings, combined to produce very limited success. Many Mk 14s were seen to detonate prematurely, allowing the enemy ship to escape. Since the outbreak of the war, the US submarines had managed to sink only 10 enemy vessels. The 31 American boats in Manila deployed to Freemantle and Brisbane in Australia, out of range of enemy aircraft on Formosa.

1942   The Fall of Singapore

On land, the Japanese military successes across the Pacific seemed unstoppable. The Philippines, Malaya and the Dutch East Indies were all in Japanese hands. The British were complacent in Singapore, with guns resolutely pointing out to sea to repel any expected seaborne invasion. This was contrary to the strenuous advice from the Australian army commander there. The Japanese attacked from the air, and from the Malay Peninsula. Off the coast, the two battleships *Prince of Wales* and *Repulse* were bombed and sunk within two hours, claiming the lives of 1,000 sailors. It was Britain's worst naval disaster of World War II. In February 1942, Singapore fell, and though outnumbering the Japanese three to one, British General Arthur Percival surrendered with 100,000 British fighters including the Australian 8th Division thus taken prisoner by the Japanese. It was the largest surrender in British military history. They faced over three years of brutal imprisonment. General Gordon Bennett escaped to Australia, claiming his experience would be valuable in future conflicts. His troops thought he should have stayed with them as they endured captivity. He would never hold another active command.

Four days after the fall of Singapore, the Japanese began bombing Darwin. Japan planned an amphibious assault to capture Port Moresby. Australia faced imminent invasion, and in 1942 brought its 6th and 7th Divisions back from the African desert, under Land force Commander General Thomas Blamey. The Australian 9th Division and the New Zealand Division remained in the Middle East, only because the Americans undertook to send troops to the Pacific in April 1942. Within a week, Japan had overcome Hong Kong. The Philippines were bombed and quickly succumbed. American troops surrendered in Bataan. Next, Japan invaded Burma and captured Rangoon.

The British defenders were swept away. The Japanese were triumphant.

The Allies' Response in the Pacific

In April 1942, the US Colonel Dolittle led a daring raid on Tokyo with *B-25* Mitchell bombers off the USS *Hornet*. Japan was shocked but the damage was largely psychological. It already controlled much of the Asian coast and the Philippines, and the Dutch East Indies. It decided to fortify strategic islands around the SW Pacific to create a network of forces protecting its homeland: The Solomons, New Guinea, and Midway.

Australia risked being cut off from the US. General Douglas MacArthur became Supreme Allied Commander Southwest Pacific, and to push Japanese forces north, began an "island-hopping" campaign, invading one island at a time in the Southwestern Pacific, up to Okinawa. American Admiral Chester Nimitz commanded the naval forces across the Pacific and brought his carriers back from the Indian Ocean to support land operations and win naval battles as the allies progressively strangled Japan. American and Australian forces fought fierce and costly battles, one island at a time.

Battles in the Pacific Theatre (1942-45)

The major battles in the Pacific theatre and the involvement of submarines with the numbers of lives lost (indicating the cost and size of the battles) were as follows:

1942: Battle of the Coral Sea 4-8 May. Two American naval task forces fought the Japanese force enroute to take Port Moresby. This was a strategic victory for the Allies, preventing

Japan from invading Port Moresby, though a tactical victory for Japan, who won sea control. Historically, this was the first naval battle in which the opposing ships did not come into direct contact with each other, but as aircraft carriers fought using their aircraft to bomb opposing carriers. The Japanese lost carriers *Shōkaku and Zuikaku* to American aircraft. The US carrier *Lexington* was lost, although but for 215 killed, the remainder of the 3,000 crew were rescued. *Yorktown*, though damaged, limped back to Pearl Harbour. After urgent and massive repairs, she was back at sea within days. The submarine USS *Nautilus* conducted surveillance. The US lost 543 killed in action. Japan lost 113 killed. It convinced Japan not to attempt an amphibious invasion from Rabaul and forced it to attempt a land battle from Buna south across the Owen Stanley Range, after landing at Lae, along on the famous Kokoda Track. Both sides underestimated the extremely difficult terrain. Heroic delaying action 300 Australian 39th militia at Isurava and the NSW 53rd Militia at Abuari resisted 13,000 well-equipped Japanese, With AIF 2/14th and 2/29th reinforcements, they effectively stopped the Japanese on 10 September 1942. The only partially-trained conscripted and press-ganged militia had fought courageously. A successful action by Australian troops at Milne Bay followed (25 August to 7 September 1942). It was the first time the Japanese were defeated on land. Australia could not allow Port Moresby to be lost. American reinforcements arrived, and by late 1943, the Japanese had been cleared from Papua New Guinea. Over 2,000 Australians were killed or wounded, and 9,300 went down with malaria in the harsh environment. The Japanese lost 12,000 troops.

1942: Battle of Midway 4-7 June. The Japanese plan to take Midway was known to American codebreakers in Hawaii. In one of the most consequential naval battles in history, the submarine the submarines Dive bombers from the *Yorktown*,

Enterprise and *Hornet* sank the carriers *Hiryu, Soryu* and *Kaga*. The fourth carrier *Akagi* was bombed and abandoned, to be sunk later by a Japanese destroyer. USS *Yorktown* was lost to Japanese torpedoes from *I-168*, along with the destroyer *Hammann* which had been supplying auxiliary power to *Yorktown* and broke in two with the loss of 80 lives. USS *Nautilus* was the only submarine in the battle to score a torpedo hit (on the aircraft carrier *Kaga*), but the type 14 torpedo was a dud. Torpedoes dropped at point blank range ran deep and failed to hit. Despite their failure to score any hits and their failure to detonate, American torpedoes did keep Japanese off balance as they prepared to counterstrike. All four Japanese carriers were destroyed by US dive bombers. A total of 307 Americans were killed in action. By contrast, 3,057 Japanese were killed in action. This battle was the second attempt within a year to wipe out the US fleet. In a few hours, the Japanese had lost sea control, 332 aircraft, and 3,000 men, including the bulk of their pilots. The attack on Midway achieved nothing for the Japanese. The result of Midway was the virtual destruction of Japanese naval aviation (248 aircraft and some 3.000 men). The US lost one carrier, one destroyer, and about 300 sailors.

This was the greatest defeat ever suffered by the Imperial Japanese Navy. The Japanese plan to invade Port Moresby had to be shelved. Midway was reinforced as a strategic submarine base to refuel American boats blockading Japan. Japanese media announced a great victory. The Japanese public, and its Army, were not informed of the defeat. Survivors were isolated and not permitted to see their families or friends. ADM Chester Nimitz had rebalanced the war in the Pacific in favour of the Allies.

American submarines made little contribution to the Battle of Midway. CMDR John Murphy in USS *Tambor* had failed to usefully report his sighting of four large ships which were later confirmed as Japanese cruisers. His report caused RADM Spruance to withdraw his ships east from the area. Spruance had Murphy relieved of duty and reassigned to a shore posting for misreporting, general underperformance, and lack of aggression. He was only one of many American submarine commanders treated in this way.

Summer 1942: The Japanese Empire stretched over much of the Southwest Pacific. It had captured Hong Kong, Burma, Malaya, Borneo, The Philippines, and Singapore. By the spring of 1942, Japanese soldiers were in New Guinea and the Solomon Islands. The Japanese were building an airstrip on Guadalcanal. America identified that enemy aircraft operating out of there would threaten the supply line between it and Australia. In June, Washington planned to take the island with an amphibious invasion code named Operation Watchtower. Aircraft carriers *Saratoga*, *Wasp*, *Enterprise*, a battleship, five cruisers, and 16 destroyers were deployed to support the inexperienced Marine Division landings. Douglas Dauntless SBD dive bombers and Grumman F4F Wild cat fighters provided significant carrier-borne capability. The Japanese operated the formidable Mitsubishi Zero. The US Task force commander VADM Robert Lee Ghormley was right to be worried.

1942: Guadalcanal July 1942 - February 1943. The landing was uncoordinated and uncontested, at least initially, on 8 August. Nimitz and MacArthur wanted to take the British territory of Guadalcanal so that it would allow later control of Rabaul, the major Japanese base, and Port Moresby. MacArthur wanted a land operation (Operation Tulsa) commanded by Army, and ADM King argued for naval command as the operation would involve mostly ships in conflict. The conflict between Army and Navy extended to July. The Japanese built an airstrip on Guadalcanal. GEN George Marshall put VADM Robert Ghormley, Commander South Pacific Force, in charge of an offensive on Tulagi. Operation Watchtower was begun. In August, US Marines invaded, supported by air cover, to capture the airstrip. Land forces dug in. the US lost 30 cruisers and destroyers. America lost two aircraft carriers. Japan lost a carrier and two battleships. Some 7,100 Americans were killed in action, 31,000 Japanese were killed in action. After six months of bitter fighting, in February 1943 the Japanese withdrew, leaving 24,000 dead. Two squadrons of US submarines were transferred from Pearl Harbour to Brisbane, with a submarine tender ship USS *Griffin*.

1942: Battle of Savo Island 9 August. This was a disaster for Allied forces, losing four heavy cruisers (including the US cruisers *Astoria, Chicago, Vincennes, Quincy*, and HMAS *Canberra*) and one destroyer. Australia lost 84 killed in action. The US submarine *S44* sank the retiring Japanese cruiser *Kako*. The Japanese submarine *I-2* damaged VADM Frank Jack Fletcher's Flagship aircraft carrier *Saratoga*. In September, Japan continued to reinforce its forces on Guadalcanal by sea with 6,000 fresh troops in "express runs" by fast destroyers, to retake Henderson airfield, which was of strategic value to both sides. By 14 September, the battle was over, and the Americans still held the airstrip. Their forces had grown to 23,000 men.

On 15 September 1942, aircraft carrier USS *Wasp* was lost with 193 men and 45 aircraft, to Japanese torpedoes from I-19. A month later in the battle of Santa Cruz, *Hornet* was lost to aerial attack in October 1942. By late 1942, the US had lost two aircraft carriers, six heavy cruisers, and 14 destroyers. Japan had lost three heavy cruisers and 11 destroyers. Ferocious fighting continued into October. US Marines were withdrawn in December. The US Marines had lost 1,600 men. Japan lost four times as many. By February 1943 all Japanese had been withdrawn. The tide had begun to turn. American submarines had sunk 147 enemy vessels, but only two were major warships. Frequently the notoriously ineffective Mark 14 torpedo failed to detonate, but not before many commanders were erroneously relieved of their commands for lack of success, because of torpedo attack failures.

1943 - Guadalcanal had been taken by the Americans, and submarines were tasked with interdicting Japanese supply ships in reinforcing their garrisons on various islands. Invasions of the islands of Tarawa and Makin followed. By mid-1943, the number of submarines in Pearl Harbour under the command of Admiral Charles Lockwood had grown to 53.

1943: March 5 – The Battle of the Bismark Sea off Port Moresby. This inflicted defeat on a Japanese convoy of 17 ships. RAAF Beaufort torpedo bombers and Beau fighters, with US Bostons and *B-17* Flying Fortresses kept the Japanese from resupplying their garrisons along the New Guinea coast. In June 1943, Macarthur began Operation Cartwheel to isolate the Japanese in Rabaul. The Australian 7th Division were airlifted into Nadzab airstrip near Port Moresby, and moving north caught the enemy in a pincer movement with the 8th Division moving south. The Japanese evacuated Lae and Salamaua.

1944: Saipan 15 June - 9 July. 71,000 American soldiers and marines fought 31,000 Japanese soldiers. USS *Albacore* and USS *Cavalla* damaged and sank two Japanese aircraft carriers, *Hiyō* and *Shokaku*. A total of 3,425 Americans were killed in action, with 657 missing. The Japanese lost 30,000-40,000 killed in action. Some 20,000 civilians were recorded as killed.

1944: June Battle of the Philippine Sea. Some 240 Japanese aircraft shot down for the loss of 29 American aircraft, with

123 Americans killed in action. By contrast, 4,000 Japanese were killed in action. Submarines sank two Japanese aircraft carriers. The conquest of the Marianas followed.

1944: 15 September-27 November. The small island of Peleliu was bombarded by five battleships, seven cruisers and 19 aircraft carriers.[83] One of the Palau Islands, it was then attacked by US Marines as part of Operation Forager. Dug in Japanese forces numbering 11,000 resisted ferociously and ruthlessly. Losses were heavy on both sides. The First Marine division lost 3,946 members in the first week. "For sheer brutality and fatigue, Peleliu surpasses anything yet seen in the Pacific".[84] The 73-day battle cost 9,615 American casualties, and over 10,000 Japanese. The famous Australian official war photographer Damien Parer was killed by a Japanese machine gun during the battle. Though the airstrip was captured by the Marines and used by American aircraft thereafter, there was later controversy over its strategic value and the cost of its capture.[85] Tinian, Saipan and Guam were secure by the summer of 1944.

1944: 23-26 October: Battle of Leyte Gulf in the Philippines. One of the largest naval battles in history, it involved 1,500 American carrier-based and land-based aircraft. 800 seventh Fleet and third Fleet American ships including some Australian ships led by HMAS *Australia* landed troops in the Philippines. *Australia was* attacked by a dive bomber that flew deliberately into her foremast, causing an explosion that killed her captain, Emile Dechaineux and severely wounded CDRE John Collins. Both would later be honoured with submarines named after them. In this large battle, 3,000 Americans and 10,000 Japanese

---

[83] *Unnecessary Hell: The Battle of Peleliu and the Fate of the Pacific Theater.* (warfarehistorynetwork.com) (Accessed: 27 April 2024).
[84] Time Magazine (1944). *Peleliu* October, p. 16.
[85] History Net (n.d.). Battle for Peleliu [online]. Available at: https://www.history-net.com/battle-for-peleliu (Accessed: April 27th 2024).

were killed in action. The force of 140 American submarines effectively cut off Japanese fuel supplies. The Battle of Leyte Gulf opened the way for the battle of Okinawa several months later.

1945:19 February-26 March: Battle for Iwo Jima. The island provided a base for air attacks on the Japanese homeland. USS S-44 sank the battleship *Hiei*. America lost 6,821 killed in action. Japan lost even more, with 18,884 killed in action.

1945 1 April-22 June: Okinawa. The largest amphibious assault of the Pacific theatre and the last major battle in the Pacific. The Gato class USS *Cavalla* (now in a Galveston Museum) sank the aircraft carrier *Shokaku*. With fuel shortages in Japan, the massive 64,000-ton battleship *Yamato* with her nine 18 inch guns was sent on a one-way mission to Okinawa with orders to beach herself and fight until destroyed. She was lost with most of her crew to American carrier-based bombers. US submarines *Sealion* and *Tang* rescued multiple downed American pilots. American losses were 12,520 killed in action, and Japanese losses were 77,166 killed in action.

1945 May 1 Australian 7th Division forces landed on Tarakan island off Borneo, and later Brunei and Balikpapan. ANZAC troops could come home. They had lost 23,000 Australians and 22,000 New Zealanders killed and wounded.

The several paragraphs above summarise the environment in which submarines operated in the Pacific. In the Pacific theatre 1941-45, the Japanese lost 131 submarines with 15,000 personnel killed. America lost 52 submarines, with 3,506 submariners killed in action.

American Submarines in World War II

After World War I, as in Britain, the American authorities were still sceptical of submarines, and strategically conservative about their use. For centuries, the long-established practice of "commerce-raiding" had been seen as justifiable for combatants to attempt to starve the enemy out of the fight by attacking their sources of supply. In his iconic book *The Influence of Sea Power Upon History 1660-1783*,[86] the esteemed American historian and strategist Captain Alfred Thayer Mahan had promoted the influential view that sea power could be used to break the enemy's will and then one could invade the enemy country only if necessary. He had little sympathy for commerce raiding and the use of small fast vessels to conduct war in this way. Fast frigates were discarded in favour of large heavily armoured battleships. This suited the industrial leaders of the time, who saw great profits to be made in building large warships.

The prevailing preference was for the massive battle between major capital ships, shooting big guns at long range. The mighty *Dreadnought* class was thought of as the principle method of projecting power. The submarine was perceived by the admirals as useful in a support role only, to scout ahead of the main fleet and clear the path for cruisers and destroyers and destroyers. However, it gradually became clear that the silent service could achieve superior benefits by stealth and cunning.

The strategy emerged slowly as old antisubmarine prejudices dissolved in the face of evidence that the submarine could become a decisive lethal weapon. The Germans had been among the first to see that the submarine could wreak havoc. In 1916, the U-boats had almost defeated Britain by sinking its

---

[86] Mahan, A T. (1890). *The Influence of Sea Power upon History 1660-1783*, Little Brown and Co, Boston.

supply ships, effectively commerce raiding. Only the belated introduction of the convoy system saved Britain. However, after World War I, this lesson was forgotten, and the *Plan Orange* that prepared for the climactic battle between surface fleets made little reference to submarines.[87]

In the 1930s, Americans still tended to see submarine warfare as vaguely uncivilised. The US had been a signatory to the London Naval conference of 1930 that prohibited unrestricted sinkings. American caution and isolationism took years to recede, and influenced their training of commanders, and their operations. The US produced nine V-boats between 1919 and 1934. These were large 2,700-ton long-range reconnaissance vessels, capable of 18 knots on the surface and 11 knots submerged. One (*SS168*) was given the name *Nautilus*, (the next boat so named in 1954 was nuclear powered). The diesel-powered V-boat in 1931 had the distinction of being fitted with air conditioning, mainly to keep electrical systems dry, which were otherwise prone to failure because of condensation.

The United States had entered the war in December 1941, only after the attack on Pearl Harbour. American Admiral Chester Nimitz broke with tradition when appointed to command the US Pacific fleet on 30 December 1941 by hoisting his flag not on a battleship but on a T-class submarine, USS *Grayling*. It may have signified a prescient shift in thinking from the primacy of the battleship to the submarine as the tip of the spear in maritime conflict. Unfortunately, American boats were then constrained not just by official US doctrine, such as with an order to remain submerged within 500 miles of an enemy airfield, but by their frequently defective Mk 14 torpedos. More malfunctioned than exploded. The Mk 6 magnetic detonator

---

[87] Miller, E. S. (2007). War Plan Orange: *The US Strategy to Defeat Japan (1897-1945)*. Naval Institute Press, Annapolis.

was described by one officer as "ingenious but utterly useless". Gradually, as the technology improved and torpedos became more effective, the American captains were able to act more independently and aggressively.

For all this, the organisational culture in the USN submarine service was inexplicably one of undue caution. American captains were threatened with loss of command if their periscope was even sighted during an exercise. One harmless mistake or deviation from doctrine could scuttle a career. Captains stayed deep and those who were not detected were commended, whether they did anything or not, and those who made attacks on opposing forces and were detected, faced disciplinary action. This inadvertently encouraged defensiveness in strategy and tactics, instead of decisiveness and initiative.

It took the Japanese attack on Pearl Harbour on 7 December 1941 before US Admiral Stark would release the powerful long-range fleet submarine to commence unrestricted submarine warfare. Though 2,403 personnel died, the attack was not as destructive as it might have been. The battleships sunk on 7 December were World War I vintage and obsolete. Had they been at sea they could have been lost and taken 6,000 sailors down. The submarines in port were not touched, and fortunately the American carrier USS *Enterprise* was undergoing an overhaul in Bremerton, Washington. *Saratoga* survived. *Lexington* was undergoing repairs and refit. It was eventually lost in the battle of Midway in June 1942. These carriers would play a major role in later battles. Eventually, after the unrestricted warfare order had been given, American submarine commanders were given wide latitude in operations. In the Atlantic, the Germans had already sunk 400 merchant ships off the American eastern seaboard, exceeding two million tons, with the loss of 5,000 seamen. *Gato*, *Balao*, and *Tench* classes of submarines were deployed in the Atlantic against the U-boats. However, relatively few U-boats were sunk by US vessels in the Atlantic, compared to the British ASW efforts, sinking 37 U-boats.

Too slowly, conservative attitudes in the US Navy and industry caught up with the reality of the situation. An overdue sense of urgency grew. Submarine development in the 1930s had been rapid. As against the smaller distances to be covered in the Atlantic theatre, the Pacific theatre required long range and thus bigger boats, with high reliability. The *Tambor* Class (such as the USS *Trout*) was able to make long range war patrols, with cruise speeds over 20 kts. The P-class had a speed of 19 kts and a range of 10,000 miles. It was the last of the riveted boats. Welded hulls became the norm. In the Pacific in 1941, the cautious but restrained lack of planning and coordination had America's 44 submarines scattered across a vast ocean.

By March 1942, Japan had achieved control of Burma, Malaya, Thailand and Java. The American fleet had dispersed to safer havens in Australian harbours in Freemantle and Brisbane. By April 1942, there were 31 American submarines deployed to Australia, from where they could interdict Japanese supply routes as well as support land operations to its north.

In 1942, the impact of the submarine in naval warfare was still only beginning to be appreciated. Held back by an official strategy to sink only warships, and not transports, the American submarines still sank 180 Japanese merchant ships. Had those ships been available to the Empire, these may have effectively resupplied forces in Guadalcanal, stopping that battle's becoming an American victory that turned the tide of the war. It was mid-1943, the same year that technology and airpower combined to defeat the German U-boat fleet in the Atlantic. By 1943, a new generation of American captains were pushing their boats and crews with innovative and bold tactics.

They used their superior speed of over 20 kts to get ahead of an adversary's convoy and then submerge, awaiting the targets. Radar allowed captains to run and attack on the surface at night. Their SJ search radar could detect ships at five miles range.

Neither Japanese submarines nor their escorts had radar of any kind and so were at a disadvantage. In 1944, more than 600 Japanese ships were sunk. Lost tankers cut off Japan's critical oil supply. Comprehending the loss of life and of ships strains the imagination. Japan had been isolated from her sources of energy and raw materials. Though her eventual defeat was inevitable, Japan remained a tenacious enemy.

1942-45   American Submarines in Australia

The victories in the south-west Pacific by the Imperial Japanese forces forced a strategic repositioning of American submarines from their base in Cavite in the Philippines to Bataan, Java, Hawaii, and then to Australia. Fremantle and Brisbane were used, to support a major submarine offensive. Brisbane offered suitability of location, close enough to allow boats maintained there to patrol waters around New Guinea, yet far enough away to be out of range of Japanese bombers operating out of New Guinea and Rabaul.

Brisbane also had a large dry dock. Headquartered in Fremantle, the Commander Submarines Southwest Pacific was CAPT Charles A. Lockwood, an experienced submariner with 18 years' service in boats. Lockwood arrived in May 1942, and relieved CAPT Wilkes, and then immediately RADM Parnell as Commander Allied Forces, with the rank of RADM. He immediately began leasing buildings for engineering maintenance and rest camps for returning submarine crews who were exhausted from their 70-day patrols. Lockwood's deputy was CDRE John Collins RAN. Decades later in the 1990s, the lead submarine of the Australian Submarine service and the class would honour him and take his name.

In 1942, the American surface units repositioned to Fremantle, Australia, followed by the old S-class submarines. There were 20 fleet submarines in Fremantle, and the 11 *S*-class boats in Brisbane. The Brisbane squadron was commanded by Captain Ralph Waldo Christie, USN. These 11 arrived alongside in the Brisbane River at the fashionable suburb of New Farm, with their invaluable submarine tender USS *Griffin* on 15 April 1942. Within days, four were on patrol. One, *S44*, commanded by Lieutenant Commander "Dinty" Moore USN became the first US submarine *S-44* to sink a major enemy warship when it torpedoed the heavy cruiser *Kako* off Kavieng, New Britain, on 10 August 1942. Lockwood's commanders were beset by the enduring problem of faulty torpedoes, either running deep under enemy hulls, exploding too early, or not exploding at all after impact. "In the Bureau of Ordnance it was believed that these stories from submarine captains were merely alibis for misses." [88] RADM Lockwood took the initiative and ran test firings into a fishing net to prove to American authorities that the torpedoes were a serious detriment to crew morale. The British and German submariners had abandoned the magnetic detonator early in the war, but to the frustration of Lockwood and his captains, the USN clung stubbornly to the old ineffective design. To extend the range of his boats, Lockwood established a refuelling base in Exmouth Gulf. It was a short short-lived experiment, until with Japanese bombers operating from Ambon against Darwin, it was thought prudent to consolidate US submarines in Brisbane which quickly became a major base for American boats.

---

[88] Lockwood, C. A. (2008). *Sink 'Em All*, Middletown, Delaware, p. 12.

Over a three-year period, 89 submarines were dry-docked for repairs in Brisbane, supported by submarine tenders USS *Griffin, Sperry* and *Fulton*. They proceeded on war patrols and attacked Japanese merchant ships in the Indian and Pacific oceans. The *S*-class were gradually replaced by the radar-equipped fleet submarines, with their greater speed, range, and payload of torpedoes. RADM Lockwood had studied the wolf pack strategy of German Admiral Karl Dönitz, and adapted it for the American boats that were interdicting the Japanese convoys. The Japanese convoys were smaller than those used in the Atlantic, with 80 or more ships being attacked by German wolf packs of 15 or 20 U-boats. Lockwood reasoned that Japanese convoys averaging 10-15 ships needed only smaller wolf packs to attack them. Still, he was critical of the cost in lives and materiel imposed by the shortage of fleet submarines to attack Japanese shipping off Indochina: "100 instead of the 39 we had would have shortened the war by perhaps six months, saving billions of dollars and thousands of American lives".[89]

The Battle of the Coral Sea in May 1942 turned back the Japanese force, but at the cost of the aircraft carrier USS *Lexington* off the north Queensland coast. Only a month later, in June 1942 the Battle of Midway was a major victory for the Americans, destroying the core of the Japanese carrier force. On 31 July 1942 Admiral King ordered 82 ships and 19,000 marines to attack Guadalcanal and Tulagi. Soon after, on 9 August 1942, the Battle of Savo Island in the Solomons showed the Japanese under Admiral Mikawa were a force to be reckoned with, in a night attack that resulted in the sinking of three cruisers: one Australian (HMAS *Canberra*) and three American cruisers (USS *Quincy, Vincennes* and *Astoria*). It was the Allies' worst naval defeat of the war, with the loss of

---

[89] Lockwood, C. A. (2017). *Sink 'Em All: Submarine Warfare in the Pacific*, Rocky Mountain Textbooks, Middletown, DE, p. 22.

1,077 sailors. Flawed intelligence and poor communication from American submarine *S-38* reporting the position of the Japanese fleet were held as contributing, along with delayed communications from a RAAF Hudson reconnaissance aircraft that had spotted the Japanese ships.

Late in 1942, American submarines seized the initiative. One commander in particular became famous. The USS *Wahoo*, based in Brisbane under its legendary CO Dudley W. "Mush" Morton, had been particularly effective in the battle of the Coral Sea. As a submarine commander, he was reputed to be "unorthodox but deadly". He was the first captain to sink an entire convoy. At one point the *Wahoo* sank eight cargo ships and one transport in 10 days. His tactics were to take his submarine in close to his target, often on the surface, rather than to mount a sonar-directed attack from a safe distance. An aggressive commander, and a charismatic and relaxed leader, Morton captained *Wahoo* to sink 19 ships in the nine months before he was lost when she went down with all hands, off Japan, after sinking a final four ships.[90]

One patrol from Brisbane became especially noted: Controversially, on 26 January 1943, Morton was ruthless in ordering the shooting with his deck gun of reputedly 7,000 survivors of a sinking freighter, the *Buyo Maru*, as they floated in crowded lifeboats and in clusters in life jackets. Morton argued that they were the hated enemy, who if allowed to live would go on to New Guinea later to kill Americans.[91] "His superior officer's endorsement of his actions tacitly approved his actions.

---

[90] Jones, D and Nunan, P. (2005). *US Subs Down Under, Brisbane 1942-45*, US Naval Institute Press, Annapolis.
[91] Padfield, P. (1995). *War Beneath the Sea: Submarine conflict 1939-1945*, Random House, London, p. 343.

However, few US captains followed Morton's example," [92] Lockwood wrote that submarines approaching survivors were often met by rifle and machine gun fire, and they tenaciously refused to be rescued.[93] The submarine's defensive response was seen as regrettable but inevitable. The episode continues to ignite ethical debate in submarine ranks. The massacre was neither reported nor questioned in staff endorsement of his report. Morton was awarded the Navy Cross, making a total of four Navy Crosses recognising his service. Morton's trusted XO was Richard O'Kane, who was said to be a genius at estimating a target's speed and angle on the bow.[94] Though the normal procedure was that only the captain used the periscope, Morton trusted O'Kane to use the periscope, to allow Morton to stay in overall charge of the attack. O'Kane later became famous by later writing a book about Morton.[95] O'Kane went on to command his own submarine, USS *Tang,* and was credited with sinking 31 ships.[96] His fifth patrol ended when his 24th torpedo circled back and sent the *Tang* to the bottom. O'Kane survived and was captured. He is acknowledged as one of America's most successful submarine Commanders, along with CMDR Gene Fluckey.

Individual aggression and competitiveness within the submarine community contributed to the culture of American submarine commanders' behaviour. Autonomy in decision making featured in countless acts of individual bravery and daring. This was so, whether attacking enemy ships, inserting

---

[92] Jones, D and Nunan, P. (2005). *US Subs Down Under, Brisbane 1942-45*, US Naval Institute Press, Annapolis, p. 104.

[93] Lockwood, C. A. (2008). *Sink 'Em All*, Middletown, DE, p. 42.

[94] Sturma, M. (2006). *Death at a Distance: The Loss of the Legendary USS Harder*, Naval Institute Press, Annapolis, p. 18.

[95] O'Kane, R. H. (1998*). Wahoo: The Patrols of America's Most Famous WWII Submarine*, Ballantine Books, New York.

[96] O'Kane, R. H. (1977). *Clear the Bridge: The War Patrols of the USS Tang*. Presidio Press. New York.

special forces in clandestine operations, supporting the very courageous Australian Coastwatchers behind the enemy lines, or rescuing downed fliers.[97] Another American submarine based in Brisbane was the USS *Growler* (*SS-215*), commanded by Lieutenant Commander Howard Gilmore USN. In an action in February 1943, Gilmore was wounded by enemy machine gun fire when he was on his bridge after his boat collided head on at 17 knots with the ship *Hayasaki* which was attempting to ram him. Two of his crew were killed and two wounded lookouts were pulled back inside the pressure hull. Eighteen feet of *Growler*'s bow was bent at right angles to port. Gilmore ordered his XO to dive the boat and escape, choosing to sacrifice himself. In the tradition of the navy, he was the last to leave the bridge. Gilmore's famous last words were "Take her down!" When the *Growler* resurfaced, there was no sign of the enemy, or of the submarine's wounded captain, presumably killed by small arms fire. His XO, LCDR Arnold (later Captain) Arnold Shea took the badly damaged submarine on a slow 10-day transit back to Brisbane for repairs. Gilmore was posthumously awarded the US Congressional Medal of Honor, the first to be awarded to a submariner.[98] On 8 November 1944, on patrol in the South China Sea, *Growler* was lost with all hands.

By war's end, Brisbane-based submarines had sunk 117 enemy ships, including three heavy and two light cruisers. With a combined tonnage of 115,000 tons. Of the Brisbane-based submarines, 11 were lost to enemy action. There was already an exclusivity to this elite group of naval officers who commanded submarines. Well-known commanders Chester Nimitz Jnr, John McCain Jnr., Manning Kimmel, and Edward Spruance

---

[97] Lee, B. (2019). *Right Man, Right Place, Worst Time: Commander Eric Feldt, His Life and His Coastwatchers*, Boolarong Press, Brisbane.

[98] Jones, D and Nunan, P. (2005). *US Subs Down Under, Brisbane 1942-45*, US Naval Institute Press, Annapolis.

were among those who were the sons of navy admirals. By all accounts, American submarine captains were of mixed quality. In 1942, nearly a third of the 135 skippers serving in the Pacific were relieved of their commands, mainly for poor performance and "lack of aggression".[99]

Paradoxically, the USN penalised trainee commanders if they demonstrated initiative by making a surface rather than deep attack with sonar. Those commanders who were successful were by 1942 more innovative and offensive, and showed greater aggression. Everyone in the boat needed to know everyone else's job. One mistake could lose all 80 their lives. Training was very thorough, and a posting to a new boat meant having to requalify. Conditions were arduous. It took five men to surface or dive the boat, and 20 to operate it, all working in perfect interdependent coordination. For this, submariners were paid twice the rate of surface crews, to reward their willingness to take on the demands and the risks of submarine service.

On 1 July 1942, USS *Sturgeon* sank the Japanese freighter *Montevideo Maru*. Over 1,000 died, including 208 civilians. Of the 1,450 prisoners on board the *Montevideo Maru* lost, 979 men and boys were Australian, making it Australia's worst maritime disaster. The wreck was found in 2023, at a depth of 4,000 metres. There was still a 24 percent casualty rate for American boats. By contrast, American submarines were particularly effective against Japanese merchant vessels. The results were 1,178 merchant ships and 214 naval ships sunk, amounting to 5.25 million tonnes. The number of American submarines grew quickly. The US Navy commissioned 65 submarines in 1943 alone. American submarines in 1943 effectively strangled the enemy trade, preventing resupply to its ground forces in

---

[99] Sturma, M. (2006). *Death at a Distance: The Loss of the Legendary USS Harder*, Naval Institute Press, Annapolis, p. 18.

Guadalcanal. The battle became a war of attrition. The *Gato* class was succeeded by the *Balao* and *Tench* classes, with thicker hulls and able to dive to 400 and 600 feet, against the 300 feet for the *Gato* class. These displaced 2,415 tons and could achieve 20.25 knots surfaced and 8.75 knots submerged. Other developments in technology brought improvements in effectiveness and safety. Better SJ radar gave better protection from air attack by giving range and bearing of enemy aircraft and ships. The Mark 14 was replaced by the Mark 18 electric torpedo, which did not leave a telltale track of bubbles that revealed the submarine's position to ASW lookouts. With better torpedoes in 1943, the number of Japanese ships sunk increased to 333, twice that of the previous year. Wolf packs became more common for commerce raiding north of Luzon. Submarine tenders supported boats with provisions and repairs from advanced bases such as at Milne Bay in New Guinea, closer to operational areas. Boats were equipped with 5-inch deck guns and 40-mm anti-aircraft Bofor guns. The preference was to stay on the surface as much as possible to maximise speed and manoeuvrability, and to run the diesels to charge batteries, but the submarines could be dived within a minute if required to avoid attack by aircraft or surface ships. With a high operational tempo, improvement followed with tactical innovations, and 1943 was a better year, with double the number of sinkings in operations more aligned with strategy. Of the 100 US boats in the Pacific, 60 were based in Pearl Harbour and 40 in Australia.

In 1943, the American submarines were being used for different missions, and only some had the traditional single boat heading off on a war patrol to sink enemy ships. Other missions had the *Gato* and *Balao* class boats carrying supplies of food and ammunition, and even gasoline to troops already ashore. Others were sent to rescue troops and downed fliers, and others again transporting special forces to contested islands. This meant that boats designed to carry 55 crew might have up to 200 people packed on board. Cramped and uncomfortable, they made for dangerously low oxygen levels as the carbon dioxide absorbent became exhausted. The level would rise to the limit of 3 percent. The submarine then had to surface sufficiently to get the air induction valve out of the water to run the diesels and recharge the batteries, but also to "blow out" the boat with fresh air for the humans. In an environment of enemy ASW ships and aircraft, this was not always a safe manoeuvre.

On 17-18 February 1944, the powerful Japanese garrison on the island of Truk was destroyed, and the American attacks following on the Mariana islands of Saipan, Guam and Tinian were supported by submarines. In the Battle of the Philippines in 1944, known as the "The Great Marianas Turkey Shoot" because of the 250 Japanese aircraft so easily shot down, as the US had air superiority. Two Japanese aircraft carriers IJN *Taiho*, and IJN *Shokaku* were sunk by American submarines, permanently crippling Japanese aviation. The effect on the Japanese war effort was catastrophic. In July 1944 alone, American submarines accounted for 100 sinkings of enemy ships, representing many thousands of tons of Japanese shipping.

In September 1944, American submarines rescued Australian and British prisoners of war who were being shipped back to Japan, having been captured at Singapore and used for two years as slave labour to build the infamous Burma railway. When the two freighters were sunk by USS *Sealion*, Japanese vessels picked up their own sailors but left Allied survivors to die. The attacking American captain was not to know these prisoners of war were crammed into the holds of the ships he had just sank. One escort was the *Rakuyo,* which sank slowly, giving the Japanese crew time to launch their lifeboats, and survive. They kept the 1,350 Australian and English POWs at gunpoint and prevented their rescue. Some POWs found rafts to keep them afloat for five days until US submarines *Sealion*, *Pampanito*, *Queenfish*, and *Barb* arrived. Eventually 159 men were rescued. By this time, they were in very poor condition and many died pointlessly. It was a tragic incident. RADM Lockwood lamented: "Had the Japanese so desired, diplomatic arrangements could have been made to permit transfers in the name of humanity. The barbarous unconcern of our enemy for the lives of prisoners is now so well known that his failure to make any such attempt is not surprising."[100] To the Japanese warrior code, to be captured was dishonourable, and death was preferable to dishonour. It was an ethic applied to both their own troops, and to Allied POWs.

The captain of one of the rescuing submarines, *S220* (USS *Barb*, was to become famous. CMDR (Later Rear Admiral) Eugene B. Fluckey (nicknamed "Lucky Fluckey") sank more Japanese ships in 1944-45 than any other American captain (17, including the aircraft carrier *Unyo*, with six ships sunk in one day). Notably, he brought all his crew home from five war patrols with no loss of life or serious injury.[101] However, by mid-1945, few targets were presenting themselves in the *Barb*'s allocated station in the Sea of Okhotsk, just outside La Perouse Strait. Fluckey took his submarine closer to the Japanese island of Karafuto. He observed freight trains moving along a track that hugged the coast. He reasoned that if he could land a demolition squad ashore at night to lay a 55lb TNT charge on the track, he could not only damage what he saw to be a

---

[100] Lockwood, C. A. (1984). *Sink 'Em All:Submarine Warfare in the Pacific*, The Rocket Press, Middletown, Delaware, p. 146.

[101] Fluckey, E. B. (1992). *Thunder Below!* University of Illinois Press, Urbana and Chicago.

munitions train but could also disrupt rail traffic and force the Japanese to move their war materials by sea, where he would be waiting to attack them. He called for unmarried volunteers in his crew and put ashore eight sailors with explosives to place on the rail lines. The large explosion blew the locomotive into the air.

Fluckey has the distinction of commanding the first and last Americans to conduct operations on the Japanese home islands, and of "sinking" the train, that rolled down the slope into the sea. *Barb*'s victory pennant has the unlikely symbol image of a railway steam engine among other images representing ships sunk. Fluckey's four Navy Crosses and Medal of Honour were undoubtedly deserved. He denied luck was involved in this unique record and credited his successes to his careful meticulous planning and calculation. Certainly, he lived up to his nickname, but more particularly he was renowned for his strategic and operational thinking about how submarines should be used (as torpedo boats to attack rather than the prevailing doctrine of waiting to ambush), and tactical skill in targeting enemy vessels. He was humble, decisive, and cautious, yet flamboyant. President F. D. Roosevelt asked for all his war reports after his patrols to be copied to him personally. Eugene Fluckey is remembered as an unusual but successful submarine captain. His attention to planning became a model to many other commanding officers. Fluckey was by any measure a remarkable submariner. Fluckey was promoted RADM by Eisenhower in 1960 and would later retire from active duty aged 69. He died at the age of 93, in 2007.

The American Submarine Blockade of Japan

By 1944, America had 100 boats in the Pacific. In the October 1944 Battle of Leyte Gulf, 30 submarines participated, sinking six enemy ships including cruisers - *Atago, Takao, Maya,* and *Aoba*. Four Japanese carriers were sunk. The submarine force had played a key role in the victory. In 1944 alone, American submarines sank one battleship, seven aircraft carriers, two heavy cruisers, seven light cruisers, 30 destroyers and seven submarines, with numerous other vessels sunk or damaged beyond repair. By April 1945, only four Japanese attack submarines were still operational, and had minimal effect as mules, blockade runners supplying the harassed army. "By the end of 1944, American submarines had sunk five million tons of Japanese shipping, crippling her combat resupply capability and starving her industries of raw materials."[102] There were few enemy ships left afloat, and only four submarines. As the air war intensified, American submarines were tasked with "lifeguard duty" and rescued more than 50 downed aviators. In April 1945, there were 145 boats operating out of the captured island of Iwo Jima. By this time, the USN had reduced the Japanese merchant to near obliteration, virtually isolating the country. The Japanese merchant fleet had been decimated by submarines. Submarines were based in Guam and Subic Bay in the Philippines. Lifeguard duty was common, with coordinates of carefully positioned submarines were given to *B-29* crews in case they needed to ditch. Over 500 downed airmen were rescued by American submarines.

Though there is a common belief that World War II in the Pacific was ended by the atomic bombs dropped on Hiroshima and Nagasaki in 1945, it has been argued that the Japanese empire

---

[102] Frame, T. (1992). *Pacific Partners: A History of Australian American Naval Relations*, Hodder & Stoughton, Rydalmere, p. 59.

had already been virtually strangled by the American submarine blockade around it, cutting off its supplies. Japan had lost seven aircraft carriers, one battleship, two heavy cruisers, seven light cruisers, 30 destroyers, and seven submarines.

Whether the Japanese would have surrendered without the demonstration of destruction by the atomic bombs is still a matter of debate. The argument runs that the American fleet of submarines had effectively destroyed all Japanese tankers and merchantmen, such that the use of the atomic bombs might not have been necessary: Japan's economy was already on the point of collapse. The contrary view was that Japan showed no likelihood of surrendering, and an American invasion of Japan to end the war would have needlessly resulted in hundreds of thousands of casualties on both sides. In overview of the naval conflict, less than two percent of American naval personnel had sunk 65 percent of the enemy ships sunk. It was the American submarine force that made the major contribution to the allied effort in the Pacific theatre. Submarines are rightly described as the most significant ships in World War II. The American submarine force suffered the loss of 52 of 336 submarines, and 3,500 men who served in them. In World War II, submarines and submariners were extremely important for the outcome, and their legacy lives on. The successful submarine captains were required to be stealthy yet prepared to take risks in attack. Training for American commanders was paradoxically conservative. Allowing their periscope to be detected could spell the end of command. This led to excessive reliance on passive sensors and caution in attack. Significantly, about half of all US commanders were relieved of their commands in the first eighteen months of the Pacific war. Partly, responsibility for this lay with training in ASW in combination only with friendly forces, and the poor performance of torpedoes. Eventually, in World War II, American captains were increasingly hungry for victory and drove their submarines and crews hard to achieve remarkable success. The then CMDR Eugene Fluckey, arguably the best of the submariners, commented on the ideal age for commanders: "At the time of the Pearl Harbour attack, the average age of sub skippers was 42. Ten percent produced good results; 90 per cent were too cautious, probably due to restricted training in peacetime- which prohibited attacks on merchant ships – and faulty torpedoes. The age group did not cut the mustard, so maximum age was lowered to 35, with entry as low as 30. The British had identical trouble and lowered their maximum age to 36. The *kriegsmarine* had the same problem and dropped its maximum age to 33 years".[103]

On reflection, in critical circumstances, leadership can demand service and competence above and beyond the call of duty. Success, as in many areas of life, assumes technical competence as a threshold variable. Similarly, high performance usually goes beyond mere technical ability. Factors of individual personality, in combination with organisational culture, including attitudes to risk and reward, appear to be the key differentiator of the successful leader. This is a risk that leaders take - that their efforts may one day be seen to have saved a civilisation, giving meaning and consequence to their sacrifice. Their success depended on teamwork and professionalism, notably in the crews of submarines.

The End of World War II

On 16 December 1944, Hitler's last gamble was a surprise attack with 200,000 troops against what became 500,000 Allied troops through the forest of the Ardennes to capture

---

[103] Fluckey, E.B. (1992). *Thunder Below!* University of Chicago Press, Urbane and Chicago. p.153.

Antwerp, resulting in the Battle of the Bulge. His plan relied on capturing Allied fuel dumps. In 1945 American forces advanced beyond the Rhine into Germany. By January 1945, the German offensive had failed. By April, the Red Army raced to take Berlin, with now well-known long-term consequences. The war in Europe came to an end in June with the suicide of Hitler and the unconditional surrender of Germany on 8 May 1945, Victory in Europe was declared.

The war in the Pacific was to run another fourth months, costing thousands more lives on both sides. On 9 March 1945, 300 *B-29* Superfortress long range bombers from Tinian in the Marianas had unleashed tons of incendiary bombs in the most destructive bombing raid in history. Tokyo's industrial heart was in flames in a massive firestorm. The ashes from the acres of fires fell like black snow. Still, the Japanese under General Tojo refused to lay down their arms. Hirohito remained silent. Japan stubbornly refused to accept the humiliation of defeat and fought on, knowing it would lose. It maintained a vain delusion.

Faced with massive privation and staggering losses of its warriors, the Japanese population had to question the lies they were being told by their naval and military leaders. In the Pacific theatre, the Japanese economy was effectively stymied by American submarines. The Empire's navy was at the bottom of the sea. Its soldiers had been outfought by American and Australian soldiers. Its airforce had been destroyed by Allied air power and its homeland bombed into starvation. It had no petrol, no electricity, and no rice. It had lost the Philippines, Borneo, Burma, Iwo Jima and Okinawa, but still occupied Indochina and Manchuria. Even though Stalin had a non-aggression pact with Japan, Russia was moving 1.5 million troops east in preparation to invade Japan on 15 August, for

Russia to reclaim the islands of Kuril and Sakhalin. As in Europe, Russia evidenced a bite-and-hold strategy, expecting to retain territory where it had its troops. It was hurrying to invade before America could do so. Russia declared war on Japan on 8 August to ensure it would acquire territory after the inevitable defeat.

In 1945, American troops continued to suffer heavy losses on the ground, pressuring President Truman to bring the war to an end. America was faced with an agonising decision: To invade Japan and lose 400,000 more troops in so doing, and to kill hundreds of thousands of Japanese civilians, virtually flattening the nation, or to use its weapon of mass destruction against one or two cities to break Japanese intransigence and bring the war to an end. On 31 July and reluctantly, President Truman chose the latter and gave the order to drop bombs on Hiroshima on 6 August and Nagasaki on 9 August. Within days, Stalin declared war on Japan and the Red Army invaded Manchuria. The *B-29 Enola Gay*, named after its pilot's wife, became famous. Justified tactically, the atomic bombs were also argued as justified politically for post-war stability, to demonstrate to Stalin that America possessed such a weapon. Air power had eventually brought Japan to its senses on 9 August Hirohito finally broke his silence, speaking on radio to his people for the first time ever, with the memorable understatement: "The war situation has developed not necessarily to Japan's advantage". Japan finally surrendered unconditionally to the USA. World War II was ended. On 15 August 1945, the Americans declared VJ Day (Victory over Japan). Australia acknowledges VJ Day as VP Day, for "Victory in the Pacific". Allied sinkings of enemy submarines in the Pacific theatre of World War II totalled 30, recognised as follows:[104]

---

[104] Lockwood, C. A. (2008). *Sink 'Em All*, the Rocket Press, Middletown, Delaware, p. 233.

US submarines accounted for 23 Japanese submarines and 2 German U-boats.

Netherlands submarines accounted for 1 German U-boat.

British Submarines accounted for 2 Japanese submarines and 2 German U-boats.

In summary, in the European theatre, by 1943, the Royal Navy and airpower had defeated the U-boat. Germany was losing 15 each month. By 1945, British and American airpower had shot the Luftwaffe out of the sky. Allied armies had reduced Germany to ruins. Japan had lost three million people, about 300,000 in Hiroshima and Nagasaki, but the land mass of Japan was not invaded. The Japanese armed forces had become extremely efficient in combat and had killed nine people for every person they lost. After the war, Japan prospered under a benign American occupation. Italy was not occupied and emerged from the war relatively unscathed, losing 1.1 million. There were no war crimes trials or expensive reparations. German soldiers killed seven enemy for every one of its own that it lost. Germany had spent lavishly on battleships such as the *Bismark* and *Tirpitz*. *Bismark* sank only two ships (HMS *Hood* and *Prince of Wales*) before being sunk herself after being at sea only 10 days. A result of Hitler's egotism, the *Tirpitz* was the most expensive ship Germany ever built. Ironically, she fired only one salvo during the entire war. The expenditure to build *Tirpitz* would have funded 30 U-boats. After the war, Germany was occupied by Allied forces and split into East and West. In the years following, Britain, France and America shared Berlin with the Soviets until reunification of East and West Germany and the destruction of the Berlin Wall in 1989.

In finally overwhelming Germany with its 90 million people, Russia with a population of over 200 million had lost 27 million people, but Eastern Europe was by then communist, and it had taken over Crimea and the Ukraine. It kept the territory it stole from Finland and kept the Baltic states. It got Eastern Europe as a buffer zone. Yet, for all its suffering, the Soviet Union ended the war in an economically stronger position than when it entered it. Britain was the only country that fought from the first day until the last day of the war and fought Nazi Germany by itself for over a year. It out-produced Germany in every category of war materiel except for tanks. It emerged from the war victorious but economically battered. It nationalised its coal, steel and power, becoming less powerful than countries it fought. The war over, it quickly reduced its defence spending. America had lost 425,000 troops out of 12.1 million enlisted, relatively light casualties for a country of the size. Its industrial capacity was overwhelming and pivotal. It had built 145 aircraft carriers and ended the war with 100 submarines on order. It had built one B24 bomber every hour and a liberty ship every three days. After the war it entered into a series of treaties that balanced opposing force in Europe. The goal for Europe appeared to be to keep Russia out, America in, and Germany down.

Early in the war, Germany and Japan had convinced themselves that their victories over unprepared smaller countries in the 1930s meant they were major world powers. They made the mistake of going to war with the world's three most powerful nations - Britain, Russia and the USA, and they lost. Because of American isolationism, British appeasement, and Russian collaboration with the Germans, it took the lives of 65 million people in the most lethal war in human history to settle the question of who were the strongest nations.[105] As the graffiti slogan has it: "War doesn't show who is right, only who is left." The submarine was shown to be a formidable weapon

---

[105] Hanson, V. D. (2020). *The Second World Wars*. Basic Books, New York.

for Germany, Britain and America. The Allied victory over the German U-boat in the battle of the Atlantic and the American submarine victory in blockading Japan in the Pacific theatre were decisive for World War II. This was the legacy left to submariners and force planners in the current era.

4

The Cold War (1945-90) and Post-Cold War

Based on the German *Type XXI,* the Americans built the *Guppy* class and in 1949 the Soviets detonated their first nuclear bomb. The Soviets built the Project 613 *Whiskey* class. In the 1950s, the British built eight T-class boats. This type had an endurance of 11,000 miles and a submerged speed of 15 knots. Primitive by the standards of today, and without air conditioning, serving for the 61 crew in these submarines was arduous. They were designed for 42-day patrols. They sailed alone, able to receive radio signals but not to transmit. High temperatures in the engine room made life for the crew very uncomfortable. Over a period of 15-20 hours, the air in the submarine became gradually fouled in spite of absorbent chemicals to reduce the build-up of exhaled carbon dioxide. The use of the 14-inch diameter "snorting" mast fed air to the diesels and the interior of the boat, as well as exhausting gases below the surface. The T-class was replaced by the *Porpoise* class attack submarines, delivered between 1958 and 1961. The *Oberon* class followed. Eight of these were destined for the Royal Australian Navy, with six 21-inch torpedo tubes for their 30 weapons carried. These boats were air-conditioned, designed for long endurance.

With diesel engines, they still needed to snort each day. The American *Tang* Class became influential in defence thinking in the 1950s and were based in part on captured World War II German designs, such as the *Type XXI*.

Diesel electric submarines enjoyed popularity because of their relatively low cost to build, their ability to operate quietly at low speed in shallow water, and their ready supportability. The limited capacity of batteries meant that the diesel-powered submarine had to spend most of its time on or near the surface, running its air-breathing engines, and diving only to attack or evade attack.

Nuclear power enters the Submarine Arena

The alternative form of propulsion to diesel electric is the nuclear reactor, famously powering the first American nuclear boat, the *Nautilus*, in 1954. This ushered in a new era in propulsion and capability. The technological breakthrough that came with the advent of nuclear power was principally associated with passed-over USN captain but eventually Vice-Admiral Hyman G. Rickover. He became the Chief of the Naval Reactors Branch of the Atomic Energy Commission, and a personal legend in nuclear submarine history. The first nuclear-powered submarine, the USS *Nautilus,* displacing nearly 4,000 tons, was launched in 1954. It has six torpedo tubes, air conditioning, and to add to crew morale, a juke box and an ice-cream machine, in anticipation of long periods submerged. The Electric Boat Company (now a subsidiary of General Dynamics) built the USS *Nautilus* in 1954, in Groton, Connecticut. It is still proudly on display alongside there, with an enthusiastic young naval crew maintaining it, and welcoming visitors. It is a significant artefact in submarine history and heritage and gives an insight into nuclear submarines to a public not normally able to board current submarines.

The submarine *Nautilus* was twice the displacement of the World War II *Gato* Class and had six torpedo tubes in the bow. *Nautilus* broke records for endurance and speed with 23 knots submerged and was the first of the many nuclear submarines operated by the USN. With nuclear power on tap, speeds of some 40 knots were attained even by early nuclear boats. However, the boat's own noise precluded effective use of sonar at speeds above 7 kts. In 1958, the Polaris missile was fitted into a Skipjack hull, which became America's first ballistic submarine as USS *George Washington*, with 16 Polaris missiles in the category of boats known as SSBN. These are known colloquially as "boomers" because early boats were very noisy. The SSBN is distinguished from the SSN, the attack submarine, whose role is to hunt other submarines and surface ships. Ballistic missiles with nuclear warheads were developed.

Also in 1958, the Soviet Union also launched a nuclear-powered submarine. By 1967, it had produced the first of its *Yankee* class boats, with 16 missiles with a range of 1600 miles. The first Soviet nuclear boats were the *November* and *Echo* class, designed to sink surface ships. The *Whiskey* class appeared, and the largest class built was the *Typhoon* class displacing 48,000 tons (larger than many World War II battleships). It carried 52 ballistic missiles. Incredibly, it even had an internal swimming pool for the crew. Only one example remains, and is alongside, reputedly now decommissioned, as a training asset. In 1960, USS *Triton* circumnavigated submerged the world nonstop in 60 days. The technology developed quickly. The Soviets built the *Alfa* class in the 1970s. These were large (length 81 metres, displacing 2,845 tonnes) and at 12 kts surfaced and 41 kts submerged, very fast nuclear boats. They could launch conventional or nuclear torpedoes. The *Kilo* class appeared in the 1980s, diesel-powered yet capable of 24 knots. China acquired several of these, in addition to its *Han* class nuclear submarines, in the 1970s.

Sea Denial and Sea Control

Australia cannot match the size of China's defence forces or in particular its navy. Australian strategy must by its nature be asymmetric in capability and deterrent in effect, with the aim of undermining any adversary's will and decision making. The strategy of sea denial is based on the submarine's stealth, reach and lethality, and make it potentially highly effective in deterrence against a superior enemy, preventing it from gaining sea control. One former CN emphasised the operational value of submarines' ability to conduct sea denial: "The presence of a submarine completely changes the dynamics of a naval operation. The threat of a no-notice attack can keep ships or other submarines in harbour or unable to go where they desire."[106] As detailed in chapter three, the history of the submarine in both World Wars demonstrated the disproportionate impact that submarines can bring to a conflict, in sinking warships and in requiring extensive ASW resources to counter them. The alternative strategy of sea control is more comprehensive and requires far greater investment of forces. In 1940, Germany had only two battleships against Britain's 15. The *kriegsmarine* pursued an asymmetric strategy of sea denial without needing sea control, that almost defeated Britain in 1940-43.[107] A similar strategy was followed by the Soviet Union in the cold war, building 300 *Whiskey* class diesel-electric submarines and threatening North Atlantic Sea lines of communication. Between 1958 and 1966, the Soviets built some 280 attack submarines,

---

[106] Shackleton, D. (1922). The Hunter Frigate: An assessment. *Strategy*, April. Australian Strategic Policy Institute, Canberra, p. 13.

[107] See Chapter 3.

many of them nuclear-powered and armed, with antiship cruise missiles to counter the massively powerful American aircraft carriers. The Soviets had the largest submarine force in the world. Between 1945 and 1991 the Soviets built over 200 submarines.

For comparison, American and Soviet submarines built between 1945-1991 were as follows:

	USSR	USA
Diesel	492	212
Nuclear	235	169

Soviet strategy was effectively sea denial, against NATO forces, with the Oscar II class cruise missile submarine. In the Cold War in the 1960s (1963-83), the U.S. and her allies (notably Britain and France) engaged in a quiet way by stealth, with hundreds of submarines operating in the Atlantic alone. For most of the cold war, the *Sturgeon* class (SSN) served from the 1960s until 2004, when they were replaced by the *Los Angeles*, *Seawolf* and *Virginia* class boats. The British launched the *Astute* class of attack submarines in 2007.

The Cold War faded with Soviet submarines' becoming progressively obsolete, British submarines becoming far fewer in number, and tasked with strategic deterrence, while small nations began acquiring numbers of diesel-powered submarines. Other than in the US, the leadership of submarine forces changed its requirements from heroic attacking to patient surveillance and special operations. Only the US, the UK, France, Russia and China maintained nuclear-powered and nuclear-armed submarines. The US, India, Russia and China are now building larger fleets. The smallest class of nuclear submarines is the *Rubis* class, built for the French Navy. In 1982, the *Churchill* class HMS *Conqueror* torpedoed the aging

Argentinian and former American cruiser *General Belgrano* during the Falklands War in 1982. This was the first ship sunk in conflict by a nuclear-armed submarine. The Argentinian navy kept its fleet in harbour. This one sinking swung the balance of seapower to the British. After that war, and reflecting its relative economic decline, the UK reduced its defence expenditure as a proportion of its GDP and maintained only a modest capability that saw its naval mastery decimated, including its submarine-based sea power. However, since 1968, the RN has maintained a nuclear deterrent with at least one ballistic submarine SSBN always at sea. Britain's *Trafalgar* class of SSBNs are being replaced by the *Dreadnought* class. The *Astute* class SSN attack submarines provide the RN with an offensive capability. The US is replacing its *Ohio*-class SSBNs with *Columbia* class, while increasing its fleet of SSNs with new *Virginia* class and its successor, known as the SSN (X).

This historical overview suggests that submarines will continue to be relied on in defence, with most countries opting for small and efficient conventionally powered boats, primarily for short range coastal or littoral operations. Germany, Sweden, and France are among the world's best-known builders and exporters of submarines, especially to Asian navies. Only the US, Russia, Britain, France and China, and more recently India, carry the weight of building extremely expensive nuclear submarines. The American and British fleets are all nuclear boats. Russia, China and India operate joint fleets of nuclear and diesel electric boats. The capital and operating costs of nuclear boats are very significant. Comparing the capital costs and the operating expenses of nuclear-powered boats with diesel-electric powered boats, nuclear boats costing at least double that of a conventional boat, it has been observed that the nuclear boat "has become more of a financial millstone than an indispensable asset to the five nations that deploy it.

The diesel-electric submarine soldiered on, deadlier than ever". In 2023, although it has operated only six diesel-electric boats since the 1960s, Australia announced its plans to join this exclusive group of navies with nuclear powered submarines. It is a huge leap forward in technology and in naval capability.

Losses of conventional and nuclear submarines Since 1945

Most losses of submarines since 1945 were attributed to technical failure and severe weather. None was associated with a nuclear submarine's reactor malfunction. This list of lost submarines is given as background information.

10 April 1963: Skipjack class USS *Thresher* SSN593, the first nuclear boat lost, with 129 crew. Wreckage found at 8,500 feet, off Boston, USA. The loss was thought due to design faults, with seawater being used as coolant. This loss led to "Subsafe" rectifications such as using a heat exchanger and fresh rather than sea water for cooling.

8 March 1968: *K129* (Russian) SSK ballistic submarine was lost 160 miles NW of Hawaii.

A very expensive secret operation code named *Azorian* conducted by the CIA (ostensibly prospecting for oil drilling) recovered some of the Russian hull in 1974, using a specially built deep sea drilling vessel called the *Glomar Explorer* in a remarkable engineering feat, from a depth of 17,000 feet. The diesel-powered *K-129* was carrying three nuclear missiles and torpedos. The Russians alleged the loss was due to *K-129*'s colliding with the USS *Swordfish*. What the US learned from what it salvaged remains classified.

27 Oct 1981 The Soviet Whiskey class *K-137* went aground 30 kms off neutral Swedish coast, to intense media scrutiny.

Divers from the submarine were found to be Russian. Rumours circulated that NATO submarines had also been operating in Swedish waters without consultation.

24 January 1968: *INS Dakar* (Israeli) lost east of Crete, with 69 crew. In 1999, wreckage was found at 9,800 feet near Cyprus. Cause of sinking unknown.

27 January 1968: *Minerve S647* (French) lost with 52 crew. Wreckage was found in 2019 at 7,000 feet.

May 27 1968: *Skipjack* class (US) SSN *Scorpion* SSN589 was lost SW of the Azores, with 99 crew, cause believed to be a torpedo malfunction. Wreckage was found at 8,500 feet.

Questions have re-emerged after 40 years silence, about whether *Scorpion* was deliberately sunk by a Soviet torpedo from a following Soviet boat, in retaliation for its 1967 loss of *K-129*.

12 August 2000: *K-141 Kursk* (Russian) was lost with its 118 crew. A hydrogen peroxide powered torpedo exploded, presumably because of poor maintenance and a second bigger explosion was caused by the heat. Soviet admirals refused British and Norwegian offers to assist with superior technology to rescue 23 survivors trapped in the hull. Russian Prime minister Putin was criticised for remaining absent on holidays. The Russian government delayed 10 days before admitting to the crew's families that the boat was lost. Submariners worldwide were appalled. Three admirals were fired. The massive *Kursk* was named after the famous World War II victory of the Russians in the largest tank battle in history. Its loss remains an emotive icon in submarine stories.

However, even into the 1960s, the dangers in operating submarines were tragically apparent. In 1963, the USS *Thresher* imploded at crush depth exceeding 1000 feet, in 1968, one of four submarines to disappear that year, and the second USN nuclear submarine was lost (the others being the Israeli INS *Dakar*, the French *Minerve*, and the Soviet *K-129*). SSN589 *Skipjack* class USS *Scorpion* sank in the North Atlantic, with the loss of its 129 crew. Tensions between the US and the Soviet Union spurred the building of ever more advanced submarines in the 1960s and onwards, during the so-called Cold War. In 2000, the loss of the Russian *Oscar* class submarine *Kursk* with all its crew of 114 reminded the world that submarines are dangerous. A leak of hydrogen peroxide through a faulty weld produced explosions equivalent to 47 tons of TNT, that were heard by seismographs across Europe.

15 November 2017: *San Juan* (Argentinian) a West German-built boat launched in 1983; lost in severe weather in the South Atlantic with 44 crew. Wreckage was found at 2,976 feet.

21 April 2021: *Nanggala* (Indonesian) lost with 53 crew near Bali.

5

Australian Submarine Service; Past, Present and Future

Under current Royal Australian Navy doctrine, the Submarine Service has the following responsibilities as part of the Australian Defence Force strategy to "shape, deter, and defend":

- intelligence collection and surveillance – loitering undetected in areas of interest, gathering acoustic, visual and communications intelligence.

- maritime strike and anti-ship warfare – equipped with the Mk 48 long range homing torpedo, the submarine is capable of sinking surface combatants, and an adversary's submarines.

- covert land strike – carrying long-range submarine to surface missiles capable of striking land targets.

- barrier operations;

- advanced force operations inserting special forces covertly.

- containment by distraction; and

- support to operations on land

To undertake these responsibilities, the RAN currently operates a fleet of six 3,300-ton *Collins* class diesel-electric submarines. Built in Australia, they are all homeported in Fleet Base West in Fremantle, West Australia. They are to be replaced by a fleet of up to eight nuclear-powered boats in the coming decades. The strategy of deterrence relies on a potential adversary's perception of lethality and capability. It is the decision of the Australian government to support Australia's submarine service as part of it is deterrence strategy. To do this, it has decided to acquire nuclear-powered submarines. This begins a new chapter in Australian submarine history.

Australian Submarine History

Australia's turbulent history of acquiring submarines goes back a century. After the formation of the Australian Navy upon Federation in 1911, a period of uncertainty had followed as the size of the force to be established was determined. Eventually, this was set at 13 vessels, including three submarines. Initially, it had been intended to purchase three small submarines, but this order was later changed and instead Australia's first submarines were the larger British E-class submarines *AE1* and *AE2*. This acquisition was driven by Australian Prime Minister Alfred Deakin's government against the advice of Naval Commandant, later VADM Sir William Creswell KCMG KBE (1852-1933). These submarines were built by Vickers Maxim in Britain at Barrow and arrived in Australia in 1914. The Captain of AE1 was Lieutenant Commander Thomas Besant RN, born in Liverpool, and an experienced submarine Commanding Officer. The Captain of *AE2* was Lieutenant Henry Dacre Stoker, RN. born in Ireland, he was also an experienced submarine CO, and on loan to the RAN. "He had a great love of sports, a wicked sense of humour, and was a man of enormous ability and courage".

He would need these characteristics to lead his crew.

The two submarines, AE1 and AE2 made the long and arduous voyage from Britain to Australia in company with HMS *Eclipse* to Singapore and HMAS *Sydney* for the final leg, via Batavia, Darwin, and Cairns, to an elaborate welcome in Sydney. Each submarine had steamed about two thirds of the 12,000 mile voyage and been towed the remainder. In such primitive craft and beset by bad weather and failures of many technical parts, it was regarded by a population worried about the prospect of war as a significant beginning for the Australian Submarine Service.

Perhaps indicative of the situation decades later, there was little understanding and apparent indifference by surface ship officers to the benefits and needs of submarine operations, and there were problematic gaps in planning, maintenance, and provisioning for the newly acquired submarines, even down to determining a suitable home port with accommodation for the crews.

Within months, three Australian destroyers (*Yarra*, *Warrego* and *Parramatta*) were deployed to New Guinea, expecting conflict with the German Pacific fleet cruisers *Gneisenau and Scharnhorst*. Both Australian submarines took part in responding to the occupation of Rabaul in German New Guinea in September 1914.

During this operation, *AE1* disappeared with LCDR Besant and his 33 men crew on 14 September off Cape Gazelle, New Britain. It was thought probable that she was wrecked on a reef during a practice dive. Australia was shocked at its first loss of a warship. Despite many attempts over the years to find any wreckage, it took until 2017 before her exact final location was established off Duke of York Island.

HMAS *AE2* remained in the South Pacific until December 1914, when she was ordered to the Mediterranean to support the British-led operations off the Gallipoli Peninsula in Turkey. *AE2* was the first British submarine to penetrate the Dardanelles, achieving this task on 25 April 1915. *AE2* operated in the Sea of Marmora for five days and made four unsuccessful attacks on Turkish ships before being damaged by fire from a Turkish gunboat and had to be scuttled by her crew on 30 April. LCDR Henry Stoker and his crew escaped the sinking submarine but were captured and spent the remainder of World War 1 in the harsh conditions of a Turkish POW camp during which four sailors died. Stoker was awarded the DSO for gallantry in making the passage of the Dardanelles.

The courageous actions of *AE2* made a positive contribution to the ANZAC landings on the western side of the peninsula, by diverting enemy attention away from the invading forces, and tying up several major Turkish fleet assets which had been firing across the peninsula at British ships anchored off the landing beaches. These attacks by *AE2* are the only occasions an Australian submarine has fired in anger. Stoker sailed from Australia to Turkey, and to have been the first to penetrate the Dardanelles. It was unarguably an incredible feat of seamanship, and leadership.

The Australian Submarine Service 1919-1945

The Australian submarine service was reformed in 1919, when the British government transferred six J Class submarines to Australia. These submarines arrived in Australia with their tender HMAS Platypus in April 1919. However, the boats were in poor mechanical condition and spent most of their service life in refit. Due to Australia's worsening economic situation, all of the *J*-class boats were decommissioned in 1921, and were sold for scrap in 1922. The Navy began to consider whether submarines could be built in Australia, concluding with a decision to buy two O-class boats (not to be confused with the later *Oberon* class) from Britain.

The Australian submarine service was established a third time in 1927, when the British *O-Class* submarines HMAS *Oxley* and HMAS *Otway* were commissioned. These submarines sailed from Portsmouth for Sydney on 8 February 1928, but did not arrive in Australia until 14 February 1929. Numerous mechanical problems had delayed their delivery voyage. They were stranded in Malta for eight months. Such delays and mechanical failures did little to enhance the reputation of submarines in public and political opinion.

Insufficient volunteers were forthcoming from the RAN for these submarines, and for a period there was compulsory selection of officers. Lieutenants Frank Getting and Norman Shaw commenced their Command "Perisher" courses in 1926 at Devonport, and spent time posted to RN submarines to gain further experience in the larger O boats. However, due to Australia's poor economic situation, the O Class boats proved to be unaffordable and "as in the early 1920s, Navy leadership was determined to maintain its surface ships and quickly agreed to sacrifice the submarines" to this end, as the preferred option. HMA submarines *Oxley* and *Otway* were placed in reserve in 1930, before being transferred back to the Royal Navy in 1931.

It was a lean time for the Australian submarine service. Even Rear Admiral G.F. Hyde RAN, Commander of HM Australian Squadron, made public his opinion that "there would be no call for submarines in Australia". The O boats had suffered morale-sapping engine breakdowns, and the crews dispersed. Lieutenant Frank Edmund Getting became the first Australian naval officer to pass the Submarine Command course, run by the Royal Navy, in 1926, and went on to command HMAS *Oxley* in 1928. Lieutenant S. Barwood RAN attempted but failed the Submarine Perisher course in 1930. He has the distinction of being one of only a very few submariners allowed to repeat the course. He passed on his second attempt, and became First Lieutenant in HMAS *Otway*, under Lieutenant Commander N.H. Shaw, RAN. Getting was promoted to Captain and was tragically killed in August 1942, while in command of the heavy cruiser HMAS *Canberra*, during operations in support of Allied troop landings at Guadalcanal.

World War II saw several Dutch submarines escape from Indonesia to Australia and regroup in Fremantle, with some success in damaging two Japanese cruisers in 1944. Other than six Australians serving in Royal Navy midget submarines (X-craft), notably damaging the German battleship *Tirpitz* in Norway), the Royal Australian Navy did not operate any submarines during World War II. The obsolete Dutch submarine *K.IX* was commissioned as HMAS *K9* on 22 June 1943, and was used for anti-submarine warfare training purposes. Owing to the boat's poor mechanical condition, HMAS *K9* saw little service with the Royal Australian Navy and spent most of her time in commission under repair, before being decommissioned on 31 March 1944, because of a lack of spare parts.

The Australian ports of Fremantle and Brisbane were important bases for Allied submarines during World War II, after the Philippine base was taken by the Japanese. A total of 122 United States Navy, 31 Royal Navy, and 11 Royal Netherlands Navy submarines conducted patrols from Australian bases between 1942 and 1945.

With its dry dock on the bank of its river, Brisbane became a major maintenance base for the American submarines.

Fremantle was the second largest Allied submarine base in the Pacific Theatre, after Pearl Harbor, Hawaii. Other than several Australian officers serving in British boats, and the extensive involvement maintaining American boats in Brisbane and Fremantle. (See chapter Three on American Submarines in Australia during World War II). Australia did not have a sovereign submarine service to contribute to the war effort.

Australia's Submarine Service in the 1960s

Following World War II, the Royal Navy's Fourth Submarine Flotilla (a total of 10 submarines) was based in Sydney from 1949 until 1968. The flotilla, which varied in size during these years between two and three boats, was used to support the Royal Australian Navy and Royal New Zealand Navy in anti-submarine warfare training, with the operating cost split between the two nations. Curiously, the RAN showed little interest in establishing a submarine arm for offensive operations, preferring to emphasise their role in training surface combatants in ASW.

In the early 1960s, the British Government advised the Australian Government that with building larger nuclear-powered submarines, reductions in the Royal Navy conventional submarine force meant that the Fourth Flotilla was to return from Sydney to the United Kingdom. The impending withdrawal of the British submarine flotilla from Balmoral in Sydney Harbour sparked the fourth attempt to establish an Australian submarine service. The final Royal Navy submarine to be based in Australia, HMS *Trump*, was withdrawn in 1969. However, the close relationship that had formed between British and Australian submariners endured over years, with many officers and sailors serving in the other's boats in exchange postings, including in command positions, and undertaking the Perisher command course in Britain.

While the Department of Defence advised the government that three to six submarines should be purchased for training purposes, following the intervention of then-Senator Navy Minister John Gorton, in 1963 the Government instead approved the purchase of four *Oberon* class submarines from Britain to form a submarine strike force, for delivery between 1966 and 1968. It revived the decades-long argument about Australia's capability to build its own submarines.

Industry held that Australian skills were adequate to the task and building submarines in Australia would support nation-building and provide employment for workers and support Australian ship building. Others were cautious about the complexity of such a project. The Navy was more impressed with the proven design that *Oberons* to be built in Britain offered. The possibility of acquiring nuclear powered boats was considered by the Chiefs of Staff in 1959 but decided against on the basis of cost.

Perhaps ironically in view of Australia's more recent debate about where its nuclear-powered boats are to be built, or based, Gorton stated then: "defence funds are intended to provide defence for Australia, not to meet the needs of some Australian shipyard owners".

It was assessed that building these *Oberon* class boats in Australia would be slower and more expensive than building them in Greenock, Scotland. It was the fourth attempt by the Navy to establish an Australian Submarine Service.

Submarine Basing in Australia in 1963

The RAN established its submarine base in HMAS *Platypus* at Neutral Bay in Sydney Harbour. Those members selected for submarine service were posted to HMS *Dolphin*, the Royal Navy training base at Gosport, opposite the surface ship base at Portsmouth. Trainees were then posted to billets in RN submarines, to gain experience. Many then stood by their new *Oberon* class boats as they were being built in Greenock. The boats were worked up in Faslane, Scotland, prior to being commissioned and then sailed for Australia and their base at HMAS *Platypus* in Sydney Harbour. In retrospect, it was the beginning of a substantial and durable Submarine Arm of the RAN.

Oberon Acquisition and Operation

Eight British Oberon class submarines were ordered in 1964, to be built in Scotland in two batches of four boats. The *Oberon* class submarines for Australia displaced 2,070 tonnes surfaced, 2,410 tonnes submerged, and had a length of 89.9 metres. They were capable of 15 kts maximum submerged and had six forward and two after tubes (later sealed off). The crew numbered seven officers and 56 sailors. The first four boats were *Oxley* (1967), *Otway* (1968), *Ovens* (1969) and *Onslow* (1969). The original purpose was for the Oberons to serve as targets in training the fleet in ASW. In 1975, the Australian government decided to use the submarines for covert intelligence collection in conjunction with Britain and the United States.

The introduction of the *Oberon* class boats into the Australian Navy was well regarded. Two more were ordered for delivery in 1975-76. These were named *Orion* (1977) and *Otama* (1978), and were fitted out to undertake special intelligence collection operations. Between 1978 and 1992, Australian submarines undertook some 22 secret intelligence collection patrols in areas north and west of Australia. Continuing upgrades and maintenance of the O-boats was carried out at Cockatoo Island in Sydney. However, only these six O-boats originally ordered were delivered; the seventh and eighth were cancelled by the government in 1971 to fund the acquisition of ten A-4 Skyhawk aircraft for the Fleet Air Arm. The Oxley's First Lieutenant was Ian MacDougall, who went on to become Chief of Naval Staff, as Vice Admiral Ian MacDougall AC RAN.

With the decision to acquire *Oberons* came an era when many Australian submariners trained with the Royal Navy and crewed British boats. Four Australians passed the Perisher course there and served on exchange as captains of Royal Navy submarines. This provided valuable *Oberon* command experience, and suited the RN, who needed to post officers to train on the nuclear submarines to which Britain was moving its force structure. A close relationship between Australian and British submariners formed through the RN Fourth Submarine Flotilla in Sydney until 1969, and the exchange postings between each other's services and boats. It appears likely to continue with present and future nuclear British design submarines, along with the potential deployment on rotation of an *Astute*-class submarine to Australia. It remains a significant element in Australia's submarine service organisational culture.

All of the *Oberon* class submarines were based at HMAS *Platypus* in Neutral Bay, Sydney. In retrospect, the *Oberons* proved very successful and saw extensive service during the last decades of the Cold War. This service included conducting secret high risk surveillance missions against India and Communist nations in South-East Asia. The patrols by HMA submarines *Orion* and *Otama* were very effective in their intelligence gathering missions, but these were extremely dangerous and arduous for the crews. When told that one boat had come perilously close to being detected, the continuation of the 16 patrols over 14 years was canceled by Defence Minister Robert Ray in 1992.

In 1998, the Australia Service Medal with a clasp prescribed "Special Operations" was awarded to 15 crews, recognising service in what became colloquially referred to as "mystery tours". Only a few politicians knew of them, and most of the navy and the crews' families were unaware of their activities or the danger they faced. The skill and daring exhibited was recognized and acknowledged by those who know about these patrols, but generally these patrols are still not generally known even within the Navy today. Some of the details of these operations are still classified.

The intelligence gathered was highly regarded, particularly by a grateful USN, whose larger submarines were not suitable for such taskings in confined waters. They built Australian submarines' reputation for its intelligence gathering capability. The 1980s saw increased Soviet interest in southeast Asia, with up to 30 Soviet warships including nuclear submarines deployed to the large formerly American facility in Cam Ranh Bay, Vietnam. In 1985, HMAS *Orion* was able to obtain video footage of a surfaced Soviet *Charlie* class nuclear submarine, exposing many previously unknown underwater technological secrets of the Soviet boat. This was said to be very impressive to the USN, and was influential in Prime Minister Bob Hawke's support for the *Collins* class program. The patrols were discontinued in 1992, under the direction of the then Defence Minister Robert Ray. As part of the Government's Two Ocean Navy policy, submarines were homeported at HMAS *Stirling* at Fremantle in West Australia from 1987, and the headquarters of the Australian Submarine Squadron was moved to HMAS *Stirling* in 1994. The *Oberon* class boats were gradually decommissioned and replaced with six new *Collins* class submarines during the 1990s. HMAS *Otway* was decommissioned in 1994. Her casing and fin were sold to the Holbrook Submarine Museum in country New South Wales. HMAS *Ovens* also paid off in 1994 and became a tourist attraction in Fremantle. HMAS *Onslow* decommissioned in 1999, and now attracts visitors at the Australian National Maritime Museum in Sydney. HMAS *Platypus* was decommissioned in 1999. The last of the *Oberons*, HMAS *Otama*, was decommissioned on 15 December 2000.

Australian Losses during the O-boat era

During the O-boat era (1967-2000) there were several tragic deaths. One was due to inhalation of toxic gas, and another when a visitor fell from the gangway when the boat was alongside.

In 1987, two sailors were drowned when working in HMAS *Otama*'s fin, unknown to the crew inside the pressure hull. The submarine dived off Sydney in extremely adverse gale force sea state 8-10 weather. Conditions were appalling. Later criticism was that the command decision to sail was ill-advised. Over-crowding combined with a lack of experience in the crew in which a significant number were trainees. As reported by the coroner, the captain admitted that 31 errors were made and procedures were not correctly followed.

The accident was tragic, and precipitated four separate investigations. Courts martial and criminal charges were contemplated. The Navy Board of Inquiry recommended a number of systematic changes to Submarine standing orders, to ensure no such event would ever recur. An admission of civil negligence was given in a confidential financial settlement with the parents of the drowned sailors. The Navy continues to view the regrettable incident and its sequelae very seriously. Though historically the O-boat era is remembered as a demonstration of Australian submariner professionalism and the submarines' effectiveness, it also saw the decline in numbers in the submarine branch, as experienced submariners separated from the Navy for more rewarding work (often employed as contractors to the Navy), where they could be guaranteed more time ashore with their families.

Evolution from the *Oberon* Class to the *Collins* Class

The six O-boats were in service in Australia from 1967 until 2000. As they aged, refits became more difficult, with spares parts from the UK often unavailable. The combat system originally supplied by the British for the *Oberons* was virtually a relic from World War II and was upgraded at Cockatoo Island in a series of projects over a decade. Meanwhile other developments took place, with the establishment of the Submarine Warfare Systems Centre (SWSC) at HMAS *Watson* in Sydney. This offered computer-driven simulators and training courses for crews. The *Oberon* boats had performed beyond expectations, and a replacement was sought, potentially the British Type 2400 (later known as the *Upholder* class).

In 1981, a Department of Defence report proposed that a replacement for the *Oberons* could be built in Australia.[108] The Navy wanted the O-boat replacement to be faster, deeper diving, stealthier, and crewed with fewer people. The 1980's saw intense discussion about the capability specifications of the future submarine. The planned acquisition of HMS *Invincible* to replace the aircraft carrier HMAS *Melbourne* had fallen through when the British retained it for the Falklands War, and it

---

[108] Vickers Cockatoo Dockyard Pty ltd (1981). *Submarine Construction Feasibility Study*. NAA CRS, M3080 item 10.

had effectively taken the fleet air arm's fixed wing aircraft with it. The Fleet Air Arm now serves by operating helicopters off the small aircraft carriers (HMA Ships *Canberra* and *Adelaide*) and embarked on RAN frigates and Air Warfare Destroyers, in an ASW role.

In 1985 a Minute from the head of the submarine project office CAPT Graham White summarised capability requirements based on the submarines' role in intelligence gathering in peacetime and as a deterrent to any enemy in war.[109] It was thought that Long range (10,000 nmls), a submerged endurance of 10 weeks, and the demand for a large weapon load, plus towed array and flank array sensors, would require at least a 2,000 ton design. The question of basing in Darwin (with shorter range smaller boats), versus basing in less vulnerable southern locations was a precursor to an enduring debate, settled perhaps only temporarily by later moving the Submarine squadron from Sydney to Fremantle. Advocacy for a submarine base to be established on the east coast has continued through the decades since the Sydney Harbour base in HMAS *Platypus* was decommissioned in 1999.

The future submarine project began with great ambition on the part of the Navy for what was needed, and considerable doubt that Australian industry could deliver. Australia had no history in designing or building submarines. The project came to be seen as a challenge for national industrial maturity, much like another Snowy Mountains Scheme.

---

[109] White, G. (1985). *Justification of capability for the new construction submarine.*

Collins Program History

The six *Collins* class vessels were the first submarines ever built in Australia, prompting widespread improvements in Australian industry and delivering a sovereign (Australian controlled) sustainment/maintenance capability. Planning for a new design to replace the RAN's *Oberon*-class submarines had begun in the late 1970s and early 1980s. Defence Minister Kim Beazley argued for the building of eight boats, but only six were approved. Proposals were received from seven companies; two were selected for a funded study to determine the winning design, which was announced in mid-1987. Swedish ship builder Kockums became the partner with the Australian Submarine Corporation, to build the boats in Australia.

The submarines of Kockums' Västergötland class, originally referred to as the Type 471, were constructed between 1990 and 2003 in South Australia by the Australian Submarine Corporation (ASC). The boats cost a billion dollars each. The *Collins* class is an enlarged version of the Västergötland-class submarine designed by Swedish firm Kockums. At 77.42 metres (254 ft) in length, with a beam of 7.8 metres (26 ft) and a waterline depth of 7 metres (23 ft), displacing 3,051 tonnes when surfaced, and 3,353 tonnes when submerged, they are among the largest conventionally (i.e. diesel) powered submarines in the world. The hull is constructed from high-tensile micro-alloy steel, and is covered in a skin of anechoic tiles to minimise the chance of detection by an adversary's sonar sensors. The depth that the submarines can dive to is classified but most sources claim that it is over 180 metres (590 ft).

Each submarine is equipped with three Garden Island-Hedemora HV V18b/15Ub (VB210) 18-cylinder diesel engines, which are each connected to a 1,400 kW, 440-volt DC Jeumont-Schneider generator. The electricity generated is stored in batteries, then supplied to a single Jeumont-Schneider DC motor, which provides 7,200 shaft horsepower to a single, seven-bladed, 4.22-metre (13.8 ft) diameter skewback propeller. The *Collins* class has a speed of 10.5 knots when surfaced or at snorkel depth, and can reach 21 knots underwater. The submarines have a range of 11,000 nautical miles (20,000 km; 13,000 miles) at 10 knots when surfaced, 9,000 nautical miles (17,000 km; 10,000 miles) at 10 kts at snorkel depth. When submerged completely, a *Collins*-class submarine can travel 32.6 nautical miles (60.4 km) at maximum speed, or 480 nautical miles (890 km) at 4 kts. The submarine has an endurance of 70 days at sea.

Following the December 1984 federal election, Kim Beazley MP at 36 years of age became Australia's youngest Defence Minister. He proved a strong supporter of both the Navy and the relationship with the US, particularly in relation to intelligence gathering as demonstrated by the *Oberons*.[110] Designing and building the *Collins* boats stretched everyone's skills, along with the budget. They are big and complex diesel-electric submarines, as noted among the biggest in the world. By 1989, there were problems coordinating the integrated ship control and monitoring, with the Australian Submarine Corporation (ASC) experiencing difficulties in the contracting relationship between sub-contractors Saab and Kockums.

These and other safety issues were resolved by the early 1990's. HMAS *Collins*, the lead ship of class, was launched on 23 August 1993. It was delivered in 1996. The last boat was delivered in 2003. The whole project cost $5bn. The Navy found there was an issue with the welding, even with that done by Kockums in Sweden. Delays in the delivery of combat system software and

---

[110] Yule, P. & Woolner, D. (2008). *The Collins Class Submarine Story: Steel, Spies and Spin*. Cambridge University Press, Port Melbourne.

industrial disputes combined to delay the *Collins* taking her place in the fleet. She had been lifted out of the water a week after her launch, and remained on the hard stand while remedial work was done and contractual duels were fought. Three years of trials and rectifications were to follow.

However, tests of HMAS *Collins* after she was provisionally commissioned in 1996 revealed serious shortcomings in the submarine's performance, including excessive hull noise and an ineffective combat system. These problems were subsequently rectified. The original Rockwell International-designed combat system had been cancelled, but because there wasn't enough time to evaluate the replacement system to include it in the "fast track" program, the two submarines were fitted with components from the old Rockwell system, which were augmented by commercial off-the-shelf hardware and software. Even with the enhanced Rockwell system, it was believed that the capabilities of the fast-tracked Collins boats were only equivalent to the Oberons. Crew training and the documentation for operation were seen to be deficient.

In 1997-99, the media frequently criticised what it claimed to be prohibitively expensive "dud subs". Every minor incident or defect was enthusiastically reported in the media. Public support for the Collins class waned. The shape of the casing (and therefore its design) and the water flow over it was held responsible for the fact that the boats were noisier than expected. Cavitation from the propellor was also a major concern. This cavitation phenomenon is common in most of the world's classes of ships, reducing the efficiency of the propellor, and may produce noise that reveals the position of the submarine to passive sonar. Both HMAS *Collins* and the second boat of the six to be built, HMAS *Farncomb*, experienced unacceptable levels of vibration in the periscopes. An adversarial relationship developed between Navy and ASC, each blaming the other for performance defects. Eventually the mechanical and technical problems were worked through and the remedies applied to the later boats.

The issues with the *Collins* class were highlighted in the McIntosh-Prescott Report, along with the pressing need to have combat-ready submarines in the RAN fleet with the pending decommissioning of HMAS *Otama* in 2000. This was the final Oberon-class submarine in Australian service. Its departure from the fleet prompted the establishment of an A$1bn program to bring HMAS *Dechaineux* and sister boat HMAS *Sheean* up to an operational standard as quickly as possible, referred to as the "fast- track" or "get well" program. The fast-track program required fixing hydrodynamic noise issues by modifying the hull design and propeller, and providing a functional combat system.

In 1998, DSTO director of combat systems research Dr Todd Mansell determined that the Boeing release 2.0 software was not able to deliver the capability promised. Navy chief VADM Don Chalmers asked the US for assistance with both the combat system software and the noise problem. The advice proved effective. However, the Navy then refused to accept the next boat (*Waller*), because it had not met all the requirements. Relations between the ASC and its customer were not in good shape. Also in 1998, John Moore became Minister for Defence. He was disappointed with the management abilities of senior military leaders, and thought the practice of short postings meant that few had a firm grasp of their jobs.[111] A number of reviews followed. Moore viewed as superficial the various reports by Defence Department Secretary Paul Barratt and

---

[111] Yule, P. & Woolner, D. (2008*). The Collins Class Submarine Story: Steel, Spies and Spin.* Cambridge University Press, Port Melbourne, p. 274.

Chief of Defence Force Admiral Chris Barrie. Moore appointed Sir Malcolm McIntosh, chief executive of the CSIRO, to investigate, working with John Prescott, formerly managing director of BHP. McIntosh and Prescott reported in 1999 that the submarine's combat system should be replaced by a proven off-the-shelf product. The report expressed surprise at the apparently minimal testing of design, while the navy asserted that comprehensive tank testing program had been undertaken. The McIntosh-Prescott report was released on 1 July 1999. It broadly agreed with criticism previously made to Navy in 1997 by Commodore Michael Dunne AM RAN, that noise from turbulence was a problem and needed to be rectified before deployment on operations could be considered.[112] The report detailed defects in the engines, propellors, periscopes and masts, and centrally, the combat system. It went on to describe ways in which the problems could be fixed. While observing that in terms of engineering excellence and production management, the construction of the *Collins* class submarines by the Australia Submarine Corporation (ASC) had been a national achievement in the tradition of the Snowy Mountains Scheme, as an ambitious one-off project. However, the future of the Australian submarine building industry remained unresolved. It had been a saga of design, mismanagement, build issues, and political intrigue.[113] The McIntosh Prescott report opened the way for a fast-track program to fix the faults in the *Collins* class. Minister John Moore appointed Rear Admiral Peter Briggs AO to cut through red tape and address the enduring problems with the diesel engines and the manpower shortages. The McIntosh Prescott report recommended scrapping the combat system. Chief of Navy VADM David Shackleton advocated an American

---

[112] Yule, P. & Woolner, D. (2008*). The Collins Class Submarine Story: Steel, Spies and Spin.* Cambridge University Press, Port Melbourne, p. 280.

[113] Yule, P. & Woolner, D. (2008*). The Collins Class Submarine Story: Steel, Spies and Spin.* Cambridge University Press, Port Melbourne.

Raytheon system to ensure interoperability and cooperation.[114] As in the 1960s when the RAN moved from British designed vessels (the destroyer escort *River* class and *Majestic* class aircraft carrier to the American design *Charles F Adams* Class DDG destroyer and the Adelaide class FFG frigate), the RAN has moved from British *Oberon* class to the Australian *Collins* class and on to the American *Virginia* class submarines.

Signing agreement with the US

VADM David Shackleton and Australian Prime Minister John Howard in the White House, Washington DC, in 2001, for the first formal signing of the Submarine Cooperation Agreement between the US Navy and the Royal Australian Navy. As Chief of Navy, VADM Shackleton AO was the Australian signatory, with his USN counterpart, ADM Vernon Clark, the US Chief of

---

[114] Yule, P. & Woolner, D. (2008). *The Collins Class Submarine Story: Steel, Spies and Spin*. Cambridge University Press, Port Melbourne, p. 303.

Naval Operations, the signatory for the United States.[115]

The agreement provided an overarching framework for a wide range of hitherto unavailable cooperative activities between the two navies associated with submarine warfare, associated technologies, weapons, and personnel. It was of direct and immediate use in obtaining USN support for improving the Collins combat system as well as assistance in aspects of hull and propeller design. The agreement contained a clause concerning renewal, and it has since been renewed several times. It remains in place. The importance of the agreement is reflected in the presence of Australia's Prime Minister, John Howard, and the United States Secretary for Defence, Donald Rumsfeld. Mr Howard was in the US to meet with President Bush, and also participate in a ceremonial transfer of the bell of the USS *Canberra* from the President to the Prime Minister. The events of 911 occurred the next day.

HMAS Waller (2017)

---

[115]. Photo provided with permission by VADM Shackleton).

The *Collins* class submarines have been the subject of many incidents and technical problems since the design phase, including accusations of foul play and bias during the design selection, improper handling of design changes during construction, major capability deficiencies in the first submarines, and ongoing technical problems throughout the early life of the class.

These problems were compounded by the inability of the Navy to retain sufficient personnel to operate the submarines by 2008, only three could be manned, and between 2009 and 2012, on average two or fewer were fully operational. The resulting negative press led to an undeserved poor public perception of the *Collins* class. After 20 years of service issues, the boats have finally provided high availability to the Navy since 2016. However, wounds from reputational damage are slow to heal, and irrational prejudice persists in some quarters.

Each *Collins* boat was named after a distinguished former member of the RAN, some of whom have made the ultimate sacrifice for their country. One, HMAS *Sheean*, carries the name of the only seaman to be so honored, Able Seaman Teddy Sheean VC. The boats are considerably better equipped to conduct operations than were the predecessor *Oberon* class.

The six *Collins* class submarines were the first Australian-built submarines, and the most expensive ships to have been built in Australia. The *Collins* class submarines were built by the Australian Submarine Corporation at Adelaide, South Australia and entered service between 1996 and 2003 following extensive trials and modifications to the early boats. Their launch dates were: HMAS *Collins* (1996); HMAS *Farncomb* (1998); HMAS *Waller* (1999); HMAS *Dechaineux* (2001); HMAS *Sheean* (2001); HMAS *Rankin* (2003). Like the *Oberon* class before them, the *Collins* class submarines have conducted surveillance patrols. These patrols have included collecting intelligence on East Timor ahead of the Australian-led intervention into the then-Indonesian province in 1999. While the *Collins* class submarines' performance has improved over time, their maximum diving depth was permanently reduced following the near loss in February 2003 of HMAS *Dechaineux* when a seawater pipe burst during a practice dive. The submarine's emergency systems, and the crew, performed to standard, and the boat returned to base for repairs.[116] In retrospect, building the *Collins* boats was the most ambitious and complex military project ever undertaken by Australia, and was eventually though expensively very successful. The *Collins* class was expected to be retired about 2026. The 2016 *Defence White Paper* extended this into the 2030s. The *Collins* class life will now be extended and will receive a capability upgrade, including sonar and communications.

The Future Submarine

A replacement for the *Collins* class was under discussion early in the current century, but successive governments procrastinated in making a decision. The 2009 Defence White Paper called for a larger fleet of more capable submarines to replace the in-service *Collins* class submarines. The thinking in 2012 was that 'the lifecycle costs of a nuclear program would place unacceptable pressure on other elements of a balanced force'.[117] Rather, considering their cost, range and endurance, a fleet of 12 evolved *Collins* class boats was favoured. The *Collins* class was expected to retire beginning in 2024. The government determined that its wholly owned ASC would

---

[116] Scott. P. (2023). *Running Deep*. Fremantle Press, North Fremantle, p. 181.

[117] Pacey, B. (2012). *Sub Judice: Australia's Future Submarine*. Kokoda Paper no. 17. Kokoda Foundation, Canberra. p. iv.

not build the *Collins* replacement. Without building work the ASC focused on maintaining the existing fleet of the six *Collins* class. It contracted to build three new *Hobart* class Air warfare destroyers. The cost went over budget by $1.3billion and the commissioning date slipped by three years. This left the ASC without recent submarine building experience, lost during a period when the US had built the *Los Angeles* then *Seawolf*, and then *Virginia* classes. The Australian government was concerned that a boat built by ASC would not be available until well after the scheduled retirement of the *Collins* class. Instead, the government of Prime Minister Abbot expressed interest in acquiring boats of the Japanese *Soryu* class. In 2015, a competitive evaluation process had Japan, Germany and France in contention for the $50billion future submarine project. All agreed on the desirability of building the boats in Australia.

The *Attack* Class Submarine

In 2016, the Australian Turnbull government committed to designing and building 12 diesel-electric submarines in Australia. It was to be the nation's largest ever defence procurement, variously estimated at about $50B. The first boat was expected to be delivered in the 2030s. The design was based on the French *Barracuda* shortfin class, offering extended range and stealth. The RAN has been persistent and resilient in operating a submarine branch, from its first venture into the field a century ago. Leadership has flourished, or been inhibited, at various stages of its history, from the primitive beginnings with *AE1* and *AE2*. the effective hiatus of the world wars, and the rebirth with the *Oberon* and later the *Collins* classes. The new *Attack* class was seen as representing a giant leap forward. Time was passing and the Collins boats were becoming older and likely to become less effective and more easily detected by a potential adversary. If capability is the product that the submarine force contributes to the Navy as a whole, then the *Oberons* and *Collins* boats delivered to Australia a national asset of professionalism and warfighting potency. The turn of the century saw Australia embark on an ambitious ship building program to design and deliver 12 conventional submarines based on the French Barracuda class design, and to be built in Australia. The first of these *Attack* class boats was scheduled to enter service sometime after 2025. Meanwhile, it became clear that with an increasing threat from a newly assertive China with the largest navy in the world, Australia needed a submarine with greater range, speed, endurance, and stealth capability.

On 15 September 2021, in the face of growing delays and cost increases, the Australian government announced the cancellation of the contract with the French Naval Group, and that the replacement will be a nuclear-powered submarine fleet to be built in partnership with the United Kingdom and the United States. In the interim, up to five *Virginia* class boats were to be acquired (the first to arrive in 2033) while the AUKUS submarine is designed and built, to be delivered from 2045. The estimated cost was given as AUD268-368bn.

Australian Submarine Warfare Strategy

History has shown the lethality of the submarine in the role of enforcing a blockade. Examples are the blockade of Germany by the British in World War I and of Japan by the Americans in World War II. It has shown the effectiveness of submarines in collecting intelligence and in hunting and sinking an adversary's submarines, and thousands of merchant ships. The debate about Australia's need for submarines as weapons in its defence force and the class of submarine required hinges on the debate about the threat being confronted. Strategy follows objectives in defence planning. The strategy of sea control requires superior forces to overwhelm an enemy by destroying or neutralizing his assets so that he is incapable of offence or effective defence. Sea denial prevents others from gaining sea control.[118] Sea denial can be undertaken with less force since its aim is less comprehensive. The aim of denial is to defeat local aggression, not to subjugate an adversary. [119] The threat faced by Australia is assessed not as an invasion by enemy forces landing on beaches but more likely coercive control over Australian territory and that of allied nations. This threat is thought significant because of possible blockading ports and bringing Australia to its economic knees through fuel shortages. Without imported fuel, Australia's fuel reserves would exhaust within a few weeks.

In view of its massive naval and military buildup in the 21st century, the likely aggressor posing this threat is China. It has the ways, the means, and it espouses the ends: "Xi's China is pursuing a long-term strategy to break the US alliance with relevant countries, and drive America out of Asia."[120] China's claims that virtually any territory it wants (including Tibet, Taiwan and the South China Sea) "have been part of China since ancient times" are palpably without historical foundation. For example, Taiwan, formerly the island of Formosa, was declared part of the Manchu empire in 1885, without the consent of its inhabitants - only to be ceded in perpetuity to Japan in 1895. Japan ruled the island with great effectiveness for 50 years, and

---

[118] RAN (2010), *Australian Maritime Doctrine*. 2nd edn, Seapower Centre Australia, Canberra p. 71.

[119] Colby, E. A. (2021). *The Strategy of Denial: American Defense in an Age of Great Power Conflict*. Yale University Press.

[120] Evans, M. (2023). Who Denies Wins: How to Prevail in a War against China in Asia. *Quadrant*. No. 601, vol. LXVII, November, pp. 19-26.

developed it into a thriving colony, whose inhabitants rebelled in 1947 against the against the imposition of Chinese nationalist rule. Many thousands were executed.[121]

Now, Chinese President Xi Jinping has stated clearly that the PCP "reserves the right to use force to "reunify" under Chinese control what he calls the rogue province of Taiwan. The inhabitants describe themselves as Taiwanese but not Chinese and have built a sophisticated defence system to guard against the routine threats and incursions by Chinese ships and aircraft. Chinese control of Taiwan would give China virtually total control of the South China Sea, through which passes a third of the world's trade, and unchallenged access to the deep ocean waters of the Pacific.

In response, America insists all other nations' right to traverse international waters in the Taiwan Strait between Taiwan and the Chinese mainland. The US cautiously warns that armed invasion by China would prompt American defence of the island under a treaty obligation. It has contingency plans for a Chinese blockade.[122] It is of course critical in the assessment of threat to understand the intention of the likely protagonists. The Chinese aim is avowedly regional if not global supremacy.[123] Though wildly extravagant, this is not historically unknown. Hitler wanted it, and Putin appears still to want it. In an age of nuclear weapons, a peace-loving country like Australia typically underestimates threat, and may find it alien and thus difficult to comprehend the unthinkable. By contrast, "American aims in Asia remain limited to upholding the current status quo. There is no messianic desire in American statecraft to try to overthrow

---

[121] Fitzgerald, J. (2018). About China. *Weekend Australian*, Inquirer Mar 3-4, p. 21.
[122] Campbell, J. and Martin, J. (2022). Prepare the Logistics to break a Chinese blockade of Taiwan. *Proceedings*, October, pp. 59-63.
[123] Hamilton, C. and Ohlberg, M. (2020). *Hidden Hand*. Hardie Grant Books, Melbourne.

the Chinese state by regime change."[124] It is unclear how long this standoff can last, as both China and the US say they do not want war but China openly claims the territory of Taiwan, an effective democracy with a 23.6 million independently-minded population, producing 90 percent of the world production of advanced computer chips – a very attractive strategic prize for China, whose president is saying that he wants the "Taiwan question" answered soon. The PLA(N) the People's Liberation Army Navy (PLA(N) has taken over from USN as the largest navy in the world, and the US admits that historically, in the event of naval warfare in only three possible cases in the last 1,200 years has a smaller fleet overcome a larger fleet.[125] All this leaves Australia asking what threat it faces from a China-US conflict in the SW Pacific. In 2023, the National Defence Strategic Review formally adopted a strategy of denial as the central pillar of its defence strategy. This invites a consideration of the concept of deterrence. Fundamental to its effectiveness is the perception by a potential adversary of a credible warfighting capability, and a willingness to use it if necessary. If an envisaged scenario has China blockading Taiwan to starve it into subjugation, the US must be seen as having the capability to break the blockade.

Perhaps the argument that Australia need not and should not participate in an antihegemonic coalition supporting America will prevail. But what if for various reasons, it does not? Will our submarines be expected to undertake blockade duties against China? Will we need submarines with the range and payload of nuclear-powered boats, or would cheaper, more numerous, and more easily crewed and conventionally powered boats be a more realistic and affordable deterrent? To answer this question, the

---

[124] Colby, E. A. (2021). *The Strategy of Denial: American Defense in an Age of Great Power Conflict.* Yale University Press.

[125] Tangredi, S. J. (2023). Bigger fleets Win. *Proceedings.* pp. 57-63. January, pp. 57-69.

next chapter examines nuclear-powered submarines. To do so effectively, we need to keep in mind the priority emphasized by the great military theorist Carl von Clausewitz in his 1892 masterpiece *On War*: "The first, the supreme, the most far-reaching act of judgment that the statesman and commander have to make is to establish the kind of war they are embarking; neither mistaking it for, nor trying to turn it into something that is alien to its nature. This is the first of all strategic questions and the most comprehensive."[126]

---

[126] Clausewitz, In Evans, M. (2023). Who Denies Wins: How to Prevail in a War against China in Asia. *Quadrant*. No. 601, vol. LXV11, November, p. 26.

6

Nuclear-powered Submarines

A Brief History of Nuclear-Powered Submarines

The experience of World War II left the Allies acutely aware of the need for protecting its carrier task groups. The submarine was seen as a manned picket that could steam with it. The US opted for very long-range sonar in nuclear-powered boats that could achieve the necessary sustained speed submerged. The USS *Nautilus* was built by General Dynamics and introduced in 1955 as the world's first nuclear powered warship, displacing about 4,000 tons and with a submerged speed of 23 kts. The *Skipjack* was designed in 1956. The lead ship of her class, she had a tear-drop shaped hull based on her predecessor *Albacore*'s design, and offered superior performance at speed, with the only protrusions providing drag being her fin and diving planes. She was capable of 30 knots submerged. *Skipjack* and *Skate* became the shape that influenced all subsequent submarine design. By 1962, the US Navy had 26 nuclear submarines operational and 30 under construction. Nuclear power had revolutionised the Navy. The US shared its nuclear technology only with the UK. Russia, France and China developed their own nuclear capability independently. The US nuclear ship program was driven relentlessly by ADM Hyman G. Rickover, one of America's longest-serving naval officers, finally retiring from active service at the age of 82 years.[127]

The Soviets also had nuclear boats operational in the early 1960s. The 5000/6000-ton *Hotel* class was the first in the world to claim to be ballistic missile submarines (seven were built in 1959-61). The nuclear-powered Victor *I* class (14 built 1968-75) of specialised ASW submarine followed. 'The Soviet Navy lagged behind the US Navy by about three years in nuclear attack submarines, with the *November* class (15 built 1958-64)'.[128]

The World's nuclear Submarines

The approximate numbers of nuclear submarines were reported in 2024 as follows:

USA 70 (28 out of 62 SSN *Los Angeles* class, 22 up to 48 SSN *Virginia* class, 18 SSBN *Ohio* class, 3 SSGN *Seawolf* class). Four have been converted to guided missile submarines (SSGNs): *Ohio*, *Michigan*, *Florida* and *Georgia*. The 14 nuclear-armed boats are planned to be replaced in 2031 with 12 SSBN Columbia class submarines in 2031.

Russia 40 (5 *Borei* class, 3 *Yasen* class, 5 *Oscar* class, 4 SSN *Akula* class, 5 SSBN *Delta* class, 4 SSN *Sierra* class.

China 19 (11 Type 094 *Jin* class, 6 SSBN, 6 Type 093 *Shang* class, 17 SSK *Yuan* class, 12 *Kilo* class, 13 *Song*, class, 13 *Ming* class).

UK 10 (6 SSN *Astute* class, 4 SSBN *Vanguard* class

---

[127] Tyler, P. (1986). *Running Critical: The Silent War, Rickover and General Dynamics*. Harper & Row, New York.
[128] Friedman, N. (1984). *Submarine Design and Development*. Naval Institute Press, Annapolis, p. 106.

France 9 (3 SSN *Rubis*, 1 *Triomphant* class, 1 *SSN Suffren* class

India 3 (2 Arihant SSBNs, 16 SSNs 4 *Akula* class, 4 *Shishkumar* class, 8 *Kilo* class.

Categories of submarines

The different types of submarines now serving can be clarified. The first difference between submarines is their propulsion: diesel-electric as against nuclear power.

Differentiator	*Diesel-electric*	*Nuclear*
Speed	17 kts surfaced 20 kts Submerged 7 kts transit	15 kts Surfaced 25 kts Submerged 25 kts transit
Endurance	Limited by fuel capacity	Unlimited
Weapons	Torpedoes Cruise missiles	Torpedoes Cruise missiles Ballistic missiles
Sensors	Limited due to space	Full array
Cost	$600M	$2.7B

The difference in cost makes the diesel boat look so much more attractive, but the comparison is not realistic, because the types of craft are fundamentally different. Diesel boats are cheaper; nuclear boats are faster bigger, typically carry more powerful weapons, and have much longer endurance. The choice is up to the particular country and its defence needs. The various types of submarines can be grouped as follows:

Attack submarines (SSK/SSN)

These vessels designed specifically to hunt and kill enemy submarines, surface combatants and merchant vessels. These submarines also serve a protective role, escorting major naval strike groups, logistics and troop convoys and merchant vessels.

Recent advances in propulsion, power generation and weapons systems have also enabled these vessels to conduct long-range land strikes using torpedo or vertically launched cruise missiles.

Ballistic missile submarines (SSBN)

Significantly larger than their smaller, more nimble hunter killer cousins, ballistic missile submarines serve as the seaborne leg of a traditional nuclear deterrence triangle, armed with submarine launched ballistic missiles capable - these submarines serve as the ultimate in strategic insurance for great powers like the US and China.

Cruise missile submarines (SSG/SSGN)

Often modified ballistic missile submarines (such as the USS *Florida*), cruise missile submarines leverage the unlimited range of nuclear-powered vessels combined with advances in weapons technology to pack vast numbers of land attack and anti-ship cruise missiles into specially modified vertical launch systems to provide immense levels of conventional strike capabilities. The *Florida* can carry up to 66 special forces to insert covertly into contested areas. For both the US and China, these vessels serve as powerful platforms critical to tactical and strategic planning, forcing both sides to consider the availability, location and number of these force multipliers in the Indo-Pacific. The US Navy operates a number of different submarines in the Indo-Pacific region, including fast-attack submarines, ballistic missile submarines and cruise missile submarines, which are responsible for providing surface fleet ASW cover, strategic deterrence and long-range strike capabilities.

Limited comparisons of Attack submarines

Factor	Collins	Astute	Virginia
Builder	ASC (Australian Submarine Corporation)	BAE Systems UK	General Dynamics Electric Boat and Newport News Shipbuilding
Cost	0.64bn	$2.2bn	$3.2bn (block V)
Displacement		7,400 t	7,900 t
Size	77 m	97 m	115 m (block V 140 m)
Speed (submerged)	10 kts	30 kts	25 kts
Crew	58	98	135
Tubes	6	6x 21in Spearfish torpedoes	12 Tomahawk 4 VLS tubes for Mk 48 torpedoes
Weapons	22	38	37 (65 in block V)

Wider Comparisons

Type	Entered service	Armament	Cost
Astute (UK) SSN displacing 7,100 tonnes	2010	Tomahawk cruise missiles, 38 torpedos in 6 tubes	1.8bn
Kilo (Russian) type 877	1980s	18 torpedo SAMS	$300M
Soryu (Japan) diesel electric 4,200t	2009	Type 89 torpedos; antiship missiles	536M
Borei (Russian) SSBN to replace typhoon class	2012 (5 in service)	Antiship missiles	$713M
Los Angeles class SSN (US)	62 built 1980s	23	$1.5Bn
Seawolf class replacing the LA class	3 built during the Cold War	Tomahawk missiles harpoon missiles	$5bn
Ohio (US) ballistic missiles 18 built	1981-1997	Trident missiles	$2.86bn
Virginia Class 7,900 tonnes block V 10,200t		Tomahawk missiles 65 torpedos in 5 torpedo tubes	$3.2bn
Akula class SSGN (Russian) 12,700t	4 in service	32 Cruise missiles	$1.55bn
Yasen class (Russia) 13,800t length 139 metres	2013 (3 in service, with 10 planned)	cruise missiles with 500-mile range; 10 torpedo tubes, anti-ship and land attack missiles with 500-mile range	$1.6bn

Both China and the US are increasing research and development into developing these potent tactical and strategic platforms, while also focusing on expanding acquisition quotas for the vessels. Submarines play a critical role in the strategy for maritime and even more broadly, multi-domain dominance planning for both nations. Nevertheless, the regional submarine race will see approximately half of the world's combat submarines operating in the Indo-Pacific by the mid-2030s, challenging the capabilities of the major powers to effectively use submarines in a congested and contested operating environment.

Australian Procurement Strategy

In 2021, the Australian government was still planning to build 12 "regionally-superior" *Attack*-class diesel-powered submarines based on the French *Barracuda* class, to replace the six *Collins* class currently operating These were to have been about 94 metres long, displacing about 5,500 tonnes, with a capacity for 20-30 mk 48 MOD 7 torpedoes, also used by the USN. They would have been the world's largest diesel-electric submarines. They were to come with a price tag exceeding A$50billion, making them by far the most expensive defence project in Australia's history. The purpose of building these large conventionally powered submarines was to address the challenges emerging from a more assertive China, with its clear focus on taking over Taiwan and increasing its reach in the Pacific region. Unsurprisingly, this strategy has not gone uncontested. Arguing against AUKUS and instead for a military alliance with Indonesia, Defence analyst Sam Roggeveen noted "The Australian Defence Force, including its nuclear-powered submarine fleet, is designed to defend Australia and our maritime approaches, and not to pose a threat to China's territory and near seas."[129] Reluctantly, he urges contemplation of a future era of American decline in its domination in Asia. Instead of unrealistically preparing for conventional confrontation, he supports strategies of sea denial over sea control, and a balanced force development that reduces the risk of catastrophic war.[130] This apparently conciliatory approach is not universally held.

Rightly or wrongly, the Australian public in 2024 perceived Chinese trade tariffs and its extraordinary naval shipbuilding industry output as constituting a threat to national security and the balance of power in the Australian sphere of influence, summarized by one observer as follows: "The course of events shows that China is on being the dominant world power. Indeed, it has unwaveringly and determinedly followed a plan and a process to that effect for almost fifty years".[131] The Australian government agonized over the cost and ethics of nuclear-powered submarines to meet the threat. Effectively, Australia wanted conventional submarines that would do what other nations accomplished only with nuclear-powered boats. The *Attack* class, based on the French *Barracuda* class, though not yet operational, was proposed as the appropriate diesel-powered submarine.

However, informed opinion developed to the point that the proposed diesel-powered boats "do not provide the value for money capability that is provided by nuclear-powered submarines".[132] Nuclear-powered submarines can deploy quicker, pursue targets more aggressively, and were seen to

---

[129] Roggeveen, S. (2024). Australia needs a military alliance with Indonesia. *Australian Foreign Affairs*, Iss. 21, June, pp. 6-25.

[130] Roggeveen, S.(2023). *The Echidna Strategy*. La Trobe University Press. Collingwood, Victoria.

[131] Nance, C. (2023). China's Great Plan, Coming to a Country Near You. *Quadrant*, no. 596, vol. LXVII number 5, pp. 35-37.

[132] Mole, D. (2020). Nuclear power for submarines. In Frame, T. (ed). *An Australian Nuclear Industry: Beginning with Submarines?* Connor court, Redland Bay. p. 175.

be possibly even cheaper than the intended French *Barracuda* class.¹³³ The cost of the contract with the French had ballooned to AUD80bn. This would consume two-thirds of the Navy budget. Projects that would have to be abandoned to support the expense were not specified. In 2018, the Australian government established a small secret task force within navy to investigate what options were available.¹³⁴ The decision was made to rescind the contract to build a new class of diesel-powered submarine based on the French *Barracuda* class, and instead to proceed towards acquiring up to eight nuclear-powered submarines to replace the *Collins* class and address the changed strategic threat in Australia's Defence environment. Details of who would build these, and where, and who would supply the nuclear reactors for propulsion, were decisions left for later. After the debacle of the *Collins* decision decades before, it is not surprising that the media debate intensified. Did we need them? Can we afford them, and can we crew them? Each submarine takes about eight years to build, and with American and British builders fully committed and under pressure to increase their output for their own fleets, nuclear powered submarines are hardly easily available off the shelf purchases. Several Defence commentators and analysts have written extensively about how Australia's acquisition of a nuclear-powered fleet will impact on the regional balance of forces, and its inevitable consequences for the strategic cooperation with American and British navies.¹³⁵ It appears that the decision was unexpected by most of the stakeholders. Pacific allies were "angered (France) and surprised" (Canada).¹³⁶

---

[133] White, (2019). *How to Defend Australia*, La Trobe University Press, Melbourne, p. 185.

[134] The Economist. (2021), Enter AUKUS, *The Economist*, Sept 25, p. 16.

[135] Roggeveen, S. (2023). *The Echidna Strategy*. La Trobe University Press. Collingwood, Victoria.

[136] Dunlop, D. (2023). A Wake-up call for Canada: Rethinking our Arctic Submarine Policies. *Australian Naval Review*, issue 2, pp. 58-69.

Options for the Australian Submarine Service

Questions about schedule remain, and as to whether a life-of-type extension (LOTE) of the *Collins* will address the temporary capability gap before the nuclear-powered boats are available sometime in the 2040s. Some strategists asked whether the SSNs will later be seen to have been unnecessary after all.

Defence strategist Professor Hugh White wrote: "Australia does not need nuclear powered submarines... nor can we afford them. We need boats about as big as the *Collins*, we need a lot of them, and we need them quickly, with minimum risk and delay."[137] He continued to publish negative criticism of AUKUS for several years. [138] Alternatively, in a radical rethink of platforms, offensive capacity in the short term was proposed by others using *B-21* bombers, or LUUVs (large underwater unmanned vehicles). The idea failed to attract political or ADF support. Instead, the Australian population, still suspicious of the *Collins* class, was surprised but generally supportive of its government's far-reaching decision to build a nuclear-powered submarine force.

The AUKUS Arrangement

By late 2021, there were concerns that the changing strategic context had rendered the planned *Attack* class design unlikely to prove suitable as hoped, and after extensive reflection, the Australian government decided not to proceed with the project with the French Naval Group, but instead to create a partnership to acquire a nuclear-powered fleet, in cooperation with the

---

[137] White, H. (2019). *How to Defend Australia*, La Trobe University Press, Carlton, p. 187.

[138] White, H. (2024). Is AUKUS Plan Feasible? *Weekend Australian,* Feb 17-18. An extract from his essay: White, H. (2024). Dead in the Water: The AUKUS Delusion, *Australian Foreign Affairs*. Feb 19.

American and British governments. The proposed 9,700 ton "AUKUS boats" will be built in Australia, with American and British nuclear propulsion and a design based on the current British *Astute* class.[139] This plan to build the AUKUS boats jointly with the US and UK has its critics. The Astute was over budget and over schedule, reflecting serious deficiencies in the British construction industry.[140]

Given the increased cost and complexity of nuclear-powered submarines, comparisons were quickly addressed. Advantages of speed and endurance place the nuclear-powered boats in a separate class from diesel-electric boats. "They can stay on station for 81 days compared with 23 days for conventional boats".[141] Driving this decision was the requirement for interoperability with US boats and systems, access to American nuclear propulsion technology, and the undoubted superiority of nuclear-powered boats over diesel-powered boats in terms of speed, endurance, stealth, and payload. With the purchase of Tomahawk missiles, the effect on the balance of power in the region cannot be underestimated. It promises a significant increase in submarine capability, although at vast expense.

The likely cost and schedule received ongoing media attention. Prime among concerns expressed were whether Australia, with no history of building or operating nuclear submarines, could manage this complex task with its inherent "heroic and frankly unrealistic assumptions".[142] Then there is the question of how Australia will be able to recruit and train sufficient submariners

---

[139] A picture of an Astute class was posted by General Angus Campbell, Chief of the Australian Defence Force on Twitter on 13 March 2023 when the AUKUS pathway was announced.

[140] Briggs, P.(2024). The Sad State of Royal Navy Submarine Capability and Implications for Australia. *Naval Officers Club Newsletter*. vol. 136, March. pp. 38-39

[141] Mole, D. (2020). Nuclear power for submarines. In Frame, T. (ed.) *An Australian Nuclear Industry: Starting with Submarines?* Connor Court, Redland Bay, p. 179.

[142] Stewart, C. (2023). High Reward, but High Risk. *Weekend Australian*, Mar 11-12, p. 38.

to crew the *Virginia* class boats in the 2030s and also the AUKUS boats to follow in the 2040s. the Virginia class require 135 crew and the *Astute* class on which the AUKUS submarine design will be based have crews of about 100.

The build of the nuclear-powered submarines in Australia will be the largest Australian defence project ever. In 2021, the decision of which class of boat to build (the British *Astute* or American *Virginia*, or a third alternative) had not yet been announced. The first nuclear boat for Australia is expected to be available by 2035, about the same time as first of class HMS *Astute* (launched in 2007) will have completed 25 years in service. The seventh and final *Astute* class boat, HMS *Agincourt*, is expected to be commissioned in 2026. This class is 97 metres long and covers 7,000 tons. By comparison, and costing a billion dollars more, the American *Virginia* class is 115 metres long and displaces 7,900 tons. Each submarine takes about seven years to build, at one of two shipyards in the US. In 2024, only 22 *Virginias* had been built out of a target number of 44.

Comparison of *Collins*, *Astute* and *Virginia* classes attack submarines.

Class	Cost	Length	Displacement	Crew	Tubes	Vertical launch	Weapons
Collins		77m	3,400 Tn	58	6	n/a	22
Astute	2.2bn	97m	7,100 Tn	98	6		38
Virginia (I-IV)	2.8bn	115m	7,900 Tn	134	4	40	37

Virginia class boats are being produced in two American construction yards at the rate of about 1-2 per year. The final four of 39 Virginia class submarines planned to be built are scheduled to be delivered in 2033. The US SSN(X) class is already under construction to succeed the *Virginia* class in 2031. With both British and US yards fully committed to the fina*l*

Astute and *Virginia* boats, and in design of the SSBN ballistic submarines (the *Dreadnought* and *Colombia* class, replacing the *Vanguard* and *Ohio* Class respectively), attention has fallen on schemes of complement. *Virginia* class boats have a crew of 134, the *Astute* class somewhat less. *Collins* class boats have a complement of 58. Australia will need an extraordinary effort to field the necessary 2,300 submariners to crew eight *Virginia* class or equivalent submarines.

The expected year for the commissioning of the first *Virginia* submarine for Australia may be 2035 or later, and in the meantime and beyond Australia will continue to rely for its submarine capability on the *Collins* class. Australia's strategic options for replacing the *Collins* class are limited. A life of type extension has been approved for the six *Collins* boats while the nuclear boats are built. However, the first *Collins* class boat has been in the water since 1993, and extending their lives to provide capability for another 10-20 years will be very expensive, committing Australia to operating a fleet of two types for decades to come: both nuclear and diesel electric, differing mostly only in propulsion technology, and but with very different capabilities and thus suitable for a range of tasks between them.

Other countries (e.g. China and India) operate both nuclear and conventional submarines). The extended life-of-type *Collins* class boats could serve to maintain capability and to provide continuous training for submariners preparatory to their crewing the *Virginias* and the AUKUS boats. clear boats to be available. However, this has them training on what would already be obsolescent equipment, and on a boat which will require expensive upgrading to bring it up to Australian standards. A similar caution applies to the acquisition of two or three *Virginia* class boats, at a time when the US is building the last of the class and replacing them with a new class already being designed, although this appears to be at least 10-15 years away. The decision to enter the AUKUS defence arrangement to build a fleet of at least eight nuclear-powered boats, with American propulsion technology, opens the door for Australia to build its own nuclear industrial sector with infrastructure support for the *Virginia* and eventually AUKUS nuclear-powered boats.

The implications of the watershed decision to rescind the contract with the French builder are far-reaching.[143] In its international relations, France responded with predictable outrage that the *Attack* Class build had been cancelled in the formation of AUKUS. It left Australia scrambling to repair its relationship with France, which has numerous territories, two million of its citizens, and 7,000 troops, in the Indo-Pacific. An ally for many decades, France is a significant political and strategic force in the region. The contract with France had a "let-out" clause that allowed either party to rescind the contract on payment of a negotiated penalty. A compensation payment of AUD350 million by the Australian government to the French Naval Group was negotiated in June 2022. At further significant cost, Australia walked away from the building and infrastructure it had positioned in Cherbourg to design the new submarine.

All this indicates a perceived requirement for continuing and expanding collaboration by Australia with its partners in its defence. The AUKUS partnership includes other technology sharing, including cyber and artificial intelligence.

Confirming an increased interest by the US in the Indo-Pacific is the call by US Secretary of the Navy Kenneth Braithwaite for the creation of a new naval command to be known as the

---

[143] Mole, D. (2020). Nuclear power for submarines. In Frame, T. (ed.) (2020). *An Australian Nuclear Industry Starting with Submarines?*, Connor Court, Redland Bay.

First Fleet (which previously oversaw American operations in the Western Pacific from 1947-73.[144] Currently the Seventh Fleet, home ported in Japan, is responsible for overseeing US operations in the Indian Ocean. This indicates a significant change in posture by the US in establishing a new fleet potentially may mean a strike group of an aircraft carrier, cruisers, destroyers and frigates, an SSN, and having the shore support in a friendly and reliable ally. Darwin, in Australia's Northern Territory, and only 1,500 kms from the South China Sea, a potential no-go zone in time of hostilities, is a potential area for a base through which American ships could be rotated. Manus Island has also been mentioned. Preference for a greater buffer could favour rotational deployments of US and British submarines to HMAS *Stirling* in Fremantle. Alternatively, the US First Fleet may be configured very differently from its other fleets, to fight with a very different strategy, unique to the current and future demands of the Indo-Pacific region.

Key to understanding Australia's place in the shifting balance of power in regard to China and the US, are the strategies available to the US in relation to China. An overview suggests that preparing for an engagement aimed at securing USN Captain Alfred Thayer Mahan's concept of sea control, it would be more effective to plan for a less kinetic blockade (confining China to the South China Sea), as might be proposed by a "cruiser" strategy initially advocated by British naval strategist Sir Julian Corbett, with the objective "to secure command of the sea or prevent the enemy from securing it."[145] This Corbett-aligned rather than Mahan-aligned strategy has received recent support by American strategists, recommending disruption of

---

[144] Trevithick, J. (2020). The Navy wants to stand up a new fleet aimed at deterring China in the Indian Ocean. *The Drive*.

[145] Corbett, J. S. (1911). *Principles of Maritime Strategy*, New York, Longmans, Green & Co. p. 87.

Chinese shipping routes and its international trade on which its economy depends.¹⁴⁶ In this strategy, just as the battleship gave way to the aircraft carrier in World War II, so now the aircraft carrier would give way to the submarine and the littoral and light patrol combatants at trade chokepoints. This strategy would avoid a potentially expensive and high-risk Mahanian "decisive conflict" close to China and far from the US, and instead focus on debilitating China's stability, by forcing it to abandon its strategy of anti-access/area denial area of operations.

Other defence analysts argue strongly that Australia is best served by an accelerated acquisition of larger Offshore Patrol Vessels (OPVs), with an increased build of 18 rather than the current projected fleet of 12 OPVs providing a capability to fill a capability gap left by the delay in delivery of the SEA 5000 *Hunter*-class frigates and the future submarines:¹⁴⁷

> Despite the Navy's Mahanian ideology that the navy exists to protect sea lanes of communication, its force structure isn't designed for that and most likely couldn't do it. Its surface fleet is built around small numbers of extremely expensive platforms that are primarily designed to defend themselves... Nor does it have the quantity of vessels needed to protect against asymmetric adversaries who might seek to interdict trade on those sea lanes. Because it often regards unmanned and autonomous systems as poor replacements for traditional manned platforms, Defence tends to overlook the benefits they offer... Sensors, weapons, processors and communication systems need to be distributed across many more smaller, cheaper platforms, many of which will be unmanned,

---

¹⁴⁶ Ward, D. E. (2020). Going to war with China? Dust off Corbett! *US Naval institute Proceedings*, January, pp. 56-60.

¹⁴⁷ Shackleton, D. (1922). The Hunter Frigate: An assessment. *Strategy*, April. Australian Strategic Policy Institute, Canberra.

whether in the air, on the surface or under the water.[148]

Notwithstanding this advocacy for more numerous and cheaper assets, the principle of purchasing or building only those ships that are fit for purpose would seem to warrant priority. The apparent drift towards smaller more automated vessels with fewer crew but still confronting missions that inevitably take them beyond littoral waters and potentially into higher intensity warfare has not gone without criticism. Just as the *Flower* class corvettes in 1942 were barely adequate for ASW in the Atlantic, so the proposed corvette to substitute as a more substantially armed OPV may be an unwise retreat from a blue water responsibility being addressed with a brown water asset.[149] Similarly, it would be unrealistic to expect uninhabited underwater vessels (UUVs) to substitute for crewed submarines. The Australian Navy is not alone in being challenged by the need for greater capability in an environment of fiscal restraint and limited human resources, as indicated in the following comments about the balance between demand and supply – or requirements and capability. Five years ago this topic was addressed in *a Report on the Restructuring of US Navy forces to Fewer Large and more Unmanned Vessels.* [150] A careful review of US surface combatants concluded:

> Perhaps of most concern is the fact that the current fleet is fiscally unsustainable due to the escalating costs to crew, operate, and maintain today's highly integrated manned surface combatants. The surface fleet's shortfalls are especially problematic because the role of surface forces in Navy offensive operations will likely expand over the next few decades. Carrier air wings will be

---

[148] Helyer, M. (2020). *From Concentrated Vulnerability to Distributed Lethality*, Australian Strategic Policy Institute. Canberra, p. 7.

[149] Moffitt, R. (2023). Corvettes are not an option for Australia. *The Strategist*, 3 Aug. https://www.aspistrategist.org.au/au/author/rowan-moffitt

[150] Congressional Office, (2019). *An analysis of the Navy's fiscal year 2020 shipbuilding plan 2019.* US Govt.

constrained in the number of weapons they can deliver because they will need to operate at least 1,000 nm from significant enemy missile threats, such as those on the Chinese or Russian coasts. Submarines, which have been considered the U.S. military's most survivable platforms, are retiring faster than they are being built and may be too vulnerable in waters close to China or Russia due to the fielding of seabed sonar networks.[151]

In response to changing threats, rising costs, and the need to pair weapons with targets more efficiently, the US is restructuring its Navy to a fleet of fewer large ships, more and smaller vessels, and more unmanned ships and aircraft.[152] In 2020, an internal Office of the Secretary of Defence assessment called for the Navy to cut two aircraft carriers, freeze the large surface combatant fleet of destroyers and cruisers around current levels and add dozens of unmanned or lightly manned ships to the inventory.[153] The study called for a fleet of nine carriers, down from the current fleet of 11, and for 65 unmanned or lightly manned surface vessels.[154]

The study called for a surface force of between 80 and 90 large surface combatants, and an increase in the number of small surface combatants – between 55 and 70, which is substantially more than the Navy currently operates. The assessment is part of an ongoing DoD-wide review of Navy force structure and aligns with the US DoD intention to begin de-emphasizing

---

[151] Clark, B. and Walton TA. (2019). *Taking back the Seas*. Center for Strategic and Budgetary Assessments.

[152] Office of Naval Research Advisory Committee. (2017, Sept). *Autonomous and Unmanned Systems in the Department of the Navy*. Retrieved from https://www.onr.navy.mil/en/-/media/Files/history/nrac-reports/2017_es_Autonomous_Unmanned_Systems_Don-SEP2017: https://www.onr.navy.mil/en/-/media/Files/history/nrac-reports/2017_es_Autonomous_Unmanned_Systems_Don-SEP2017

[153] Larter, (2020). Defense Department study calls for cutting two of the US Navy's aircraft carriers, *Defense News*, 20 April.

[154] US Government. (2020). *Navy Force Structure and Ship building Plans: Background and Issues for Congress* RL32665.

aircraft carriers as the centrepiece of the Navy's force projection and put more emphasis on unmanned technologies that can be more easily sacrificed in a conflict and yet can achieve their missions more affordably. The US Navy is currently developing unmanned surface vessels that are intended to increase the offensive capability for less money expended, while increasing the number of targets the Chinese military would have to locate in a fight. Chief of Naval Operations Admiral Michael Gilday said in late 2019 that the future fleet has to include a mix of unmanned vessels: "We can't continue to wrap $2 billion ships around 96 missile tubes in the numbers we need to fight in a distributed way, against a potential adversary that is producing capability and platforms at a very high rate of speed. We have to change the way we are thinking." [155] In 2019, to save billions, the refuelling of the USS *Harry S. Truman* (commissioned in 1998) was cancelled, effectively decommissioning the aircraft carrier with half its intended 50-year hull life remaining. In 2020, the decision was reversed. In 2020, the United States Navy issued contracts for the design and development of what it termed the Large Unmanned Surface Vehicle (LUSV). A 1000-2000 tonne, 200-300 feet long autonomous vehicle the size of a conventional corvette with the capability to engage both sea and land-based targets.[156] The US intended to acquire seven of these vessels by 2025, at a cost of $3 bn in the 2020 budget. However, Congress stipulated that the two LUSVs to be built in 2020 would not have vertical missile launching systems. Given that the LUSV class will likely carry strike packages for ASW and autonomous operations, there are questions being raised as to the preparedness of international law to

---

[155] Larter, D. (2020). Defense Department study calls for cutting two of the US Navy's aircraft carriers, *Defense News*, 20 April.

[156] Congressional Research Service. (2020), *Navy Large Unmanned Surface Vehicles: Background and Issues for Congress* (CRS No. R45757, 10 November 2020), 7.

address this development of capability in lethal autonomous weapons systems (LAWS).[157] It should be noted that in 2024 the US cannot guarantee the safety of its ships out to 4,000 kms from China's coast, this being the range of China's DF26B, the world's first ballistic missile designed to hit ships at sea. The purpose of these weapons is to deter American ships with unacceptable risk from approaching close enough to strike.

The OSD assessment also called for essentially freezing the size of the large surface combatant fleet. There are about 90 cruisers and destroyers in the fleet. The study recommended retaining at least 80 but keeping about as many as the Navy currently operates at the high end. The Navy's small surface combatant program is essentially the 20 littoral combat ships in commission today, with another 15 under contract, as well as the 20 next-generation frigates, which would get to the minimum number in the assessment of 55 small combatants, with the additional 15 presumably being more frigates.

In summary, the US Navy is opting for a force structure of fewer carriers, more and smaller combatant vessels, more unmanned capability, with large, unmanned surface vehicles (LUSVs), medium unmanned surface vessels (MUSVs) and greater reliance on AI. The big change comes in the small unmanned or lightly manned surface combatants. In an interview with *Defence News*, US Defense Secretary Esper said the Navy needed to focus integrating those technologies into the fleet. "What we have to tease out is, what does that future fleet look like?" Esper said. "I think one of the ways you get there quickly is moving toward lightly manned [ships, which over time can be unmanned. We can go with lightly manned ships, get them out there. You can build them so they're optionally manned

---

[157] Parker, J. (2020). The United States Navy's Autonomous Corvette: Is international law ready? ANU Unpublished paper, Canberra.

and then, depending on the scenario or the technology, at some point in time they can go unmanned."[158] The American move to unmanned systems is reflected in the US Navy Unmanned Campaign Framework.[159] Specifically, it notes that 'autonomous systems provide additional warfighting capability and capacity to augment traditional combatant force, allowing the option to take on greater operational risk while maintaining a tactical and strategic advantage. Unmanned systems will increase lethality, capacity, survivability, operational tempo, deterrence, and operational readiness."

China's PLA(N) fleet

By comparison, The Chinese people' Liberation Army (Navy) or (PLA(N) operates the world's largest submarine fleet. Most are diesel-electric, but they carry nuclear missiles with a range of 1500 kms. China also launched two type 094 Jin-Class nuclear powered submarines in 2019, each carrying 12 ballistic missiles with a range of 4,500 kms. It is expected to have eight SSBN and 13 SSN submarines by 2030.[160] The Chinese navy is now the largest in the world, having virtually doubled in size since 2000. In 2005 China had some 220 battle force ships (frigates, destroyers, cruisers, and submarines). By 2020, this had grown to 360. The rapid naval expansion of Chinese naval power is the largest naval expansion in human history.

This Chinese shipbuilding of industries deliver a fleet of new vessels the size of the British Royal Navy every four years. In

---

[158] Larter, (2020) Defense Department study calls for cutting 2 of the US Navy's aircraft carriers, *Defense News*, 20 April.

[159] US Department of the Navy (2021). *Unmanned Campaign Framework*. US Department of the Navy, Washington DC.

[160] Senate Armed Services Committee (2020). *Update China: Naval construction Trends vis-à-vis U.S. Navy Shipbuilding plans 2020-2030*.

2005 the PLA(N) deployed 16 major surface combatants larger than frigates (cruisers, destroyers and aircraft carriers) by 2020 this had increased to 43.[161]

In the same period, Minor war vessels went from 38 to 102. The new ships offer better capability than those they replace. For example, with S-band advanced radar and towed array sonar, and 64 cells for vertical launch of HHQ9 surface-to-air and YJ-18 supersonic antiship and CY-5 land attack cruise missiles, the 25 operational 7,500-ton Type 52D DDG air warfare destroyers are each on a par with Australia's three *Hobart* class AWDs. The even more heavily armed 12,000-ton Chinese Type 55 large destroyers, of which eight have been built, are classed as cruisers in the West. Their 112 VLS cells can fire a range of long-range missiles. Such capability clearly goes beyond what might be required to defend China or fight a local conflict. With two and shortly three aircraft carriers (*Liaoning*, *Shandong* and 80,000-ton *Fujian* embarking J-15 fighters), they allow force projection to distant theatres in expeditionary warfare. The intention of the CCP seems clear and goes beyond coastal defence. This poses a significant strategic risk for Australian defence. Australia has no ambition to become a dominant world power or to threaten or coerce its neighbours. Its purpose is to ensure as far a possible that nations are able to share the high seas in mutually beneficial trade, and to defend its borders against invasion. The intention of the Chinese Communist Party is explicitly the converse of this and has made it clear that it seeks domination by coercion or invasion of its neighbours. It has claimed the entire South China Sea and has openly committed to bringing Taiwan directly under Beijing's control.

---

[161] Senate Armed Services Committee (2020). *Update China: Naval construction Trends vis-à-vis U.S. Navy Shipbuilding plans 2020-2030.*

Class of vessel	PLA(N) Fleet	AUKUS Fleets (Totals)
SSBNs	6	16
SSNs	8	66
SSKs conventional submarines	55	6
Aircraft carriers	3	12 nuclear aircraft carriers
Large surface combatants	40	96
Medium surface combatants	102	70
Large amphibious ships	11	41
Major logistic ships	30	93
Unmanned surface and underwater vehicles	?	150

The Australian Submarine Fleet

For Australia, with nuclear-powered submarines planned to be acquired through the AUKUS arrangement, a third phase is about to begin. It is to the nuclear propulsion era that attention is now turned.

This book has overviewed the history of the Australian submarine fleet, from its beginnings in 1915 with *AE1* and *AE2*, through various classes of boats, with its two greatest phases, from *Oberons* to *Collins*, through to the planned but now discarded plans for the *Attack* class. A decision by the Australian government in March 2023 to buy five *Virginia* class boats, although this class is now about to begin its phase out period from the USN, allows Australia to train crews to operate nuclear boats in preparation for the eventual build and maintenance of its nuclear-powered AUKUS submarines in Adelaide, in collaboration with the American and British partners.

The *Collins* class are expected to be beginning to phase out in the 2030s as the *Virginia* class boats arrive, up to HMAS *Rankin*'s projected retirement in 2048. The *Collins* class boats are thought likely to undergo a life-of-type-extension (LOTE) beginning with HMAS *Farncomb* in 2026. Each boat will take two years, virtually rebuilding the boats. They are planned to remain a core of the national defence until the 2040s.[162] Australia is committed to extending the life of at least several of its decades-old *Collins* class (delivering one every two years) that were due to be decommissioned in the 2020s. This is far from cheap or simple.

To bridge the capability gap Australia intends to buy two or three *Virginia* class submarines from the US, with an option to buy two more, and it is expected that these will be operational early in the 2030s. However, many are cautious in their optimism that these vessels will actually arrive, because of training and security and regulatory concerns, and because the USN does not have any spare.[163] Also, the two US yards that build them are doing so more slowly than expected (at only 1.2 per year instead of the expected 2), so the USN is itself in need of more boats quickly to maintain its operational fleet. It was announced in 2024 that Australia would is pay $4.5bn to the USN to ease supply chain constraints in building more *Virginia* class submarines, at a time when American focus is moving on, to designing and building the SSN(X) replacement for the *Virginia* class.

Thirdly, White cautions that Australia has committed to buying a submarine that Britain is expected to build, based on the *Astute* class, as the first of the AUKUS class for the RN, "although

---

[162] Australia's emergence as a major maritime power of the 21st Century (2023). www.youtube.com/watch?v=kYEfmAJBUMI&t=746s accessed 13 Oct.

[163] White, H. (2024). Is AUKUS Plan Feasible? *Weekend Australian*, Feb 17-18. An extract from his essay: White, H. (2024). Dead in the Water: The AUKUS Delusion, *Australian Foreign Affairs*. Feb 19.

at this stage we know nothing about it."[164] The British have busy decade ahead, building the last of their *Astute* class, the first of their *Dreadnought* class to replace the *Vanguard* SSBN class, and designing and building the first of the AUKUS class for the RN, with its build eventually being done in Adelaide with American and Australian collaboration. As in the US, the UK facility for building submarines is currently stretched, as it begins to build the successor to the *Trafalgar*-class SSBN. In 2024 the Australian Government agreed to contribute A$4.7bn over 10 years to accelerate the plant in Derby in the British Midlands in building the Rolls-Royce reactor for the first AUKUS submarine.

In Defence planning, most strategic, if not operational and tactical decisions also are based on a mix of "push and pull" factors, such as an offensive capability matched by a defensive deterrence. A new Australian Submarine Agency (ASA) has been established to oversee the delivery of platforms to the submarine service. ASA Director General VADM Jonathon Mead AO outlined the pull advantages of nuclear-powered submarines: "no other capability matches the endurance and the mobility of what a conventionally armed nuclear-powered submarine provides. The push factors he alluded to in a statement "throughout the 2030s and 40s and beyond, periscope depth operations – especially snorting to run the diesels and recharge the boat's batteries – will become progressively more dangerous for submariners".[165] Given the complexity and regulatory challenges of the AUKUS arrangement to build and operate nuclear-powered submarines, "a new regulator has been established, independent of the ADF chain of command,

---

[164] White, H. (2024). Is AUKUS Plan Feasible? *Weekend Australian,* Feb 17-18. An extract from his essay Dead in the Water: The AUKUS Delusion, *Australian Foreign Affairs.* (2024). Feb 19.

[165] Ferguson, G. (2023). Navy Prepares for a new Generation of Submarine Technology. *Navy Outlook.* FairCount Media, Bankstown NSW, pp. 33-39.

and like the ASA, is part of the Defence portfolio, but with its own independent reporting line to the Minister for Defence."[166]

It is an understatement to observe that on the basis of history, the design and building of the projected eight AUKUS class submarines represents a very significant challenge in conditions of great uncertainty. The outcome will be that the RAN will be operating three classes of submarines simultaneously, two of which it has never operated before, with extensive and complex logistics personnel and training supply chain requirements, following on from a historical period of troubled operations and sustainment of just one class. It is possible that in the 2030s the RAN will be operating the *Virginia* class, planning and training for the AUKUS class in the 2040s, while also operating the extended life of type *Collins* class, and all at the same time. The Australian Submarine Service of the 2030s and 2040 will not be for the faint-hearted.

National Examples of Submarines

American Submarines

Attack submarines (SSN): Los Angeles Class - The fast attack "688" *Los Angeles* class are quiet and fast, with speeds exceeding 30 knots, modified to launch Tomahawk land attack missiles. The planned total of 62 *Los Angeles* Class (built 1962-1996) were designed during the height of the Cold War to counter increasingly quiet Soviet submarines in the north Atlantic and north-western Pacific, which would pose a threat to the US Navy's carrier battle groups. The 32 remaining operational vessels displace just under 7,000 tonnes when submerged and are reportedly capable of over 33 knots submerged. Some LA

---

[166] Ferguson, G. (2023). Navy Prepares for a new Generation of Submarine Technology. *Navy Outlook*. FairCount Media, Bankstown NSW, pp. 36.

class boats served for 40 years before being decommissioned. Maximum operating depth is 650 feet. The *Los Angeles* Class are capable carrying 37 Mk 48 heavyweight torpedoes, 12 Tomahawk land attack cruise missiles in vertical tubes, Harpoon anti-ship missiles and multiple Mk 67 captor mines.

Seawolf Class SSN - The three 9200-ton *Seawolf* Class submarines were designed to be the ultimate predators of the sea, responsible for hunting down stealthy Soviet *Akula* and huge *Typhoon* Class submarines in a deep ocean environment. *Seawolf* Class submarines range in weight from 9,140 tonnes to 12,140 tonnes (for the USS *Jimmy Carter* subclass). Commissioned in 2005, SSN-23 the *Jimmy Carter* (named for the former submariner and President) was modified to support clandestine operations by adding an extra 100 feet to the platform to accommodate up to 50 special forces. They can dive to 2,000 feet, are capable of 35 knots while submerged, and carry approximately 50 Mk 48 heavyweight torpedoes, Tomahawk land attack cruise missiles and Harpoon anti-ship missiles. The *Seawolf* Class are the most expensive boats ever built and carry twice the torpedo load of the *Los Angeles* Class. They are seven feet shorter than the LA class, though with a wider beam of 40 feet. Costs of USD3bn each forced a reduction in the planned 29 boats, and only three were built. The *Seawolf* class has a surface speed of 18 kts and a submerged speed over 33 kts. The *Seawolf* class was followed by the smaller *Virginia* class 7000-ton craft with unparalleled intelligence gathering capability, in addition to its offensive weapons. The nuclear reactor has a life of 30 years, so the limit to the submarine's patrol duration is the amount of food that can be carried for the 118 crew. Most patrols are now about 70 days, operating at depths up to 240 metres.

Virginia class SSN - The US has relied on its *Seawolf* and *Los*

Angeles Classes as its primary attack submarines. The LA class boats are being replaced by the *Virginia* class. A successor to the *Los Angeles* SSN and *Seawolf* Classes, a total of 66 of these smaller, cheaper and quieter nuclear boats is planned. *Virginia* and her projected 66 sister ships are a 21st century submarine, with a classified top speed of greater than 25 knots submerged and submerged weight of 7,900 tonnes.

Virginia class submarine

The various "blocks" of the *Virginia* Class are capable of carrying a variety of weapons, including 22-26 Mk 48 heavyweight torpedoes with a 23-mile range at 55 kts, four torpedo tubes, Tomahawk land attack cruise missiles in 12 vertical launchers and Harpoon anti-ship missiles. The *Los Angeles* class attack submarines were designed in the 1970s to hunt the large

Russian *Akula* and *Typhoon* classes of submarines. The US has embarked on a period of rapid modernisation for the submarine fleet, with 22 *Virginia* Class attack submarines delivered out of 38 planned to be built, replacing the 26 *Los Angeles* class attack boats. The S9G nuclear reactor has a life of 35 years. This means that the submarine will not have to be refuelled for its entire expected 35-year operational service life.

SSBNs - All the while since 1945, the firepower of submarines was increasing. *Nautilus* had introduced nuclear propulsion in 1954, and nuclear weapons (principally missiles) followed. In the 1960's, the nuclear warhead Regulus missile could be submarine launched with a range of 500 miles. The Polaris missile followed.

Ballistic missile and cruise missile submarines (SSBN/SSGN) Ohio Class – The *Ohio* Class was first launched in 1981, displacing 18,000 tonnes. It was then the largest submarine America ever produced. The 170 m long American *SSBN Ohio* class carry 24 Trident missiles, each with eight independently targeted nuclear warheads, capable of destroying targets at a range of 2000 miles. The US has 14 *Ohio*-class submarines, each armed with about 20 Trident II missiles, each with 8 independently targetable warheads, with a range of 6,100 nautical miles. The *Ohio* Class (with about 12 active) is expected to serve well into the 2020s.

A single *Ohio* class SSBN with Trident missiles has more firepower than all the bombs dropped in World War II, Korea, and Vietnam combined. The US commissioned 18 *Ohio* class submarines between 1981-1997. The *Ohio* class have four torpedo tubes, but their main armament is their 24 Trident II missiles, Originally designed as ballistic missile submarines responsible for carrying the sea-based leg of America's nuclear deterrent, the early-to-mid 2000's conversion of four submarines to be classed as cruise missile submarines reduced the total number of ballistic missile submarines to 14. These SSBNs displace 18,750 tonnes submerged and have a reported submerged speed of 25 knots, the *Ohio* class SSBN variants are capable of support 24 Trident I and II missiles, while the SSGN (guided missile) variant carries a payload of 154 Tomahawk land attack cruise missiles, Mk 48 heavyweight torpedoes and Harpoon anti-ship missiles.

Each *Ohio* Class boat has two crews of 154 officers and enlisted personnel. The "blue' and "gold" crews undertake 70-day patrols in rotation. Nine "boomers" are based in Bangor in NW USA, to patrol the Pacific Ocean, with five homeported in Kings Bay Georgia, on the US east coast, to patrol the Atlantic. The *Ohio* class constitute the most potent nuclear deterrent developed. Stealth became as important as weapons, and the stealth and secrecy attending the *Ohio* class is legendary. The SSBN is a first strike weapon intended to deter any aggressor by patrolling silently to keep its position unknown. Most of the crew, and all their families ashore, are unaware of their whereabouts.

The *Ohio* boats entered service in the 1980s as a replacement for five different classes of fleet ballistic submarines. With the exception of the USS *Henry M Jackson*, each *Ohio* class submarine is named after a US state. With advanced Trident missiles, they can take out an enemy's military installations. The SSBN is tasked with avoiding rather than engaging with the enemy. In 2022, the American Navy continued to operate an all-nuclear fleet of approximately 72 attack and ballistic submarines, with an undisclosed number always on patrol. The successors to the *Ohio* class will be the 12 slightly larger *Columbia* class, with 16 missile tubes (these will be approximately 560 feet long and displace 21,000 tons submerged. They will host the Trident missile system in 10 tubes, in addition to torpedoes. The *Ohio* class is being replaced by 12 *Columbia*-class SSBNs, with an estimated cost of USD100bn. These are expected to serve until 2085. America's Indo-Pacific submarine fleet is based at a number of key locations, including Naval Base Pearl Harbour, Hawaii; Naval Base Kitsap, Washington State (home port to 10 SSBNs); Naval Base Guam and Naval Base Yokosuka, Japan. On the east coast, Kings Bay in southeastern state of Georgia is home to the American Atlantic fleet.

Australian Submarines

Collins class SSK (diesel electric) - Replacing the British-built *Oberon* class, the six Australian *Collins* class submarines (built 1990-2003) displace 3,100 tonnes surfaced. In the 2030s they are being replaced initially by *Virginia* class boats and later in the 2040s by AUKUS boats based on the British *Astute* design with an American combat system. The *Collins* class are expected to be in service until well into the 2030s. they are capable of 10 kts surfaced and 20 kts submerged. They have a range of 11,500 nm at 10 kts. Weapons include 22 Mk 48 torpedos and Harpoon antiship missiles, fired from six 21-inch bow tubes. They carry a crew of 55 with an endurance of 70 days. The *Collins* class are large diesel electric powered submarines based in HMAS *Stirling* on the west coast of the continent. After technical difficulties early in their lives, the *Collins* class underwent modifications to become a successful submarine service with higher availability. The *Collins* class was expected to start phasing out in the mid-2020s, to be replaced by new conventionally powered versions of the French *Barracuda* class. However, Australia rescinded a contract with the French builder and in 2023 opted to buy three *Virginia* nuclear boats but not to nuclear arm them. The *Collins* class are to undergo life of type extensions to keep them operational well into the 2030s. These *Virginia* class submarines were intended to provide capability while a new class of boat based on the British *Astute* class, with an American combat system, initially dubbed AUKUS class in deference to the three countries collaborating in building them (Australia UK and US). The nuclear-powered AUKUS boats are expected to become operational in the 2040s.

British Submarines

Vanguard class SSBN - The *Vanguard* class nuclear powered ballistic submarines were in service with the Royal Navy from 1993. Four were built by Vickers in Barrow-in-Furness, Cumbria (1986-98) as Britain's nuclear deterrent. At 149.9 metres. They displace 15,900 tons and carry 8-16 Trident D5 SLBMs missiles with up to 8 warheads each. They will be replaced by the new *Dreadnought* class in the 2030s. The *Vanguard* class SSBN submarines were introduced in 1994, with four vessels: *Vanguard, Victorious, Vigilant,* and *Vengeance.* The first British nuclear-powered submarine was the HMS *Dreadnought,* completed at Barrow-in Furness in 1963, with an American-supplied Westinghouse nuclear power plant. Four ballistic missile submarines (SSBNs), of the *Vanguard* class each carry up to 16 Trident II missiles with up to eight warheads each, and serve as Britain's nuclear deterrent. The replacement class for the four *Vanguard*-class SSBNs was ordered in 2016 and is named the *Dreadnought* class after its lead boat. The programme will seek to replace one-for-one the current four ballistic missile submarines starting sometime during the late 2020s. One RN submarine is maintained at sea by the RN continually as a UK-owned nuclear-armed deterrent and has done so since the RN took over this task from the RAF in 1968.

The *Resolution* class (SSBNs) were introduced to carry out the nuclear deterrent role under the Polaris programme from 1968. HMS *Resolution* became the RN's first SSBN, firing the first nuclear-capable missile on 15 February 1968. The *Resolution* class carried US-built UGM-27 Polaris A-3 missiles and were later replaced by the *Vanguard* Class submarines and the Trident missile system from 1994. The four *Vanguard* class boats were responsible for the United Kingdom's nuclear deterrent, and carried the Trident missile system. SSBN submarines such as HMS *Vigilant* displace 16,000 tonnes and carry 12 nuclear warhead Trident missiles. Patrols last months, limited only by the food carried for the 130 crew.

Dreadnought class SSBN - Each 150 m long 16,000-ton *Vanguard* class boat could carry up to 16 Trident II D5 Missiles, each of which could carry up to 8 nuclear warheads. The UK Government policy to limit the actual number of warheads carried to 40 per boat and eight Trident Missiles. There has been at least one SSBN on patrol at all times for around 40 years and since April 1969, the Royal Navy's SSBNs have not missed a single day on patrol. Construction of the first of the new class, HMS *Dreadnought*, began in 2016 by BAE shipyard in Barrow-in-Furness. Expected to be commissioned in the 2030s, the British SSBN will displace 17,200 tons, the largest submarine ever built for the RN. They will have four 21-inch torpedo tubes for Spearfish heavyweight torpedoes. Main armament will be 12 Trident II D5 ballistic missiles, four fewer than in the *Vanguard* class. Four Dreadnought class submarines are planned: *Dreadnought, Valiant, Warspite,* and *King George VI*. The four boats are expected to cost over $39.5 billion and serve 30 years. Propulsion is provided by the Rolls-Royce PWR3 nuclear reactor.

SSNs *Churchill* class (1970-92). Three submarines of this

class were built: *Churchill, Courageous,* and *Conqueror*. HMS *Conqueror* sank the Argentinian obsolete and former American cruiser *General Belgrano* with two mk 8 torpedoes at 2,000 yards, during the Falklands War in 1982.[167] This was the first recorded torpedo sinking by of a warship by a nuclear-powered submarine.

SSNs Swiftsure class - HMS *Swiftsure* was the lead boat in the six-strong British hunter-killer class (1973-2010). These submarines were the equivalent of the American *Sturgeon* class and shadowed Soviet boats during the later years of the Cold War. All six built are now retired. In 1999, HMS *Splendid* fired her Tomahawk missiles during the Kosovo conflict. In 2003, HMS *Turbulent* launched 14 Tomahawk missiles in the Iraq conflict.

SSNs *Trafalgar* class Seven submarines of this class were built in Barrow-in Furness and served (1983 - present), as successors to the *Swiftsure* class. Only the HMS *Triumph* remains in service.

SSNs *Astute* class - The RN submarine service now operates six of seven fleet submarines (SSNs), of the *Astute* classes. SSN *Astute* class submarines are the largest nuclear fleet submarines ever to serve with the Royal Navy. They displace 7,100 tonnes, nearly 30 percent larger than its predecessors. Replacing the *Trafalgar* SSN class are the seven *Astute* class boats planned. By 2016, the first three boats were in service (*Astute, Ambush and Artful*), *Audacious* was launched in 2020, with *Anson,* in 2023, with *Agamemnon* and *Agincourt* to follow. The last of the *Astute* class is expected by 2026. No further *Astute* class boats are planned to be built. The replacement SSN currently in design is coded as SSNR (R for replacement).

---

[167] Woodward, J. (2003). *One Hundred Days*. Harper Collins, London.

An *Astute*'s powerplant is the Rolls-Royce PWR2 reactor, developed for the SSBN *Vanguard*-class. The submarine's armament consists of up to 38 Spearfish torpedoes and Tomahawk Block IV land-attack cruise missiles. Indicating the cost and complexity of these craft, HMS *Astute* was four years late in delivery in 2007, and 800 million pounds over budget.

HMS Ambush (2011)

© *Wikimedia Commons*

Chinese Submarines

In 1958, Mao Tse-tung told the Soviet ambassador to China that he wanted 200 or 300 nuclear submarines. It produced its first SSN of the 4,000-ton *Han* class in 1974, followed by the 7,000 ton *Xia* class. China's transition from a brown/green water navy to a fully-fledged blue water naval powerhouse has seen the nation rapidly growing its fleet of both nuclear and diesel-electric submarines, which unlike the US are not split between operational requirements in the Atlantic and Mediterranean, enabling China's rapidly developing submarine fleet to focus the entirety of its attention on the Indo-Pacific region. China's submarines are built in several different yards including Wuhan, and floated down river, with a submarine base at Hainan Island, in the north of the South China Sea. China has about 12 nuclear-powered submarines (about 8 SSN type-93 *Shang* class and type-95 *Tang* class, about 6 SSBN type-94 *Jin* class and type-96), and was building 21 more. This focus has enabled China to deploy a range of advanced nuclear and conventional attack and ballistic missile submarines, including the first fully Chinese developed conventional submarines, both the Type 039/A Class submarines are designed to supplement the larger nuclear submarines in the anti-shipping and anti-submarine operations in littoral waters. The vessels have a submerged weight of 2,250 tonnes, with a top speed of 22 knots and are capable of carrying 18 torpedoes, the YJ-8 anti-ship cruise missile or 36 naval mines.

Attack submarines (SSK/SSN): Type 039/A Class (NATO category Song Class) - The Song class diesel electric class are 74.9 metres and displace 2,250 tons. The *Song* class are succeeded by the Type 39A *Yuan* Class.

Type 39B SSK (known to NATO as the *Yuan* class) - More modern than the *Song* Class, the *Yuan* class was launched in 2006, a variant of the Type 39A, displacing 3,600 tons. Length 77.6 metres, With AIP, they are capable of 20 kts and have 65 crew with flank array sonar. They use a Chinese version of the Stirling engine. With features of the Russian Kilo class, they combine features of the previous Type 039 *Song* Class.

Type 39C Class - A new variant of the Chinese *Yuan* Class appeared in 2021. These have a towed array sonar. The chined sail is similar to the Swedish A26 class and are thought to support surface operations.

Type 49B Kilo Class - These are fast attack submarines, designed to conduct anti-shipping and anti-submarine operations in littoral waters. Larger than the Type 03/A Class vessels, the 12 Russian designed *Kilo* submarines have a submerged weight of 3,000-3,950 tonnes, a submerged speed of 20 knots and submerged range of approximately 740 kilometres. The heavily armed vessels are capable of carrying 533mm torpedoes, 24 mines and, in the case of Russian use, four Kalibr land-attack cruise missiles, eight Strela-3 or Igla-1 surface-to-air missiles.

Type 091 Han Class - China's first generation of nuclear attack submarine weighs in at 5,500 tonnes when submerged, with a top speed of about 25 knots and is capable of carrying 20 533mm torpedoes or 36 mines in their torpedo tubes. Additionally, the vessels are capable of carrying submarine launched variants of the C-801 anti-ship missile.

Type 92 SSBN - The Type 92 (NATO name *Xia* class) was built in 1993 as the PLA (N) was the first Chinese SSBN. Only one boat was built, and it is being succeeded by the Type 094 Jin class. The Type 092 displaces 8,000 tonnes and has a length of 120 m. She has a crew of 100. The *Xia* has made allegedly only one patrol, inside Chinese regional waters.

Type 093 Shang Class SSN - China's second generation of nuclear attack submarine displaces 6,096 tonnes while submerged, with a top speed of 30 knots. The vessels were designed as a replacement for the Type 091 vessels with key improvements on speed, reliability, acoustic performance and *capability*. The Type 093 carry a variety of weapons, including 533mm torpedoes, submarine launched variants of the CJ-10 missile and YJ-18 supersonic anti-ship cruise and CJ-10 land attack cruise missiles. The Type 093B was launched in 2023, with a pump-jet propulsion, and is quieter than its predecessors. It has a large increase in armament, with 18 VLS cells (compared with 40 cells in the *Virginia* class). It likely fires the long range YJ-18 anti-ship missile. A Type 95 is under development.

Chinese Ballistic missile submarines (SSBN) - Type 092 Class: China's first SSBN design, the submarine is capable of maintaining a max speed of 22 knots. Weighing in at 8,000 tonnes submerged, the vessels also carry 533mm torpedoes and up to 12 JL-1A submarine launched ballistic missiles with an operational range of 2,500 kilometres.

Type 094 Jin Class SSBN - China's second SSBN design is an enlarged design of 11,900 tonnes submerged, with a highly classified speed. The vessels are armed with JL-2 submarine launched ballistic missiles with a range of 7,400 kilometres. Two Type 094A *Jin* Class ballistic missile submarines were added to the fleet of four in 2020. China's next generation submarines will carry up to 16 missiles. The PLAN is believed to have 50 SSKs, six SNs, and four SSBNs.

Type 96 class - Little is known of the Type 96 SSBN, other than it is being built in the Bohai shipyard on the shore of the Yellow Sea near the North Korean border. It will likely carry the JL3 nuclear warhead ballistic missile, with a range beyond 12,000 kms, allowing it to strike most American cities without having to leave Chinese waters and risk detection or attack. With rim drive shaftless propulsion, it will be quieter than a Type 95, and with natural cooling instead of continuous pumped cooling, Chinese designers have boasted it will be as quiet as an American Virginia class attack submarine.

French Submarines

Scorpene class SSK - Launched in 2005, the 1,565-1,900-ton *Scorpene* class was developed jointly by France and Spain, they have a length of 62-70 metres and are capable of 20 kts, with MESMA air independent propulsion. They serve in the navies of India, Brazil, Malaysia and Chile. They have six torpedo tubes, firing the Italian black Shark torpedo and Exocet antiship missiles.

Barracuda (or Suffren) class SSN - The French attack submarine displaces 5,300 tonnes surfaced and has a length of 99.5 m. is intended to replace the four *Rubis* class. The first boat was commissioned in 2023. and the second began sea trials in March 2023.

German and Italian Submarines

25 kt speed. Type 212 SSK - The six Type 212A submarines are the mainstay of the German and Italian submarine forces. The German boats are bult by GDW in Kiel, and the Italian boats by Fincantieri. They have a length of 57 metres and displace 1,830 tons submerged. They are small submarines with a crew of only 27 hot bunking on 21 racks on 6-hour watches. Only the commander has a sole use cabin. A diesel engine produces 2,773hp for surface or periscope depth running at 12k speed, and an AIP propulsion system for quiet slow running or 20 kt submerged, uses compressed hydrogen and oxygen fuel cells from separate tanks outside the crew space. This allows it to stay submerged for up to three weeks. The export version is the Type 214, with a crew of 27 personnel. They are succeeded by the Type 216. Six larger Type 212 CD (common design) submarines displacing 2,500 tons are being built for the German and Norwegian navies. Two diesel engines provide propulsion for its maximum 12 kt surface speed. It is a very quiet submarine that can operate in shallow littoral waters and has state of the art sensors and combat systems. An export version, the Type 214, with greater range and with crews of only 21, is operated by the Greek and Turkish navies, and armed with land attack missiles as well as torpedoes. The *Type 216* evolved with a longer range (19,000 kms) was targeted as a replacement for the Australian *Collins* class. With the AUKUS boat planned, no Type 216 was ever produced, although a *Type 219* was developed for the Singaporean Navy, and was commissioned in 2022.

Indian Submarines

Arihant class SSBN - India has commissioned two of four planned locally built SSBN (*Arihant* class). (*Arihant* means destroyer of enemies, in Sanskrit.) It began sea trials in 2015.

Scorpene - India is acquiring German type 209s and French *Scorpene* class. It leased two nuclear powered submarines from the Russians. India also has eight *Kilo* class, from Russia. It is the sixth country to construct and operate nuclear submarines.

Japanese Submarines

Soryu Class - Japan commissioned its first Soryu class in 2009, building towards a fleet of 22 SSKs of this class. The class has a displacement of 4,200 tonnes submerged, a speed of 20 kts, and carries 65 crew, with a range of 6,100 nm. It is succeeded by the 3,000 tonne *Taigei* class (2018-present), 675 feet length, with six torpedo tubes and Harpoon missiles. Propulsion is diesel electric engines charging lithium-ion batteries for twice the energy output of lead acid batteries, enabling faster speed submerged and longer endurance. The time to charge the batteries has been reduced to about 1-2 hours, less than half that of lead acid batteries, allowing shorter snort times, exposing the submarine's snorting mast at periscope depth for shorter periods. The JMSDF is the only defence force using Lithium-ion batteries instead of the traditional lead acid batteries. The lithium batteries have exhibited difficulties with fire safety in the past. Japanese shipbuilders believe they have developed this technology to an acceptable safety standard now. The second boat in this class is the *Hakugei*, which became operational in 2023.

Russian Submarines

Russia operates five of the 24,000-ton *Borei* class, of 10 planned. three 8600 tonne fast attack *Yasen* class (out of 10 planned), five 12,500 tonne *Oscar* class (after the *Kursk* was lost), and four 12,700-ton *Akula* class. The huge SSBN *Borei* class, approximately the same size as the *Ohio* class, was designed to replace the formidable 48,000-ton *Typhoon* class. Six of this huge class were built in the 1980s and are now obsolete. The *Borei* class carry 16 *Bulava* ballistic missiles with nuclear warheads. These have a range of 9,300 kms. Up to 40 torpedoes are carried, to be released from its six tubes.

The *Yasen* class SSGN (1993-) has a submerged speed of 35 kts, and eight silos for weapons, and two torpedo tubes, with a crew of 90.[168]

Lada class - The *Lada* class Russian submarine is a highly improved derivative of the *Kilo* class, launched in 2010. Displacing 2,700 tons, with a length of 72 metres, these boats are capable of 21 kts with a crew of 35, and are designed for defensive littoral operations, and protecting nuclear submarine bases.

---

[168] Ross, D. (2022). *Submarines: The World's Greatest Submarines, from Eigthteenth Century to the Present.* Amber Books, London.

Improved Kilo II - The improved *Kilo II* has been introduced by Russia since 2015, based on the original *Kilo* class from the 1980s. these displace 3,100 tons, and have a speed of 20 kts, and are crewed by 52 personnel. They have six torpedo tubes firing the type 53/65 torpedo against surface targets, and the Kalibr missile against land targets. In addition to bow sonar, they have flank array sonar, and towed array sonar. These are primarily for export to countries such as China, Vietnam and Algeria.

Singaporean Submarines

Invincible class - Launched in 2023, the *Type 219* is an extensively customised version of the German *Type 214* submarines, with a length of 70 metres displacing 2,200 tons. They are capable of 15 kts, and have a complement of 28 crew.

Swedish Submarines

Gotland Class (A26 class) - The 60.4m 1,647 ton *Gotland* class launched in 1993 is recognised as an effective conventional submarine, but has not achieved export sales. They have an AIP Stirling engine, allowing submerged duration of up to three weeks. They are very quiet when using AIP. With a crew of only 27 personnel. Its torpedoes have a range exceeding 50 kms. Its maximum surface speed is 10 kts, and submerge speed is 20 kts.

Taiwanese Submarines

Taiwan is upgrading its ROCN fleet of two submarines obtained from the US in 1973 and two *Chien Lung* Class modified Dutch built boats obtained in the late 1980s. Attempts to acquire new boats have been opposed by Beijing. Construction of eight planned attack boats began in 2020, with American support. The first expected to be delivered in 2025.

North Korean Submarines

Whiskey Class - North Korea has one of the world's largest and oldest attack submarine fleets, comprised of Soviet era *Whiskey* class in the 1960s and *Romeo* class from the Chinese in the 1970s.

Turkish Submarines

Reis class - Turkey is building its own new Reis Class submarines of 1.850 tons displacment, 67 metre length and capable of 20 kts. With a crew of just over 30, these have German and Turkish technology, and eight torpedo tubes. They are based on the very quiet Type 214 U-boat of the German navy, with air independent propulsion with German fuel cell technology, enabling submerged duration of 2-4 weeks. They have eight torpedo tubes firing heavyweight torpedos and missiles.

In summary, as background, leading submarine designers and producers are as follows:

1. USA – SSN, *Los Angeles* class (first produced in 976), *Sea Wolf* class SSN, SSBN *Ohio* class, SSN *Virginia* class.

2. Russia - Type 941 *Akula* class SSN, *Typhoon* class SSN, *Delta* class SSBN, *Kursk* class SSGN, *Kilo* class SSK Sierra class *Charlie* and *Oscar* class

3. UK SSBN Vanguard class SSBN, SSN Astute class.

4. France SSBN *Triomphant* class, SSN *Barracuda* class SSN, Shortfin Barracuda SSK, Scorpene class SSK.

5. Japan conventional *Soryu* class SSK, *Taigei* class SSK

Nuclear-powered Submarines

Submarine types Compared

Country	Planned/ Completed/ active in 2024	Class and class type SSK diesel electric SSN Nuclear attack SSBN nuclear ballistic	Years	Size	Displacement (Tons)	Speed in kts Surface/ dived
Australia	6	Collins SSK	1987	77m	3,300	15/10
France	12	Scorpene SSK	2003	70m	1565	12-20
France	4	Triomphant SSN	2009	138m	12,600	>25
		Rubis SSN	1976	73m	2,400	25
Germany		Type VIIc SSK	1940	65m	769	17.7/7.6
Germany		Type XXI SSK	1943	52m	1,621	15.7]17
Germany	68	Type 209 SSK	1971	64m	1,800	11.5/22.5
Germany	10	Type 212SSK	1999	56m	1,500	12/20
Indonesia	4	SSK Type 209	2005	59m	1,800	11.5/22.5
Italy	8	SSK U212	2008	58m	1,514	12/20
Iran	18	SSK Akula	1980	154m	8.470	10/28
Japan	12	Soryu SSK	2007	84m	2,900	13/20
		Sentoku SSK	1942	122m	5,222	18.7/9.9
PRC	6	Type 094 Jin SSBN	2011	137m	11.000	10/52
Singapore	3	Invincible SSK	2020	70m	2,000	10/20
UK	5	Astute SSN	2007	97m	7,000	30
	4	Vanguard SSBN	1992	150m	15.900	>25
USA	5	Holland SSK	1897	19.46m	110	8/7
USA		Gato SSK	1940	95m	1,525	21/9
USA	62/62/26	Los Angeles SSN	1976	109m	6,082	20/>25
	12/3/3	Seawolf SSN	1995	107m	8,600	20/>35
	66/24/23	Virginia SSN	2004	114m	7,800	25/34
USA	24/18/12	Ohio SSBN	1981	170m	16,780	12/20
USA	4/1	Columbia SSBN	2030	171m	20,800	
Netherlands	4	Walrus SSK	1985-	67m	2,400	13/21
Russia	70	Kursk SSBN	1994	154m	12,000	32/16
Russia	20/13/4	Akula	1980	175m	8,450	10/35
	14/7/7	Borei	1995	170m	14,700	15/29
		Lada	2004	66m	2,700	10/21
		Yasen SSGN	2014	139m	8,600	20/35
Sweden	5	Gotland	1995	60m	1,494	11/20

7

The Future for Australian Submarines

The current decade began in 2020 with Russian aggression invading the Ukraine and increased Chinese assertiveness in the Indo-Pacific. China has the largest fleet in the world, with a battle force of some 340 vessels. Countries everywhere appear to be building up their submarine forces.[169] The waters around Australia are becoming increasingly contested. Unsurprisingly, the future for Australian submarines has become an important subject for analysis and debate by defence strategists.[170] However, they should not be seen as just bigger and faster. Given the increased complexity of the technology, and the training and regulatory requirements, acquiring nuclear-powered submarines is likely to prove extremely challenging.[171]

Over a century has passed since Australia acquired its first submarines. In that time, the Australian Submarine Service has endured wars and various roles in defending the nation. It

---

[169] Scott, P. (2023). Australia's Submarine Capability – Enduring Characteristics, Emerging features. *Australian Naval Review*, Issue 1, pp. 40-51.

[170] Evans, M. (2023). The Eye of the Storm: Future Warfare in the Indo-Pacific and its implications for Australia. *Australian Naval Review*, issue 1. pp. 22-30.

[171] Pearce, P. (2023). Fitness for purpose in Submarine Acquisition. *7th Submarine Science, Technology and Engineering Conference 2023* (SubSTECT).

has gone from near oblivion initially to modest and respected acceptance with its British built *Oberons*, and relative independence by building its own successful *Collins* class. The replacement of the current *Collins* class with nuclear-powered boats is a huge step forward in complexity and lethality. The SSN has many advantages over the SSK. Stealth is a critical factor. Depending on its speed, the SSN may be as quiet or quieter than the SSK. The SSK may need to spend up to a third of its time (the "indiscretion ratio") vulnerable at periscope depth to be able to snort. Its mast may be detected by satellite or aircraft and running its diesels to recharge its batteries emits noise that risks detection. If an SSN is detected, with 75,000 shp on tap, it can run at perhaps 15 kts, whereas the SSN can run at speeds over 30 kts. A major advantage of the SSN is its ability to transit large distances quickly, with a greater weapon payload. The role for Australian submarines continues to focus on familiar tasks:

Covert surveillance, reconnaissance and intelligence gathering, Covert insertion and recovery of special forces in contested environments, Covert land strike, Antiship warfare, and Antisubmarine warfare.

As capabilities and threats emerge, this list might be added to with UUVs, controlling UUVs, and detecting and neutralising an adversary's UUVs. The purpose of Australian submarines is summarised by an Australian former submarine commander: "The true value of Australian submarines should be in deterring conflict from occurring in the first place. If deterrence fails then our submarines need a capability that would respond and assist in bringing the conflict to a conclusion satisfactory to Australia, in the shortest possible time."[172]

---

[172] Mole, D. Nuclear power for submarines. p. 204. In Frame, T. (ed), (2020). *An Australian Nuclear Industry: Starting with Submarines?* Connor Court, Redland Bay, pp.178-205.

The history of the submarine in Australian and other navies as a weapon of war including but especially since World War I provides a backdrop that illuminates the significance of the submarine, and the critical nature of the challenges being confronted. Australian submarines are on the cusp of extraordinary expansion, change, development, and significance. The initial replacement for the *Collins* class was to be a conventionally-powered version of the Barracuda class SSN proposed by the Naval Group of France, dubbed the *Attack* class.

From French to US/UK/Australian design

On 15 September 2021, in the face of growing delays and cost increases, the Australian government announced the cancellation of the contract with Naval Group, and that the replacement will be a nuclear-powered submarine fleet of up to eight AUKUS boats to be built in Adelaide, designed in partnership with the United Kingdom and the United States. Though both Britain and the US are currently designing the successors for their Astute and *Virginia* classes, these are likely to be based on the British-designed *Astute* class and its replacement, the SSNR with an American combat system, and SG9 reactor to facilitate interoperability with US boats.

Estimates vary, but figures of $368bn over 30 years appeared in the media, in a massive project thought likely to create up to 20,000 jobs and boost the nation's skills across several industry sectors significantly. The cost is expected to be some 0.15 percent of GDP per year averaged over the program. A project of such scope, cost, and complexity can be expected to attract criticism from the start from present and aspirant stakeholders. Already there are calls for tight governance and published warnings that "the UK government and BAE Systems will be working very hard in the AUKUS program to minimise Australian industry to the benefit of British industry."[173]

The eventual March 2023 selection of three *Virginia* class boats to be followed by a jointly (AUKUS) designed boat to be built in Australia, will commit the Australian submarine service to a prominence in Defence thinking and taxpayer awareness that can only be guessed at currently. By July 2023, several RAN officers had passed the American nuclear power course in anticipation of the acquisition of the *Virginia* class boats. Australia has RAN submariners serving on exchange in American submarines.

In July 2023, the Australian government announced the creation of the Australian Submarine Agency, with VADM Jonathon Mead as its Inaugural Director General, reporting to the Minister for Defence, and responsible for the acquisition and regulation of the nuclear- powered fleet. Building the jointly designed 9,000 ton AUKUS class could be a mix of British build and Australian build. For example, BAE Systems already has a significant presence in Australia and is scheduled to build the nine new Australian *Hunter* class frigates in Adelaide.[174]

The AUKUS submarine with a Rolls-Royce reactor is likely to be a close relative of the British SSNR built by BAE Systems in Barrow in Furness. This close collaboration represents a reinvigoration of the traditional historic defence relationship between Canberra and London.

Australian-built AUKUS boats are expected to be delivered beginning in 2042, through to 2060. This is Australia's

---

[173] Briggs, P. (2023). Mandating Australian Industry content for the AUKUS SSNs. *The Strategist*. 24 August. Australian Strategic Policy Institute, Canberra.

[174] Shackleton, D. (2022). The Hunter Frigate: An Assessment. *Strategy*. Australian Strategic Policy Institute, Canberra.

continuous ship building program.

In the meantime, to minimise a capability gap, the life-of-type (LOTE) extension for some or all of the *Collins* boats will enable them to continue to serve until the 2040s, when *Virginia* class will be operational (from 2035) and perhaps AUKUS class boats will have entered service (in 2042-2068). Australian submariners are already gaining experience in exchange postings in American and British nuclear-powered boats. The *Virginia* class has large capacity vertical launch tubes for land attack missiles. The Block V boats have the capability to launch 42 Tomahawk missiles from vertical tubes. At 7,900 tonnes and 115 metres long, the *Virginia* class block 4 attack submarines are twice the size of the *Collins class* boats and are crewed by up to 135 officers and enlisted sailors. Their S9G nuclear reactors produce up to 30 megawatts, with speeds exceeding 26 kts. These boats are nuclear powered and in 2023, 21 have been delivered to the USN. They are capable of releasing nuclear weapons, Mark 48 torpedoes from five tubes, and 12 Tomahawk missiles. The later block V carry a weapons load of up to 65 weapons. It is expected that the *Virginia* submarines to be acquired by Australia will be nuclear powered but not nuclear armed. In 2023, their estimated cost was $3.2 billion each. They are expected to arrive in 2033. It represents a huge increase in submarine capability.

Questions being asked

As might be expected, this ambitious plan in 2023 produced a frenzy of questions in Australian media:

1. Why embark on an expensive life of type extension for some of the Collins boats when the focus will be on the *Virginia* class in the

first instance with the AUKUS boat based on the Astute or SSNR British boat to follow?

2. Why acquire *Virginia* boats only to go to the cost and trouble of designing and building a new nuclear-powered boat which could become an orphan unless it is acquired by the Royal Navy also? It is likely that the RN may acquire jointly built AUKUS boats? Given the history of the Astute construction, is the UK up to it?

3. The answer appears to be that the two American builders of the *Virginia* class (General Dynamics and Newport News Shipbuilding) are fully committed to the USN's current needs and will move their production from Block Vs to the *Virginia* replacement.

4. If crews in the *Virginias* are to be mixed American and Australian, who will deploy and command these boats? Information thus far is that the *Virginias* purchased by Australia will be commanded by Australians.

5. Can we afford to operate two classes of submarine, especially when the *Virginias* have crews of 135 compared to the 55 in a Collins crew? Given our historic difficulty in crewing even our *Collins* boats with 55 submariners, is it realistic to think we can recruit and train nuclear crews in sufficient time to operate the Virginias and the AUKUS boats and address Australia's defence requirements?

6   The related challenge will be for our universities to educate sufficient numbers of civilian nuclear qualified engineers. The *Virginia* class require a crew of 135. The *Astute* class require only 97.

These are questions that our government and defence planners are currently facing. They do so against a background of disquiet expressed in media publications, critical of the RAN as no longer "fit for purpose. It is older, has less firepower and is less reliable with fewer ships than a generation ago, with our ships outgunned and outmatched by Chinese cruisers with 112 missile cells against our frigates with eight."[175] Critics ascribe this to "complacency, poor decision making, a broken defence procurement system, bureaucratic inertia, and lack of political leadership in funding a viable ship building industry".[176]

Challenges and questions for Australia's Nuclear Submarine Program

What must we do?[177]

1   Establish a naval nuclear regulatory framework for Australia. This needs to be developed to secure the nuclear technology.[178]

2   Decide a procurement policy – import complete or part-build in Australia build in Australia at

---

[175] Moffitt, R. (2023). As an island nation, why do we accept such a weak navy? *Australian Financial Review*. September 13.

[176] Dupont A. (2024). A game of high stakes on the high seas. *The Weekend Australian*. Feb 3-4, p. 33.

[177] Jeremy J. (2022). Submarines for the RAN going nuclear. Technical presentation to the Royal Institution of Naval Architects, 3 August. https://youtu.be/W6blo6tY2EU.

[178] Money, S. W. (2023). AUKUS is writing checks Australian security can't cash. *Proceedings of the US Naval Institute.* October, pp. 38-39.

Adelaide where facilities are under construction or build the first one or two overseas?

3. Decide on location for submarine bases and complete all environmental safety assessments at HMAS *Stirling* in WA and on the east coast at Port Kembla
4. Define the nuclear specific facilities required for construction and support locations - secure and protected from seismic events.
5. Achieve local acceptance of a nuclear presence at these locations. WA is already accustomed to visiting nuclear submarines. The attraction of jobs will influence acceptance in Adelaide.
6. Establish a training program for civilian and nuclear engineers- scholarships for nuclear science and engineering.
7. Establish a disposal strategy for end of service life.

On balance, the future for the Australian Submarine Service It builds on a long and strong history in the service of this country. Its continuing success will continue to demand the highest levels of professionalism, and national support from this nation and our partners.

Submarines and the Navy – a wider perspective

The scope and focus of this book is on submarines in history and on the Australian Submarine Service in particular. Of course, the service exists as an arm of the Royal Australian Navy, and developments in the RAN form a context for the Submarine Service. This section examines some emerging issues in the RAN of relevance to the Submarine Service. Without doubt, the cost of the forthcoming submarine service to include the expense of extending the life of type of the Collins boats and the acquisition of Virginia class nuclear- powered submarines, through to the eventual design and build of the projected AUKUS submarines will have a huge impact within the Navy. Already in 2024 there has been the announcement from a Surface Fleet Review (SFR) that the Government intends to more than double the number of surface ships from 11 to 26, presumably in response to the 2023 Defence Strategic Review (DSR) that reported the growing level of threat being confronted.

This ambitious expansion anticipates 11 General Purpose frigates to replace the *ANZAC* class (FFH) frigates that Australia has operated since the lead ship of eight, HMAS *ANZAC*, was launched in 1995. By the 2040s, these will join the six *Hunter* Class frigates currently being designed and built in Australia, and the six Offshore Patrol vessels (OPVs) being ult to replace the Armidale class patrol boats. The three DDG Air Warfare Destroyers (*Hobart, Perth* and *Sydney* will continue to serve as will the three large ships, the helicopter landing docks *Canberra,* and *Adelaide* and *Choules*.

The Current and Emerging Threat

Australia is heavily dependent on its international trade, almost all of which is by sea. Two thirds of its trade is with the Indo-Pacific.[179] Obviously a predominant focus for the RAN is the maintenance of its sea lines of communication. (SLOCs). Views differ as to whether this is best driven by a strategy of sea control or sea denial. The former is aimed at protecting our trade without which our economy would quickly falter a fuel supplies

---

[179] Australian Government Department of Foreign Affairs and Trade (2021). Trade and Investment.

became exhausted.[180] The latter, sea denial, has an emphasis on deterrence of an adversary by maintaining capability to combat any hostile forces.[181] The strategic objective is to ensure reliable access to the maritime commons.[182]

The Royal Australian Navy (RAN) fleet is made up of 32 commissioned warships and 11 non-commissioned as of December 2023.

The main strength is the seven *Anzac* class frigates and three *Hobart* class air warfare destroyers of the surface combatant force. Six *Collins*-class boats make up the submarine service, although due to the maintenance cycle not all submarines are active at any one time. The issues have now been fixed and five submarines are available for service. Amphibious warfare assets include two *Canberra*-class landing helicopter dock ships and the landing ship HMAS *Choules*. Four *Armidale*-class patrol boats perform coastal and economic exclusion zone patrols, and four *Huon*-class vessels are used for mine hunting and clearance (another two are commissioned but in reserve since October 2011, for sale from 2018). Replenishment at sea is provided by two *Supply*-class replenishment oilers. In addition to the commissioned warships, the RAN operates the sail training ship *Young Endeavour* and eight *Cape*-class patrol boats. Other auxiliaries and small craft are not operated by the RAN, but by DMS Maritime, who are contracted to provide support services.

The majority of the RAN fleet is divided between Fleet Base East (HMAS *Kuttabul*, in Sydney) and Fleet Base West

---

[180] Goldrick, J. (2021). Australia's Essential Need: Not seaborne trade but seaborne supply. *The Interpreter*. 3 September.
[181] White, H. (2021). Australia's seaborne trade: Essential but undefendable. *The Interpreter*, 27 August.
[182] Hardman, P. (2023). Maritime trade is essential to the Indo-Pacific. *Proceedings*. US Naval Institute May. pp. 10-11.

(HMAS *Stirling*, near Perth). Mine warfare assets are located at HMAS *Waterhen* (also in Sydney), with HMAS *Cairns* in Cairns and HMAS *Coonawarra* in Darwin hosting the navy's patrol and survey vessels.

Ships Planned and under Construction

Arafura class offshore patrol vessels (OPVs) – six planned of which two are completed. These are intended to replace the Armidale class patrol boats in constabulary duties,

Hunter class frigates (32 VLS) (compared to an Arleigh Burke destroyer with 96 VLS). The sixth and final Hunter class is due in 2043. These are estimated to cost $7bn each.

Also, in 2024 it was announced that a further 11 general purpose frigates would be acquired, with the first three to be built in their country of origin and the remaining eight in Australia. Six optionally crewed missile vessels each with 32 VLS cells will be added.

Our youngest submarine is over 20 years old. Given the threat environment in relation to the perceived capability of the RAN, continuing public concern expressed in Australian newspapers is to be expected. Predictably, each major political party blames those opposite for decades of negligence, and strategists and commentators are publicly vocal in questioning threat assessment and combat capability. [183]

The doubling of the fleet size in itself is an obvious topic for debate. Irrespective of planned classes in the ship building

---

[183] Sheridan, G. (2024). Our warship fleet doubles but nation's security still at grave risk. *The Weekend Australian* Feb 24-25, p. 36.

programme.[184]

The increase in numbers of members required to crew these vessels presents a major challenge to the Navy's Human Resource Management in attraction, selection, training and retention.

Other commentary has focussed on operations, such as the desirability to maximise force capability by increased joint exercises.[185] This invites reflection on Winston Churchill's aphorism "There is only one thing worse than fighting with Allies and that is fighting without them".[186]

The Australian CN in 2024 VADM Mark Hamond AO cited ongoing grey zone activity, military modernisation coercion, and contested maritime sovereignty as challenges to international global order in Australia's region. Our increasing capability with new submarines will make for a powerful deterrent. His emphasis is on maintaining mutually beneficial cooperation with all nations.[187]

---

[184] Shackleton, D. (2022). The Hunter Frigate: An Assessment. *Strategy*. Australian Strategic Policy Institute, Canberra.

[185] Copland, M. (2023). Never Sail Alone. *Proceedings*. US Naval Institute, May. pp. 12-13.

[186] Churchill, W. (1945). Quoted in Hemmings, J. (2020). Hindsight, Insight, Foresight: Thinking about Security in the Indo-Pacific. Sep 1. The Evolution of the US Alliance System in the IndoPacific Since the Cold War's end. https://jw.jstororg/stable/resprep2666714. p. 9.

[187] Hamond, M. (2023). *Proceedings*. US Naval Institute, May. p. 28.

8

The Perisher course and Australian Submarine Commanders

The Submarine Command Course (SMCC) is known as "Perisher", and since 1917 has been the gold standard in training and assessing officers for command of submarines. In its 100 plus years of operation, since being established by the Royal Navy as the Periscope Course, it has undergone many evolutions and iterations as submarine technology developed, diesel-electric to nuclear propulsion and nuclear capable weapons. It has produced submarine COs for several navies, including British, Dutch, American, Australian, Canadian, and others. For all this, there is relatively little written about "the abstruse and arcane subject of submarine command", until the comprehensive historical research by CAPT David Parry RN.[188]

---

[188] Parry D. (2022). *Perisher: Its Evolution 1917-2017 and the Submarine Commanding Officer*, PhD thesis, Kings College, London.

The Perisher Course: Mastery and Mystery[189]

It is not so much a course about strategy, which may vary from navy to navy, but about the common elements of an officer's character, leadership skills, and judgment which serve the CO to keep a submarine safe as well as effective. There is a constant emphasis on decision making under conditions of stress. Along with 13 graduates who were awarded the VC, and countless other awards to many other graduates, Perisher has qualified just 1,165 RN and 365 officers of Commonwealth and other navies. It is known not just as a "very tough course" with a high failure rate. After four months of demanding exercises ashore in simulators and at sea in submarines subjected to attack by ASW vessels and aircraft, officers have been known to fail on the last day of the course, to be put ashore with a ceremonial bottle of scotch, never to set foot in a Royal Navy submarine again. For they must either rejoin the surface fleet or find an alternative career. Perisher is known as one of the most demanding and exclusive courses in naval and military service.[190] Over the century it has operated, it has earned a respect and mystique all its own. "To submarine ships' companies, it is a badge of confidence in their captains, and to other navies it has been coveted and copied."[191]

Originally, Perisher was run by the Royal Navy out of Portsmouth. After the Royal Navy changed from a fleet of diesel-powered boats to nuclear submarines, the course was taken over by the Dutch Navy, who continued to operate diesel boats. The RN changed the name from SSK Perisher to SMCC

---

[189] Brown, T. (2022). This section was contributed in part by CDRE Tim Brown, AM, RAN (retd) formerly Director General Submarines, to whom appreciation is expressed.

[190] Gordon, A. (1996). *The Rules of the Game*, John Murray, London.

[191] Parry D. (2022). *Perisher: Its Evolution 1917-2017 and the Submarine Commanding Officer*, PhD thesis, Kings College, London. p. 17.

to signify that the British version of Perisher was now totally nuclear. In 2022, Australia offered a Perisher course off its own coast for the first time, carefully designed to be at the same internationally recognised standard as that in the Dutch course. Prior to 2022, all commanders of Australian submarines had passed the British or Dutch Perisher, or had transferred from other navies (South African and Canadian) after having passed the British/Dutch course and commanded submarines in their navies.

"A submarine is a totally controlled, well-ordered world on which you can almost forget what's outside". This is how television producer, Jonathan Crane, described his first experience on joining the British nuclear submarine HMS *Warspite*, to film the 1980s documentary on the Royal Navy's famous submarine command course. It is this "totally controlled, well ordered world" that sets the conditions upon which officers are able to train and develop as leaders in a way that is rarely available in the outside world.

It is the Perisher course where would-be submarine commanding officers are assessed in their abilities to command a submarine in peace and war. The qualities that need to be presented are both tangible and intangible. A student must be able to drive the submarine and operate it in precarious situations that demand competencies requiring years of training. The student intent on becoming a submarine commander must also develop the skills and abilities to lead and motivate the entire ship's company, such that they are confident the officer is achieving the aim while keeping them safe—all without their knowing what is occurring outside of the submarine.

A submarine is designed for each person to be performing a specialised task, operating equipment, navigating, operating the combat system or some other tasks. All these tasks fit together. In this sense, a submarine works like an orchestra, with everyone having their specialised tasks which they must perform in a coordinated manner to produce an aggregate effect, while being mindful of a multitude of other external factors influencing every decision. Typically, most of the crew are engaged in tasks "internal" to the submarine. Only the command team (the CO, XO, watch leaders, and certain senior sailors) have their tasks external to the boat as well, and in three dimensions.

This makes commanding a submarine different from other sea-going commands. This long road begins when officers commence their initial training in submarines. Normally, this is after most officers have been in the Navy for 2-3 years and have completed their basic training to prepare them to be employed on surface warships. Initial submarine training sees these officers introduced to the basic aspects of submarine design, submarine equipment, routines, safety, operation and navigation. They get exposed to life at sea on submarines and are able to gain a decent appreciation of at-sea operations through the use of simulators. Many find this period daunting given the volume of information they need to digest in a short time.

Once this training is completed these officers will be posted to a submarine, under training. Here they will be employed to perform basic tasks expected of a junior warfare officer, while at the same time learning about the systems that go to make up the submarine hydraulics, High Pressure/Low pressure air systems, auxiliary machinery, etc. As submarine officers, these trainees are expected to be fully conversant of the submarine's systems in order to be deemed competent to earn their 'dolphins' badge, as a fully qualified submariner. This means they are deemed competent to perform the role of a junior officer without supervision, and to be an officer-of-the-day (i.e. the officer-in-charge) of the submarine when it is alongside.

This first stage of qualification is experienced as challenging for many, and it is not unusual for some officers under training to elect to pursue careers other than in submarines. The thinking is that it is better not to waste everyone's time on a road going nowhere.

The early years of an officer's career also enables their captain to observe how quickly these new officers adjust to submarines. Often the officer's performance in these early years is a good indicator of their ability to pass the Perisher and eventually to qualify for command.

From qualifying as submariners, all officers need to progress through the same steps to gain the necessary at-sea experience as they work to qualify for command. They will normally spend about two years employed as a junior officer rotating through several jobs, before completing a navigation course to qualify as a submarine navigator. This role is the first true appointment as a mariner where officers learn fundamental principles to driving a submarine and keeping it safe. It's a challenging and demanding hands-on job where a junior officer can demonstrate their aptitude for situational awareness—a fundamental trait and skill required for submarine command.

From navigator, the officer will be recommended to attend submarine warfare officer's course, which is the first major submarine course after qualifying. It takes about six months and has both theoretical and practical assessments. From here, the officers are employable as one of the submarine Watch Leaders.

When a submarine is at sea, conducting dived operations, there are normally two watch leaders that share the responsibility for operating the submarine. Normally, dived operations see the submarine crew divided into two watches that rotate duty about every 6 hours.

This places significant stress on all the crew. Sleep time is precious, and personal fatigue management is a priority. The mental effort required of everyone is constant and unyielding. When the submarine is undertaking specific operations in congested waters with other vessels or submarines, friendly and potentially otherwise, the workload on the leadership team in particular intensifies significantly. In working up a submarine to operational readiness, a graded series of evolutions and phases is undertaken to give all the crew the necessary experience for the submarine to be assessed as fully operational.

All this time, through all these phases, the officer is learning, being progressively stretched in a series of assignments and tasks, learning from each, and being assessed for their suitability for command. The ultimate consideration is the judgment as to whether a nation is to trust an officer with one of is submarines, and the lives of all on board, along with the operational mission for which all the training and competence is required.

The Reason for Perisher

To truly understand the essence of the Perisher, one must understand not just the "what" but also the "why". Why is it essential that an officer needs to be assessed in command? Why can an officer not be assessed along the training continuum that brings a prospective CO to the decision point in their submarine career?

Preparing for Perisher: The Command Recommend

For many such officers it takes an average of eight years in submarines just to gain sufficient experience to be considered for a "Perisher recommend". Some navies, such as Sweden, don't conduct a command course, but assess continually in the years leading up to the potential command decision. This works for the Swedish Navy, which is unique, as it operates to a unique Swedish paradigm.

For those navies that operate long range, ocean-going submarines where their submarines operate far from home and deploy for many months at a time—a command course is a prerequisite, to equip them for every eventuality in such specialized operations, contending with such particular demands.

When these nations' submarines deploy the commanding officer is the ultimate authority for all on board. When you are deployed it is very busy, with long hours of giving full attention to the task, and often at a high stress level. Therefore the Perisher stress tests its candidates, not just to test for weaknesses in possible command, but to give them the experience of being stressed in a supervised and relatively safe environment, so that if and when they are in command in a stressful incident, or in a low-level but long term stressful situation, they will recognize their responses to it, and having analysed and reflected on their experience, they will be able to manage themselves better in the situation. The CO needs to be comfortable and familiar with being stressed. Thus, in training they need to be assessed in stressful situations to learn their own limits, and their own coping skills.

During an officer's submarine sea career, they progress through the ranks, and gain experience across various areas of operation. Then, when they are second in command, they are assessed by their CO for the "Perisher Recommend". This recommend is the first key milestone sought by an aspiring CO. However, this is a difficult arrangement. As a second in command, an officer has specific duties which ultimately require them to be a leader, yet subordinate to the CO.

Yet, the CO is looking for their XO to be stepping up and leading with little guidance or teaching. So, it's a fine balance. To that end the CO can assess only so much of the XO's suitability. Moreover, the CO lacks the resources to set back completely and allow their XO to 'run the show'. For a CO to be in a position to just teach their XO requires additional support staff to be embarked. This is because the CO cannot stop commanding their submarines at any stage. The submarine is a constantly running machine that demands constant oversight.

This additional support is ultimately what the Perisher course provides. The officer in charge of the course is traditionally and respectfully known as "Teacher", in effect a second CO, who is highly experienced and given "conduct" during the course. "Conduct" is a unique Navy control mechanism built into the Command-and-Control arrangements during training courses such as these.

When an officer takes command of a naval ship or submarine, they are accepting a privileged and challenging appointment, of national importance. After all, they are charged with a nation's prized vessel that consumes a vast sum of a nation's treasure. Moreover, they are charged with protecting the safety of all those who serve in her. Therefore, during a course such as Perisher, additional measures are required to cater for the demanding additional requirements that Perisher demands.

The Teacher is on board to "conduct" the course, under the watchful eye of the submarine CO. While they work together, the CO still has "command" responsibility, while Teacher coordinates the day-to-day comings and goings of the submarine to fulfil the course requirements. The CO effectively reserves their right to veto and can take the submarine off Teacher if they were to be unhappy about proceedings. This allows the submarine to be placed into challenge, and even somewhat hazardous conditions, more than what can be achieved in normal command arrangements. By doing this the students can be placed in stressful and challenging conditions so their responses can be observed and assessed.

The Command Recommend is an essential part of the assessment journey. It forms the assessment of a prospective CO's potential to successfully pass the course.

It is typically given by the officer's own CO. This is in itself a demanding process. The CO must balance a close working relationship and sometimes longstanding friendship with the requirement for an absolutely clear-headed and as far as possible evidence-based determination. The CO will confer with others for their view, and will take into account the opportunity cost, the downside for the individual's career of a negative decision, and myriad other factors, but the decision will ultimately hinge on whether the officer has the experience, the intellect, and the aptitude, to pass what many regard as the toughest command course in Defence.

To train to be ready to be assessed for Perisher takes on average, eight years of at sea training. Most officers will join a submarine in the early stages of their naval career after having conducted basic submarine training ashore. As they gain experience and competencies they progress in rank and job until they are ready for Perisher. There is a fairly high rate of attrition along the way until only a few officers remain, to undertake the course, even after their 8-10 years of submarine service.

The Perisher course and Australian Submarine Commanders

It is not easy. It can't be. A submarine is a complex vessel operating in a harsh environment. The crew are what keep it safe, and the commanding officer is deemed to be that person that oversees all to keep it safe and operationally effective to achieve superior performance.

"Apart from technical skills and leadership qualities, Perisher takes officers down the road of exploring and accepting their personal limitations.'[192] Essentially, if an officer doesn't know their own boundaries, it is a mantra of the submarine service that they are dangerous to not be supervised. It has been noted that those who are successful commanding officers:

> "accept responsibility eagerly and [are] self-confident. They are strong willed, tenacious and determined; they [are] brave, and they possess great physical and mental stamina. They all care passionately for their ship's companies, had a strong sense of humour and many were surprisingly modest. Their professional experience and training had developed quick calculating brains, the ability to delegate, presence and a 'good periscope eye'—the ability to react instinctively and not lose sight of the tactical picture unfolding on the surface."[193]

What kind of course might either create or at least not inhibit such attributes in its graduates?

The History of the Perisher

Since 1917, the Perisher course has evolved over time to address the changing technology and weapons in submarines and the evolving nature of submarine warfare and its political context but retains certain elements year upon year. It also retains a

---

[192] Parker, J. (2001). *The Silent Service: The Inside Story of the Royal Navy's Submarine Heroes*, Headline Book Publishing, London.
[193] Hennessy, P. & Jinks, J. (2016). *The Silent Deep*. Allen Lane, London. p. 8.

certain mystique and communicates into submarine operations a culture of its own. To have done this through a century with two world wars and hundreds of submarine commanders undertaking thousands of missions across the decades gives Perisher a unique place in the history of submarines.

> "Notwithstanding he ultimate prize of command qualification, *Perisher* is first and foremost a teaching course, and submarine periscope safety training forms a large and integral part of it. It raises the knowledge and skills taught to periscope watchkeepers from their earliest days in the Arm to an art form and engrains them to the point of instinct. These skills are absolutely critical to the effective operation and in extremis to the survival of the submarines executing their various missions."[194] First developed by the Royal Navy to train young submarine commanding officers in the art of attacking.[195] This was associated with the rapid expansion of the force during World War 1. Parry recollects an account made by Admiral Charles Little following his development of an Attack Teacher—a rudimentary simulator. Little said that the teacher offered an opportunity to allow "novices familiar" group discussion on the matter of attacking to avoid the dilemma into which the young commanding officer often gets at an awkward juncture.[196] It is appropriate to emphasise that submarines were fairly new weapons platforms in World War I. Submarines had really been introduced into naval service only just over a decade beforehand.

However, they developed quickly. By 1917 they had become a potent weapon of protagonist navies, and they evolved quickly with technical advances being ever-present. At the start of WW1 Submarines were still very much experimental, weighing

---

[194] Scott, P. (2023). *Running Deep: An Australian Submarine Life*. Fremantle Press, North Fremantle.

[195] Parry, D. (2019). *Some Things You May Not Know About the Perisher (and Submarines) 1901-1945*. Kings College, London. p. 8.

[196] Parry, D. (2019). *Some Things You May Not Know About the Perisher (and Submarines) 1901-1945*. Kings College, London.

The Perisher course and Australian Submarine Commanders

in around 300-500 tons, but by the end of the war submarines were over 2000 tonnes and carried up to twenty torpedoes.

This technological advance demanded the personnel production equation matched, so training and competency-building in rapid time was needed. As the complexity of submarines themselves increased, the war effort very much became focussed on submarine warfare and anti-submarine warfare. It became apparent that these vessels needed their officers to be well trained in the art of submarine command. This expansion of the submarine service saw Commodore Sydney Hall, Inspecting Commodore Submarines, to establish "a ledger to circulate among other captains to comment on officers' suitability for command". In a letter to the Admiralty in 2017, Hall "identified the requirement for a school that "concentrates entirely on submerged attack by means of periscope".[197] After receiving approval from the Admiralty the school was established in HMS Dolphin, Devonport, in September 1917, adopting the colloquial eponymous name of "The Periscope School".

CAPT David Parry RN (retd), a Perisher graduate who completed a doctoral thesis on the history of the perisher, described the school as building the ability for students to look through a periscope and exhibit a "Periscope Eye"—maintaining a mental picture of the surface situation, and to manoeuvre the boat into an attacking position. He rightly states that this became *the sine qua non* for submarine commanding officers.[198]

Indeed, this trait remains central in assessing for submarine command today. While advances in technology have yielded

---

[197] Parry, D. (2019). *Some Things You May Not Know About the Perisher (and Submarines) 1901-1945*. Kings College, London. p. 11.

[198] Parry, D. (2019). *Some Things You May Not Know About the Perisher (and Submarines) 1901-1945*. Kings College, London. p. 13.

exceptional capability to support command decision making, the ability for a commanding officer to assess the situation for themselves and anticipate developments remains at the core of being a successful, safe and effective commander. To this end, the "human in the loop" remains an essential ingredient to successful submarine employment and that individual is the commanding officer. They must be able to perform the essential skills while also demonstrating the leadership to bring the crew along with them.

The Perisher course has operated non-stop through the peace and war throughout the twentieth and into the twenty-first century. While the course has constantly evolved as technology has changed, and the submarine became more and more capable, the fundamentals of the course has remained the same. "In order to pass, a candidate must prove that he is able to operate a submarine both safely, effectively and aggressively, in a hostile environment, by completing a variety of tactical scenarios that cover the complete spectrum of submarine activity: everything from attacking a task force or other submarines, gathering intelligence, or landing members of special forces"[199]

Perisher looks for those submarine officers with 'professional competence and professional honesty. It looks for leaders who have the 'ability to motivate their crew of typically 70 or so highly trained submariners. You may be very good, as an individual, at moving a submarine from A to B. and handling it dived quite competently, but unless that XO can take those seventy crews and have them work for you, then you really don't have the qualities that are necessary for command. This is the essence of submarine command that has resonated for a century.

Falklands War British commander RADM Sandy Woodward

---

[199] Hennessy J. & Jinks, J. (2016). *The Silent Deep*, Allen Lane, London, p. 9.

RN stated, "as a Commanding officer 'you're centre stage—and you have to give a command performance all the time". When a submarine is at sea for weeks on end, this is a substantial test of someone's leadership. A commanding officer needs to be approachable yet above reproach at all times. Unlike any other Navy vessel, the commanding officer is in view of the ship's company almost all the time.

While they generally have a small cabin, this cabin is mostly immediately adjacent to the control room so they can be there in seconds. The cabin door is normally open, or separated only by a curtain, so he can never get away. Eyes are always glancing, and the CO is rarely out of the picture. A small monitor in the CO's cabin continually relays the submarine's depth and heading. In most other workplaces, the leader can go home at the end of a hard day where they can remove themselves from their employees. Not so the submarine commander. They are always on show and therefore they always have to perform. Hence, they must demonstrate a sense of duty that the crew respect and trust.

A commanding officer may join a submarine that has officers with whom they have served together in more junior roles in previous years. They may have close personal friendships with some. However, the friendship is on hold the moment the captain takes command. They need to serve in their command, respected by all. They can never aim to finish their command with a hope that all friendships remain intact. Some "skimmers" will say that this is no different from in a surface ship, or in commanding an army unit in combat. In some respects, this is true. However, a submarine is different and therefore requires these skills and attributes to be tested before an officer is deemed suitable to take command for themselves. The difference obviously comes about because on a submarine there is very little ability to see—a natural human sense—and if mistakes are made then the outcome can be catastrophic, in both peace and war.

On a submarine, information is collected by sensors and analysed by the combat system before being projected on a screen—providing a plan view of the surface picture. But it doesn't mean it's right and it portrays only historical information. The captain must be able to interpret the surface picture and anticipate what is occurring. In this sense, the combat system data is just a reference to assure that picture that the commanding officer has calculated is the same. Where there is a divergence, the captain must reassess and correct or verify the solution. Sometimes this is art, sometimes it is science. Either way, it is built upon years of submarine experience and an intuition that is inherent. It is the intangible qualities of command that are the key to finding a successful submarine commander.

To pass the Perisher requires students to be able to process and hold a mental picture of what is happening on the surface, while also being totally aware of the operation of the submarine itself (trim, heading, systems performance etc), and bring the team on, at the same time. Many struggle with this. But this form of multitasking and being assessed for it in this tried and tested manner, brings the people who possess these abilities to be brought to the surface. Importantly, it delivers officers that are ready to command a submarine—ultimately managing the inherent risks of operating a submarine at sea. In submarines there is very little divide between peace and war. When a submarine deploys it is ready for high-end warfighting operations at a moment's notice. To that end, the standards of Perisher always remain high. Without it, the people system that goes to crew a submarine will not be ready for combat operations; the submarine will most likely be ineffective, and there will be a high risk of the submarine not surviving. CAPT Parry offers a valuable and nuanced insight into submarine command and the Perisher course as preparation and assessment for it:

> In accordance with BRd 9275(3) Ch 18, the aim of SMCC is to prepare Submarine Warfare Officers for challenging command assignments in submarines, the foundations of which are based on deep tactical knowledge, advanced leadership skills, and the ability to consistently achieve the highest standards of personal integrity and professional conduct commensurate with those defined by the ethos and war-fighting capability of the Royal Navy Submarine Service.[200]

At the Dutch submarine base in the north of the Netherlands at Dan Helder, CO aspirants are put through months of simulator training as well as weeks of exercises at sea, acting in command of a Dutch boat. During a visit there in 2017, I was given the opportunity of "commanding" a *Walrus* class submarine in a very realistic simulator, navigating into and coming alongside in Portsmouth Harbour. Much as Perishers learn from during their course, watched closely by Teacher, whose standards they must meet. It was, to say the least, an impressive piece of kit and a memorable learning experience.

Perisher has these two complementary elements of teaching and assessment, in the context of personal development. The teaching element builds on what an already well-experienced course participant knows. There is always room for improvement, and for adding to a vast store of knowledge and experience. However, it is not a course designed to impart content, but rather to fine-tune knowledge and offer opportunity for disciplined personal growth through reflection and experience, and to assess that subtle and difficult to

---

[200] BRd 2 The Queen's Regulations for the Royal Navy Version 6 April 2017. In Parry D. (2022). *Perisher: Its Evolution 1917-2017 and the Submarine Commanding Officer*, PhD thesis, Kings College, London, p. 64.

define or quantify characteristic of being "ready to command a submarine". This allows the recommendation that no one should be posted to undertake Perisher if there is any doubt in his or her sponsoring navy that the potential course member is not likely to prove capable of passing the course. Competence in the basics of submarine operation is assumed. What Perisher adds is structured competence for command over and above technical ability to operate the submarine. With Australia's future being oriented to nuclear powered but not nuclear-armed *Virginia* class SSNs and eventually to a yet to be detailed class of nuclear-powered boats based on a British design though with an American combat system, it is possible that Australian SM CO aspirants will again be offered the opportunity to undertake the RN SMCC, recognising that since 2017 this has been nuclear only. In the meantime, it is likely that the RAN will continue to conduct its own SMCC course using *Collins* class SSKs, as it initiated successfully in 2022.

The following section provides a synopsis of reflections on submarine command, by several Australian commanding officers.

Reflections on Submarine Command

This section is comprised of the reflections on Submarine command by several Australian Submarine Commanders.

CDRE Tim Brown AM RAN (retd) Former CO HMAS Sheean

Tim grew up in Brisbane and studied Mechanical Engineering at QUT before commissioning into the Royal Australia Navy where he served for 33 years, specialising in submarines.

During his career as a dual streamed marine engineer and seaman officer, Tim served in multiple *Oberon* class submarines and went on to command the *Collins* class submarine HMAS *Sheean* from 2001 to 2002. He was also selected to command the ANZAC class frigate HMAS Arunta from 2007-2008, during which time he deployed on Active Service operations in the Persian Gulf as the Commander Task Group 633.1.

His career then took him to Canberra where for the next decade he worked in the submarine program, naval and defence policy, engineering and operations, force structure and capability, strategic and naval industry policy, program management, strategic communications, and government relations. He was promoted to Commodore in 2016 to serve a five-year appointment as the Director General Submarines (DGSM) and the Head of the Submarine Service. This appointment was cut short in 2020 when he was asked to lead the Prime Minister's first Task Force into the feasibility of nuclear submarines for Australia. Upon its successful completion, Tim transitioned from the Navy in September 2021. He reflects on his time in submarines: As a submarine CO. you are very exposed. The buck stops with you! If something goes wrong, it can be very serious. It's a concentrated environment. So, one needs to be an expert in the submarine as a platform. One has to know where everything is and how everything works. In many ways one becomes part of the platform system and the people system. They can work only in combination. Things can go wrong in submarines very quickly. Even when you're out of the control room having lunch you have to be across everything. This means developing an intrinsic sense of what's happening 24-7, because you might have only a few seconds to respond if something was to go wrong or something unexpected happens.

There are two parts to command – the technical bit and the leadership bit. The technical bit is the job of managing the boat and the crew to get the boat to where it's supposed to be and doing what it has to do. The leadership bit is knowing what you have to do and bringing everyone along with you. Submariners are a group of people that are proud of their professionalism, so they don't like being told what to do. They must be treated with respect, so they willingly work with you Submarine command requires mentorship, motivating, and influencing.

Essentially, leadership in submarines is about knowing and taking responsibility for the job you have been given. Submarine command also means being constantly aware of one's surroundings. I've seen a CO get up hastily from a meal in the wardroom and go to the Ops room because they felt something was wrong—and it was! More often than not when things go quiet, something is not quite right. So, by the time a submarine officer becomes a CO, they have developed a sense for knowing when something's not right. No level of training is going to teach this. It becomes an inherent intuitive trait that builds over years of experience. Good captains are always plotting the picture in their head, to keep the submarine safe, as their first responsibility. You are never in a steady state. Things are constantly changing. You have to maintain the integrity of the safety system and the submarine's operational effectiveness. Systems need to be monitored all the time. There is never an end state. We are all learning all the time, so every day is a training day, and every day is an operational day. The ship's company trusts you with their lives. There is no doubt that the buck stops with the CO. the Purpose and the mission are critical, but the demand for the safety of the crew and the boat overrides every other concern!

When you go to sea in a submarine you are not in contact with the senior leadership hierarchy ashore. There's a high level of autonomy. You are solely accountable. There is no-one to bounce ideas off. You are it! Managing risk competently is routine and pervasive. There are a lot of rules, but often it's knowing how to operate safely though on the edge of those limitations that is the key to success. Demonstrating and instilling conscientiousness is vital. If one person drops the ball others have to pick it up. The XO is trained to be your devil's advocate, respectfully questioning your decisions so that your decision making continually improves. If they are always agreeing with you then that should raise alarm bells! "Yes men" are not helpful at sea in submarines.

RADM Peter Briggs AO CSC RAN (retd) Former CO HMAS *Oxley*

What appealed to me about submarines? My decision to go to submarines was impetuous. I was returning from a year with the RN in Dartmouth and a year of sub-lieutenants' courses but wanted to stay in the UK a little longer, but I found I enjoyed it. I realized I could be commanding a submarine at the age of 31 years. I joined submarines and at 22, I was navigating my way up and down the fiords in a British submarine.

Technically, a CO has to have the capacity to hold a picture in his head. A good *Oberon* commander will think much the same as a *Collins* CO, although of course the technology is different, in terms of getting your submarine within 1200 to 1500 yards of your target to fire a straight-running torpedo required excellent ship-handling and a good periscope eye, but a *Collins* CO who took his submarine in that close might get a smack on the wrist, because he's got a longer stick and should be using it rather than taking the risk. Also in my day, the CO is the only person in the boat who is command qualified. The XO is qualified to bring the boat home in an emergency. It's different in an American SSN, where both CO and XO are command qualified, and often work shift about, so leadership is more a shared thing. (The RAN is changing to have both CO and XO command qualified).

It's a solitary situation as a CO. You've got a team around you but in the *Oberon* you were heavily dependent on the periscope, and usually the only person looking through it is the CO. so you have to be careful to be aware of all the other things that are going on around you. Every time you put to sea you are taking the submarine into harm's way. Even your friends will quite happily run you over.

In my experience, I had a couple of near misses, when surface ships didn't do what they were supposed to do. In those situations, information is being fed to you, but the decision remains. yours.

Critical incidents show the need for quick instinctive decision making. I'll give you an example. During a carefully choreographed exercise in HMAS *Oxley*, a frigate had fired an Ikara missile with a torpedo and lost track of the location of the position of the torpedo. We were in the process of being brought to the surface in a normal surfacing procedure. That is, we were returning to periscope depth which is a dangerous activity at the best of times. But when other friendly warships are close in exercises, special procedures are used to help the submarine return to periscope depth with reduced risk of collision.

On this occasion, the ship was quite close on our starboard beam, about 1500 yards, and both the ship and I were steering the safety course until I got to periscope depth and could see him, and then the ship could be released and head off at an agreed speed. As I came through 90 feet the bearings broke and I felt the hairs on the back of my neck, and quickly checked the attack sonar and ordered an emergency Go deep. We did and the ship passed over the top of us ten seconds later. They had turned and put on speed without telling us and gone off to get their torpedo. What can be learned from this? The importance of good communication is obvious.

A second example was returning from New Zealand on the surface. A storm was forecast, and we became aware that one of the berthing ropes had come loose on the outer casing. This was an issue because it could foul the propeller. I made the decision to have two crew all kitted up go out on the casing to secure the rope. A major wave came and washed one guy over, snapped his safety harness and put the other one over the on his safety harness. He was at risk of being injured by the hull. We told him to press his quick release, so now we had two men overboard in the middle of the Tasman Sea.

There was a big sea running, so I made the decision to get another two dressed and we recovered them. The storm came and we dived to avoid it. It was routine from there, back to Sydney. The point is that sometimes you need quick and instinctive decision making.

In my second command in *Oxley*, I was 35, and it was stressful, but also fun and effective. There's a big difference between a first and second command. I watched first timers and second timers. Second timers had learned, and often were less cautious, and appropriately so. Measured aggression is an important part of the psyche.

The whole time you are calculating risk. You are always thinking about the battery, and what percentage you have left, whether the submarine is balanced and trimmed. Situational awareness comes through the balls of your feet, to know whether you are heavy or not. The planes help but you need to feel it.

So, we teach the three strike rule. Strike one you can absorb, but you must prepare for strikes two and three. The first you live with but then you have a defect, and you have to decide whether you can get into a crowded harbour in a fog. The answer is, don't do it. Either fix the defect or stay out until the fog clears.

You've got to train people, to get the confidence. You are trying to develop your team. As a CO you are trying to train your XO so he can pass the Perisher. You learn from your CO in every job. One distinctive feature of being a submarine CO is that the cook can tell you how good the CO is. Everyone knows. There's no room to hide. There's less room for distant leadership.

It's critically important to get the team together to go back over things and do lessons learned, not to find fault or blame but to make it better. In this sense, a near miss can be very instructive. Every time you do a major thing you take it apart afterwards. Every calamity is a series of events. You have to recognize the sequence and take positive steps to break the sequence. The leadership skills go across areas. You need to be on top of the context, and you need to communicate that to the team. If you've invested the effort to build the trust and the confidence, you bring your team with you. Tell them what the priorities are and what the indicators are. Normally you've got a broad objective against which to measure our efforts.

There have been changes of course, as the technology means you spend less time at the periscope and rely more on the screen with its information from various sensors, but you still have to make the decision, sometimes quickly, and to lead the team. You don't own them. You only lead them.

Vice Admiral Mark Hammond AO RAN Former CO HMAS *Farncomb*

Vice Admiral Hammond was promoted Rear Admiral and appointed as Deputy Chief of Navy in March 2018, and Commander Australian Fleet in November 2020. He was promoted to Vice Admiral and appointed Chief of the Royal Australian Navy on 7 July 2022, the first RAN Recruit School and Australian Defence Force Academy graduate to do so. He is also a graduate of the Royal Netherlands Navy and US Navy Submarine Command courses. He reflects:

From the moment I joined the navy I was interested in submarines, and I volunteered for Submarine service with a recruit school classmate and friend Damien Humphreys in late 1986. When Damien was tragically killed in the *Otama* accident in 1987 I became determined to play my part in preventing a future similar incident. So, after I commissioned, I pursued a pathway to service in *Oberon* and *Collins* class submarines. I completed a science degree, focused on maths and oceanography, and information systems. Unfortunately, during my first year at the Academy I suffered a spinal injury. I had a lot of opportunity during five months in and out of traction in hospital - and the following 12 months of self-paced rehabilitation - to reflect on the good and bad leadership examples I experienced as I fell behind in my academic studies. I later worked part-time as a midshipman at HMAS *Platypus*, finished my degree, spent a few days at sea in HMAS *Otway*, and then completed seaman's officer training in the amphibious ship HMAS *Tobruk* and in the frigate HMAS *Melbourne*. As soon as I achieved my officer of the watch ticket, I joined the O boats, qualified in *Onslow*, served as an operational relief briefly in *Orion*, decommissioned *Ovens*, navigated *Collins*, and was posted as flag officer to Chief of Navy. I didn't want to leave *Collins* (it was my dream job) but when the Flag Lieutenant posting fell through (owing to some uninspiring senior leadership behaviour) I ended up doing the Principal Warfare Officer course in Sydney, then straight to submarine warfare course and back to sea in HMAS *Waller* for two years. After my XO course and teaching the submarine warfare course in HMAS *Stirling* (which included a week or so at sea in French nuclear submarine *Perle*) I joined *Sheean* as XO. In 2002 we spent 225 days away from home port including 187 days underwater between February and November. We had great success in Exercise RIMPAC and made a lot of friends in Hawaii and Guam.

My CO in *Sheean* was Tim Brown. He had prepared me

exceptionally well for Perisher, so I enjoyed the submarine command course. Tim gave me good guidance, feedback and sufficient rope to learn. When I returned to Australia from the Netherlands, I completed the US Prospective Commanding Officers Course (USS *City of Corpus Christi*) but there was a shortage of command opportunities, so I was posted to Canberra for a six-month strategy job in Canberra working for Commodore Davyd Thomas and Captain Alan DuToit. Then it was off to the Australian Command and Staff Course in 2004, and then to a nuclear submarine deployment in the South China Sea with the Royal Navy in HMS *Sceptre*, and finally a command, of HMAS *Farncomb* for two years. A lot of sea time, and a great experience, deployed and working mostly in the South China Sea.

My leadership style is heavily influenced by my submarine time. In my experience some of the best warfare officers in submarines were not the best leaders. They didn't look after their people, and they achieved results at the expense of their people. You learn a lot from a bad leader.

The best leaders knew how to handle the submarine, but also invested effort in training and knowing their team. They were self-aware and knew how to drive the submarine but had a light touch and empowered their team. They worked on creating capability so they could ultimately leave the control room with confidence that the crew could handle any situation without them.

One of the strengths of a seaman officer career in submarines is that you do all the roles from Torpedo Officer to Executive Officer before you are trusted to Command. You learn to understand the equipment, the operational context, and what everyone else in the team is doing. You become tactically and technically proficient. We now call this Technical and

Professional Mastery. The human factors piece is called Social Mastery, but it essentially equates to humanistic leadership. The ability to manage risk and to fight for clarity through ambiguity while driving a submerged submarine is critical. You start to learn this at a junior level, but it is intrinsic to your entire submarine career. This strength crystallised in my mind when I was Chief of Staff to CDF, and I had to quickly come to grips with a new operating environment - something submariners do on a daily basis. In a submarine when you are deep and fast you are essentially blind and largely deaf. When you slow down you gain faint traces on sonar that give rise to a bearing. You gradually discover more information - a bearing rate, an estimation of range, and once you step through a deliberate risk management process you rise to periscope depth. You then have a quick look around, make sure everything is safely distant, do your electronic surveillance measures clearance (to detect and classify threat radars before raising too many masts), update navigation and then work to fill in the details of the tactical picture. You build awareness, then confidence…and then you start to exploit the environment (as only an undetected and tactically aware submarine can!).

This is a dangerous phase, coming up from being deep to periscope depth where there are potentially other vessels on the surface. But you step through the process deliberately and professionally leveraging the full capabilities of the submarine and the crew. Everything in a submarine is a risk mitigator. Every valve, and every member of the crew. It's all about understanding the context - risks and opportunities- in order to make good decisions that assure the safety of the crew and submarine and maximise your own performance. This approach worked equally well as I came to grips with the Chief of Staff role.

In decision making, you must trust your training and your instincts, but you always do the math. You must actively seek the right information you need to make the right decision. If you bluff, you'll get caught out and your people will notice. When you get it wrong you must admit it. Apologise and own your mistakes when you make them. It empowers others to do the same. Fatigue is a constant issue, so you have to monitor your fatigue, and the fatigue levels in others. You need to set a good example. You make poorer decisions when you're tired. On at least one occasion I raised my voice when I shouldn't have when the on-watch team had made a mistake. I reflected on my comments in my cabin then I went back into the Control Room, and I apologised for setting the wrong example. I then asked the watch leader to do a lessons learned review to understand how the submarine got into that position, and I said I would be back in 20 minutes. We had a professional discussion with the whole watch about how to do things better next time.

One of the great privileges of commanding a submarine is the autonomy but it is a bounded autonomy – it is not unlimited. You have to understand the context and how you are operating within a set of rules and boundaries. You are trusted by the crew's families, and by the government, to do the right thing. It's a great responsibility. Every time you are below periscope depth you are on your own. You need to understand the data you need to get your job done, and you need to know how to use it and how to maximise the performance of the team, and their enjoyment of the experience. My time as a senior leader has also focused my mind on other issues. From a resource perspective, we need to manage our people better. Some captains I worked for didn't have kids and they forgot that their crew had families who were anxiously awaiting their return. We need to consider their needs 'outside of the pressure hull'. I was over 35 when I was in command, and I had two children at home. That was pretty old by O-boat standards. We also had an exacting operational program slated over a two-year period. I knew that fatigue would be an issue with our program, so I focused on balancing my expectations of performance against the context of each day.

You have to allow people to vary within a performance range where the lower end is above a minimum acceptable threshold, but you can't set the bar high and expect everyone to meet it all the time - they will burn out and start either making mistakes or just behaving badly. You have to get the context right. I firmly believe that the leader's job is to train, inspire and empower. To create a professional and rewarding environment wherein our people want to get out of bed and get to work because of the important work we do AND how we do it. To get people to see how good success in a challenging environment feels, and to give them the tools and responsibility to get on with it - then to stand back and watch their success with pride. On that note, I look forward to seeing the next generation of submariners thrive!

RADM Greg Sammut AO RAN (retd) Former CO HMAS *Farncomb*

I joined the navy in 1984, and submarines in 1990, having studied engineering, qualified as a seaman officer and gaining my bridge watchkeeping ticket in HMAS *Tobruk*. I qualified as a submariner in 1991. I did a series of jobs in submarines, as a torpedo officer in HMAS *Otway* then torpedo officer in HMAS *Ovens*, and went to navigator in HMAS *Orion*, and operations officer and sonar officer in *Orion* then I went to Perisher in 1996. was told I was posted as CO to HMAS *Otama* but instead went to went to staff college in 1997, and then did

Collins conversion training before going as CO to commission HMAS *Farncomb* in 1998 till 2000 (almost three years to the day). I spent five months as Commander Sea Training, during which we worked up three submarines. Then it was to the US to the Naval command course that was a general staff course, a year-long international course at the Naval War College. I spent a year with the combat system program, and with the heavy torpedo program, in Newport. In 2011 I was Director General submarine Capability and commenced my next role as Head of Future submarines.

I think the command responsibilities are different for submariners. I wondered whether the leadership capabilities are exceptional. I reflect on leadership principles and think that in a submarine command you get responsibility early for an asset with a strategic capability. Some of the demands are important, and you are trusted to lead your people through these situations, without the ability to pick up the phone to higher authority. Other young officers have to deal with similar challenges in their situations. I make a distinction between command and leadership. Winning the trust and confidence of your people is vital, so competence in the job is essential - not just the technical skills, but knowing how and when to apply them, to keep the submarine safe.

The CO needs to demonstrate he is making the right decisions. You bring your team with you and demonstrate trust in their ability to do their jobs. The enduring thing is to be able to watch people do what you did and do it better. You need to make sure the technical aspects don't overshadow the need for leadership. In decision making, priorities are safety, remaining undetected, and achieving the mission. Making sure you take thinking time, to make better decisions, to convert data into information. In a submarine, compared to a surface ship, you have bits of limited information and you're working hard to build the tactical picture.it might take only a couple of minutes, but you need to keep all the elements of the plan in mind. You need to keep asking your team what they think too and what are their recommendations from what they are seeing. You are training them to think as if they are the CO. lessons are learned all the time. Getting the team together afterwards and undergoing the discomfort of admitting you've made a mistake, so it could be talked about, and we can all learn from it. Transparency is important. Purpose is important. Otherwise, why do it? You have to keep explaining it to your people. Autonomy is something we treasure because it's how we operate best. We need to be trusted to go and do it. You have to genuine as a leader, and you have to know yourself and be yourself – know your values, and these determine how we approach issues. You have to live with yourself after you've made the decision. In a submarine your people see you up close all the time, whether you're on watch or not. They need to know what your values are.

Also, as a submarine CO you have to be your own mentor and not need the applause of others. There's no one else there to pat you on the back, or even to tell you that you could have done better. I suppose it's about being confident with what I've done. You just have to live with it.

In resource allocation, the question is how do you steward your resources? You have to understand what is important rather than what you want to do. This is critical when you ask people to dig deep, when the resources are scarce. Your tactical picture is a set of probabilities making the most out of the information you have.

CDRE Michael Dunne AM RAN (retd) CO HMS Finwhale and HMAS *Otama*

The most important character of a good submarine commander is competence. It's probably essential for any leader in any organisation. In submarines, because the operating environment at sea is always inherently dangerous, it's understandable that the crew look for it right from the start. Of course, they know that the CO would not have been posted in had they not done the command course, and passed it, so they expect that they will, above all else, know how to keep the boat safe. If the crew suspect that the CO is deficient in competence, they will not want to risk their lives by going to sea with that captain. Thankfully I had been well trained, and I never had a situation in which I did not know what to do, but I know of some commanders who experienced challenges in this regard, and had to work hard to regain the trust and respect of their crews. Building on this, when I had a role in recommending people for particular jobs, I always ensured that as far as I could tell, they would be competent to do the job. There is no sense in tasking people with work that they might not be able to carry out. If they fail, it impacts their self-confidence and their subsequent decision making. In submarine leadership, especially in command, it could be fatal.

CDRE Sid (Stephen) Dalton RAN Former CO HMAS *Onslow* and *Sheean*

My motivation to join the Navy was about securing a job and a tertiary education, but my professional attraction and commitment to submarines turned this vague notion of employment into a rewarding career. After 35 years full-time and another three in the Reserves, I still have a deep passion for and commitment to submarine service, the Navy, sea power, undersea warfare and a keen interest in every other aspect of the sea service, Defence and the people of our service. Having joined the Navy in 1982 and completed the first Dutch Submarine Command Course (SMCC) in 1995, roughly the first third of my career was spent preparing for submarine command, the next third applying my knowledge in submarine command and related roles, and the latter third applying everything I had learnt through knowledge, experience and education to roles supporting the operational and strategic management of Defence.

When Paul Davidson asked me to write some personal reflections on submarine command and leadership, my first thoughts were "I could write a whole book on that topic myself." The harder task was to concentrate my thoughts into something much more compact, which is a real challenge but a good exercise in being concise. So, I have limited my reflections to what I consider the most valuable lessons: the importance of professional mastery, building and leading a team where you respect the contribution of everyone, taking charge in command, how to leverage stress and manage fatigue, and how to plan and manage priorities.

Submarine command is a unique blend of command and leadership. At its core submarine command requires a professional mastery of all things submarine – warfare beneath the sea, knowledge of your vessel and its many systems, a deep understanding of operating procedures and dealing with emergencies, as well as an ability to think and plan ahead. With a science background and a general interest in how things work, submarines were a natural fit for my thirst for knowledge.

Although I earned my submarine qualification in *Oberon* class submarines, a natural curiosity for all things submarine meant it was not difficult to learn how other classes of submarines work and operate and apply that knowledge to new situations and threats. I learnt early in my career that you never stop learning – you draw on the knowledge and skills of others, and they f/rom you. Later in my career, I had to use ALL my professional expertise built throughout the preceding 32 years of my career to lead the team that developed the requirements for what was to become the *Attack* class submarines. More importantly than professional mastery, submarine command demands an ability to build, train and lead a team of individuals into a motivated and professional crew that you must rely on and who trust and support you, no matter what happens. During sea training, I have seen the submarine's captain pull the crew out of a disastrous emergency depth change and after-planes failure – stepping in at exactly the right time, he pulled the boat out of a huge bow-down angle and had it under control at safe depth within the standard time. But more often than not, in extreme circumstance, it will be someone else in the crew that saves the day – calling a close contact, a dangerous radar transmission, stopping a flood, alerting the crew, performing their emergency operating procedures, isolating the dangers, searching through smoke haze for casualties or diving into the water to rescue people who've fallen overboard.

All submariners know they are all in the same boat; as a team means they must all look out for each other, learn from mistakes, do their duty as they expect others to do theirs but at the same time respect the contribution that every member of the team makes. As the captain you may well be one of the most important people on board – you are in command – but you cannot and should not do everything yourself. So, investing in your people as a team, knowing their strengths and weaknesses, being open with your plans, expectations and standards engaging and speaking with each individual, every groups and the entire ship's company is critical to success. Not infrequently, the most junior or least experiences crewmember can save the day – knowing and appreciating this fact will also stand you in good stead in any team situation.

A crew needs its captain to be in charge and they look to the CO for leadership, guidance and direction. Taking charge in command is a very personal thing, you are on your own. As a junior officer, this is not necessarily something you get to experience until you are preparing for command – generally, there is someone else looking over your shoulder who can step in if you do something wrong. Building the professional mastery, self-confidence and self-reliance necessary for command takes time, and is best done driving submarines around in addition to the necessary training and mentoring. From my experience, it was not until I was ten miles from Sydney heads on the way to New Zealand a week into my first command of *Onslow* that I truly felt full responsibility of command – what we call "the weight". You must embrace the weight of command – no-one else is accountable, you have your orders and your guidance, and you alone must step up and make the decisions. The weight never leaves until you are relieved by the next commanding officer, but you share the load with your officers and crew through delegation, clear guidance and communications, teamwork and shared responsibility for the functions and standards that make the submarine work, keep you safe, undetected and achieve the aim.

Managing stress and fatigue are important skills to learn to function in any sort of demanding workplace or situation over an extended period. Few workplaces are as demanding or stressful as a submarine. While not pretending to be an expert on stress or traumatic stress, in the period before submarine command I found it helpful to make a distinction between normal stress, the stress that improves your response when faced with potential danger, and harmful stress, which is best thought of as stress induced by other things that do not pose an immediate danger. By this simple definition, harmful stress can be anything from the stress felt from a pressing deadline to post-traumatic stress years after a critical incident.

In the case of normal stress, this would be the stress from a potential danger such as a shipping contact that gets in too close, a submarine at close range or a submarine emergency such as a fire, flood or collision – in these cases I would leverage this normal type of stress-response to potential danger to heighten my response to the situation, which for trained submariners are sets of orders, procedures, reports or responses you train for and anticipate. In the case of harmful stress, at the lower end you need to remind yourself or others that the stressor is not an immediate danger, and work through the issues.

At the upper end of the stress spectrum – post-traumatic stress disorder (PTSD) – though there may be no immediate danger this is a serious condition that can cause self-harm in those afflicted and clinical intervention by professionals may be necessary. As a commander or even a manager of people who have been exposed to critical incidents, it is important you can recognise the signs and know how to respond. Every person has a different perspective of the same incident, depending on their place in an organisation – as the captain you are probably better informed than anyone else in the crew and can keep things in perspective, but you need to remember that there are those with less experience and less knowledge of what is going on who will respond to incidents in different ways, including elevated levels of harmful stress, and you need to watch out for each other. After any sort of stressful situation, knowing how to relieve stress, talk things through with your team and let off steam to relieve stress at an appropriate time is an important skill set.

Closely related to managing stress is managing fatigue – this means looking after yourself as well as your team. As the captain it is critical that you are as well rested as possible. If everyone else is tired, they are more likely to make mistakes, so it is important that the captain can be relied on to make the right decisions at any time. I found I was better at managing fatigue during my second command of HMAS *Sheean* – being a little older, wiser and more experienced helped, but I was also better at knowing when to catch extra sleep and devoted more time to planning days and weeks ahead to ensure I was well rested and alert when I needed to be. Likewise, you need to manage the routines of the crew so that they are as well rested as they can be - you need to protect the sleep periods of watchkeepers from out-of-routine activities, and make sure non-watchkeepers are not overused. In command you need to understand the fatigue status of your crew as much as the status of your battery – they work in a similar fashion and need regular re-charging to maintain function. Good leaders will recognise when they need to pull back and cancel things when they or their crew are too tired to function, though good planning can minimise this as a risk.

My final reflections concern planning and managing priorities. Things rarely turn out as expected, so military plans need to consider as many possible outcomes as possible, plan for the worst and detail how to respond. During my second command I applied a style of planning based on the joint military appreciation process (JMAP) used for Joint operations that I'd learned on Navy staff course. It meant that every activity was approached with an open mind using a modified JMAP rather than applying a set of pre-conceived routines or responses. Starting with a main planning session before the start of a major activity, I derived a concept of operations and produced a set of operations orders, then used the daily sessions of the 'S Club' to test assumptions, update our situation both internally and externally, then adjust. I even had a crisis planning procedure for adjusting things quickly, working from the control room around the plotting table, though never really needed to use it. What I did find though, was that I had few surprises and nothing that had not been thought of or planned for beforehand.

This leads me to managing priorities – most plans include a set of priorities. In submarines we use a hierarchy of priorities: safety of the submarine and crew, remain undetected and achieve the aim. Most submariners are familiar with these, and they work well up to a point. They are treated as steps, assuming that only if the first two of these are achieved can you think about the mission – achieving the aim – and submariners will move between these steps depending on the situation. However, on SMCC you are taught to examine these steps more closely, adding additional steps as required, thinking more deeply about what these mean in practice, and challenging yourself to plan for risk managing the worst-case situations.

For example, there are different degrees of safety – a grounding can be less dangerous than a collision, losing a periscope or incurring damage to the submarine's fin is less dangerous than a collision with the pressure hull. With respect to remaining undetected, being counter-detected is better than being recognised as being a threat submarine, which is better than being engaged with a torpedo, and the worst case is being hit by a torpedo. As a submarine commander you need to think through and plan for the worst case, and everything in between, that way you will always have a response you can apply. Sometimes this means you need to have thought more deeply about how to manage conflicting priorities and apply a more sophisticated and calculated approach to managing risks.

CDRE Peter Scott CSC, RAN (Retd) Former CO HMAS *Dechaineux* and *Collins*

There was a day when I was at sea in command of one of our submarines. We were preparing for a major, four-month deployment into Southeast Asia. We were dived, in a very deep part of the ocean, of the coast of Western Australia. In fact, we were at our 'Deep Diving Depth'. Think the red line on your car's engine: you can go past it, but you're pushing your luck. Things were going very smoothly, until a pipe in Lower Motor Room burst, flooding the submarine at the rate of a tonne a second. Emergency Stations – Alarm!! A tonne a second! To paint a picture, that's the same as one hundred crates of beer ripping into your submarine, through a hole the size of your clenched fist, every second. Imagine the shock, the noise, the damage! At the moment of a flood such as this, everything changes. You go from knowing the state of your submarine in intimate detail, to endless unknowns. Where is the water? Are my people drowning? Are they dead? And, of course, we are all in the same boat! We knew one thing – we had to get to the surface and stay there! Because if the submarine went down in that depth of water, it would be crushed before it hit the bottom. There was no coming back! I vividly recall one particular moment during that melee. Standing between the periscopes in the centre of the packed control room I felt the eyes of one the sailors rigidly fixed on me. Have you ever looked into the eyes of a person who respects and trusts you – a colleague, a friend, a child - when they are searching earnestly for answers – for leadership? Now I did not know if we would survive that flood. In fact, I remember seeing myself in my mind's eye floating, face down, through a dark, cold submarine. But hey, I had survived tough days before. I had trained the crew to know their stuff. And I knew that if I could remain calm, hold back my fear and offer them the courage they needed, then we had half a chance.

Survive we did. And when we sailed for that deployment two weeks later, every man and woman who was onboard that fearful day joined with me and went back to sea. So, that's a sea story, but it's not the story. What I have continually found is that "people can learn to lead" - and some people can learn to lead really well. I am not a born leader. When I joined the Navy as a young lad, I couldn't lead myself, unless it was into strife, let alone lead others through a life and death crisis. Yet, over time, I successfully commanded two submarines. I served in twenty different command and leadership appointments over 34 years. I progressively discovered and realised my true and full leadership potential, time and time again. So, to those who dare imagine themselves as leaders, I encourage your absolute determination in the unending quest to discover and realise your full leadership potential. It's the class that never ends. Good hunting!"

Leadership insights from Submarine Command

Of making many books there is no end, and much study is a weariness of the flesh. (Ecclesiastes 12:12)

The author of these words in the Bible thousands of years ago appears to be proven correct, if only by the number of books about leadership on sale in almost every bookstore and airport terminal. There seems to be an infinite appetite for theories on how to understand the process of leadership, and the knowledge and skill needed to become a leader, so that leadership can somehow be taught and the benefits of good leadership realized.

The Nature of Leadership

Being a leader, or being perceived by others to be a leader, is seen as being influential in determining the behaviour of others. They may be known as followers, thus conferring on them a certain status in the group. Sentiments of loyalty or envy and antipathy may be aroused in this process of group formation. Leadership is also often related to power and authority in decision making. By implication, rightly or wrongly, because of the significance of the leader's decisions, leaders are thought to matter more than other people. This may explain the general interest in the concept of leadership. Of course, there is the view that leaders are born and not made, but they are not born made. So, we have a huge leadership "industry" that offers courses of various durations, costs, and content, which will make participants into better leaders. This is parallel to and part of the growth of knowledge and skill-based management courses in business.[201] In this view, leadership is a combination of knowledge, skill, and behaviour, that can be taught over weekends or months. The logic runs that if leadership is what leaders do, then students of leadership need only study what leaders do and teach these behaviours to would-be leaders. The better the leader is judged to be, the more effective any learned behaviours are likely to be in leadership development courses. This line of thinking encourages analysis of leadership as it is demonstrated by recognised leaders. The result of this analysis usually concludes that leaders are both person-centred (to meet follower's needs for affiliation) and also task-centred (giving directions and coordinating resources to get the outcome desired). There is also usually reference to charismatic leadership based on the personal qualities of the leader, democratic leadership based on the participation by those led, and authoritarian leadership based on the use of coercion and power. Military figures such as Montgomery, Douglas MacArthur, Eisenhower, Patton. Chester Nimetz, Erwin Rommel, and Adolf Hitler are frequent candidates for attention as variously charismatic egotistical, and toxic.

---

[201] Schermerhorn, J., Davidson, P., Woods, P., Factor, Simon, A., MacBarron, E., and Junaid, A. (2020). *Management* 7th edn, John Wiley & Sons, Brisbane.

Finally, there are alternative models and styles of leadership such as leaderless groups and laissez-faire leadership in the absence of an appointed leader. At heart is the notion that leaders are influential in others' behaviour, and their effectiveness is essential in achieving group tasks. Unsurprisingly, there are mediating factors in the context or environment of leadership. In this situational leadership thinking, the leader adapts to the demands of the situation, rather than using the same style across all different situations. If the context is that the leader is appointed as an externally validated expert, it is likely that some group members subject to that authority will be relieved and willingly confer authority on the leader. Resistant others may be less impressed and conspire to create situations that will test the competence and thus acceptability of the appointed leader. Can anything of value be learned beyond this? Reviewing the history of submarine warfare and the reflections of several Australian Submarine Commanders in preceding chapters allows a number of insights to be drawn about leadership in submarines and leadership in general. In summary they are:

1   *Know your Product.* Be clear about the purpose and meaning of the group's activities. Give as much information as appropriate, to promote inclusiveness and genuine participation. Explain your mission and why it is justified.

2   *Know your platform.* A threshold requirement. Be technically competent in commanding a submarine.[202] Be technically knowledgeable "enough" about what it does, what can go wrong, and what to do about it.

---

[202] See Product, Platform, Processes and People: Management Questions for Submarine Service planners, in this Appendix.

3 *Processes* - What processes need to be created or modified to enable this? What are the legal and engineering processes that need to be established? What processes need to be undertaken to maintain and operate them? What upside and downside risk attaches to these processes?

4 *Know your people.* Know and be concerned about the welfare of your crew. Understand what your employees need and want. he emphasised that the leader's first obligation was and always will be to his crew and their welfare. The leader is well advised to remember - They are not there for you. You are there for them. The challenges in recruiting, training and retaining crews may pose the most complex questions of all. The high-level matrix below for member category represents an applied design thinking model in conceptualizing the human resource management planning for the nuclear submarines. It is not exhaustive, but only a model for thought. Given the differences in *Astute* and *Virginia* platforms, different HR planning will be required. This matrix should be read from right to left. The next level of abstraction to enable planning is to insert numbers required and years when required as a further column to the right to stimulate future HR planning.

REFLECTIONS ON SUBMARINE COMMAND

Category	Role	Recruitment	Training	Retention	Competency	Effect
CO	Command	Command selection	Perisher qualified Nuclear power course graduate	Advanced leadership course	Critical for strategic and tactical management	Mission success
XO	Admin	CO aspirants	Nuclear power course graduate 8+ yrs experience	Regular updating exchanges	2ic, ship organisation	Ship organisation
NO Navigator	Navigation	Navigation training	Nav course	Exchanges	Positioning	Effectiveness Safety
OPSO Operations officer	Operations	SWO experience	Seaman specialists	Exchanges	Weapons, sensors, Intelligence	Coordinated operations
SWO	Submarine Warfare officer (SWO)	From seamen specialist officers	Mariner skills	ASW course	Warfare skills	Combat effect
EO	EO Engineering officer	Engineering graduates	Nuclear power courses	Exchanges	Propulsion	Reliable power
CISM	Information Mgt	Comms quals	Comms	Exchanges	Comms systems	Communications
WEO	Weapons electrical officer (WEO)	Electrical engineering quals	Engineering	Exchanges		Maintenance of Weapons and electrical systems
SO	Sonar Officer	Sonar training	Sonar	Exchanges	Sensors operations	Accurate Threat assessment

TO	Torpedo Officer	Torpedo training	Engineering	Exchanges	Torpedoes		Mission success
MO	Medical officer (MO)	Medical practitioner	Specialist undersea medicine/ emergency medicine	Regular updating courses, exchanges, shore postings	Health care of crew		Effective crew
Coxswain	People mgt		Admin		Coordination Regulator		Morale and discipline
Steward	Catering	Supply officers and Sailors			Catering services		Crew sustenance

Appendix: Selected Submarine Class specifications

Class	Displacement (tons)	Length ft	Propulsion	Speed kts sur/sub	Crew	Weapons
Holland (1920-23)	113	63	160hp petrol 70hp electric motor	7/5.6	7	
B class (1905-06)	280	142	600hp petrol	12/6	16	Two 18-inch tubes
E class (1913-16)	660	81	1,600hp diesel	16/10	30	Five 18-inch tubes
J class (1916)	1,210	275	3,600hp diesel	19.5/ 9.5	44	Six 18-inch tubes
Shark class (1934-37)	670	202	1,550 hp diesel		40	Six 21-inch tubes
O class (1926-28)	1598	270	4,400hp diesel	15/9	50	Eight 21-inch tubes

Gato Class (1939)	1525	311	5,400hp	21/9	60	10 21-inch tubes
Type VII (1939-45)	769	220	3,200	17.7/7.6	44-52	14 torpedoes
Oberon (1960-67)	2030	295	3,680bhp diesels	12/7	68	Eight 21-inch tubes
Swift sure (1973-81)	3,500	272	15,000shp	25/30	97	Five 21 inches
Collins SSK (1990-2003)	3,100	254	7,200hp diesels	10/20	58	Six 21-inch tubes
Seawolf SSN (2005)	8,600	353	Nuclear	25/35	140	Eight tubes
Astute SSN 2007)	7,400	318	Nuclear	30	100	Six 21-inch tubes
Virginia SSN (2000)	7,900	377	Nuclear 280,000hp	25+	135	12 VLS tubes
Ohio SSBN (1976-97)	18,750	560	Nuclear	20+	155	24 missile tubes Four 21-inch torpedo tubes

Bringing Projects from Initiation to Completion

A hierarchical stepwise process of decision making can usefully guide thought and action.

STEP	Definition	Questions for action
1 Vision	the desired end state resulting from an organisation's activities.	What do you want to see?
2 Mission	This is the organisation's statement of its purpose and reason for being in its operating environment and its justification for committing resources and effort) to attain goals and achieve objectives.	Why do you want to see it?
3 Goals	These are **attained** as outcomes through their influence on behaviour and resource deployment	What goals does your mission require?
4 Objectives	These express the purpose of the organisation's lines of effort in terms of what is to be achieved. They are **achieved** as end states in the service of goals, which in turn serve the mission.	What objectives will serve these goals?
5 Achievements	These are expressed by scores or results on **Key Performance Indicators (KPIs)** which are **satisfied** to a greater or lesser extent by the **implementation of strategy**.	What indicators need to be satisfied to confirm objective achievement?
6 Strategy	The **strategy** is the statement of how the objectives are to be achieved by resource allocation and undertaking of activities in lines of effort, to produce specified deliverables. Alternatively, if the (high level) strategy is developed directly from the mission, the objectives may be formulated to **fulfil** the strategy.	How will these objectives be achieved? What activities are necessary?
7 Deliverables	These are the intended products or end states that result from undertaking activities. They may be evaluated by KPIs.	What products or end states are delivered?
8 Implementation	The **Implementation** of strategy through **activities** is the application of resources and effort in undertaking the strategy. Risk Management and stakeholder engagement are critical drivers in planning implementation.	How can resources be applied in activities to undertake the strategies?

9 Outcomes	**Outcomes** or **effects** are **produced** as the results of implementing the strategies to achieve the objectives and produce deliverables.	What outcomes are there from implementing the strategies?
10 Benefits	**Benefits** are **realised** as the positive effects or outcomes that flow from the outcomes. **Disbenefits** are the undesirable consequences (outcomes or effects) resulting from undertaking activities.	What benefits are realized by implementing the strategies?
11 Evaluation	**Evaluation** is the process of assessing the achievement of objectives, attainment of goals, and effectiveness of strategy in the service of the vision and mission.	Were the objectives achieved? Did they serve the goals? Did this meet mission requirements?
12 Feedback	**Feedback** allows correction as continuous improvement, potentially to **each step**.	What changes are needed for the future? Who should now be told of the whole process?

Threat Assessment in Defence

The accurate and appropriate assessment of threat is arguably a necessary survival skill for all sentient beings and has been so since pre-history. Knowing what in one's environment poses a hazard is critical for decision making about how to manage the risk involved in life itself. This section proposes perception and learning as central processes in threat assessment, applied to the process in the defence environment.

> *'If you are a fish, swimming in the ocean, there are things in the ocean that are alive and dangerous and there are things that are good to eat. The rest is just water.' Knowing the difference between these is a matter of survival.*

Submarine crews must become critical decision makers about the threats they confront, both rarely and frequently.

Distinguishing the noise of an enemy or potential enemy from the routine noise of the ocean is critical to staying alive. Unrealistic hyperresponsivity is expensive.

Most people and most cultures throughout history have lived their lives knowing that the accurate and appropriate assessment of threat is a necessary survival skill. From infancy, animals and humans are taught by parents or others, painfully or otherwise by events, about what in their environment is dangerous, and what is not. Survival depends on being able to recognise threat realistically, and to respond with either avoidance or counter force.

It may be argued that some external threats are so obvious as such that recognition of the danger they pose is unavoidable. Other threats are more subtle, less obvious, and recognised to be such only in painful hindsight. The reflection "what were they thinking?" is testament to our amazement that "they didn't see it coming". We ask why they did not, because with the benefit of hindsight, it seems so obvious, and we are puzzled that they did not take some evasive action. We ask how they missed the signs of danger. However, while knowing to avoid a dangerous part of town might be straightforward for the individual, a nation's ability to assess threat to its safety and existence is more complex and may appear on a grand scale. This points towards an examination of the process of threat assessment based on learning and risk taking.

Learning is critical because it is the process that brings relatively long-term behaviour change consequent on experience. If the experience is pleasant and the outcomes believed to be positive, the learning may encourage repetition in circumstances judged to be sufficiently similar allowing the belief that they will be pleasant again. If the experience is painful, operant conditioning theory predicts that the behaviour will be less likely to be repeated. Children and adults have been punished for their misdeeds over the centuries on this basis.

The commonly espoused theory is that of the pleasure principle. In general, and other things being equal, we seek to maximise pleasure and avoid pain, so when we are in a powerful position, we are able to administer punishment, ostensibly to "correct" the offender's behaviour. When we are the ones being punished, we are expected to believe that the punishment is because of our misdeed, and the effect of this punishment is to discourage repetition of the offence. Thus, it is held that we learn from experience of what is a threat and what is not, and from this we learn what threats we are prepared either to confront or to avoid. Mostly, perhaps, we get it right, and we survive, either because we managed the threat by evasion or engaging in some level of pre-emptive action with it to lessen its impact, or alternatively we tolerated it and its effect on us was not fatal. So far, perhaps, so good.

Threat assessment

Threat assessment needs to be accurate and appropriate for several reasons. Firstly, and most obviously, getting our threat assessment wrong can have a fatal outcome. More commonly, getting it right can also be dangerous in the long run, because a subsequent threat might be different enough from our fortunate escape from it the first time to blind us to realistic danger posed, and we may fail to take the needed avoidant action based on our learning from a different situation. What worked for us last time might not always work. The consequences may be destructive. Alternatively, we may assess the threat to be worse than it actually is and expend energy and resources needlessly "jumping at shadows". Where this is done on a national basis, populations may commit vast financial reserves to building armed forces that are not needed either to create excessive deterrence or in preparation for a conflict that never actually happens.

Those responsible for planning a nation's defence have an awesome responsibility. Too little or inappropriate procurement of defence equipment, or other deficient preparation, may lead to large scale suffering and destruction. On the other hand, wrongly assessing the threat as serious or extreme may lead to irrational fear, and paradoxically bring on the conflict that it seeks to avoid, by leading the potential adversary to perceive warlike preparation by the one as offensive rather than defensive and triggering a pre-emptive strike by the other. Either way, threat assessment is a critical phase in a relationship between nations that can lead to fatal misjudgement.

Unsurprisingly, because the stakes are so high, much attention has been given to the ways by which one nation can judge the threat posed by the actions of another. Nations conduct surveillance activities on potential adversaries to determine not only the potential force that might be exerted against them, but also the intent of the potential adversary. Ships, aircraft, missiles and soldiers are counted, and because Sun Tzu emphasised that as all wars depend on deception, much effort is given either to concealing force, or to camouflaging it, or to engaging in "psyops", psychological operations to introduce doubt into the potential adversary's mind and degrade their ability to make decisions which could prove harmful if left unchecked by disruption.

What of the situation where the threat genuinely exits and is perceived but not admitted? The nation in denial may comfort itself that it did not actively provoke war by building warlike defences but may later have to face the argument that their unpreparedness manifestly encouraged the belligerent opponent to initiate war. Lack of preparedness by both Britain and the US In the 1930s almost certainly was seen by Germany and Japan as an invitation to strike in 1939 and 1941.

The Argentinians' belief that a cost-cutting British government would not have the will to defend an invasion of the disputed Falkland Islands (or Malvinas) in 1983 was a misperception that resulted in a war and state of enmity that exists still. The Argentine government was wrong, and fell, and the Thatcher government reflected that the threat posed by Argentina while not to Britain itself, was at least sufficiently significant in principle and for the lives of British citizens living in the Falklands, to take the nation into a war it would rather not have had to fight. The initial underestimation by British of the threat posed, their reluctance to engage in hostilities, and their eventual bowing to the inevitability of armed conflict only when there seemed no alternative, is now argued as being responsible in the era of post-cold war accord. Now, the situation is different.[203]

The perception of threat has been heightened in recent years by the massive arms build-up by China, to levels of force that observers see as both overwhelmingly intimidating and excessive in the extreme, since no other country is showing any significant intent to invade China. It must be assumed that the strategy being followed is coercion. Whether such a strategy has relevance, and traction depends on relative opposing forces. If America declines as a great power in Asia, it is assessed as unlikely that it will confront China over Taiwan, for example: "the costs are too high, and the stakes are too low"[204] The perception of threat is based on the position and power of the

---

[203] Barrett, T. (2017). *The Navy and the Nation*. Commonwealth of Australia, Canberra.

[204] Roggeveen, S, (2023). The *Echidna Strategy: Australia's Search for Power and Peace*. La Trobe University Press, Collingwood. p. 13.

perceiver. If "making America great again" becomes a cultural imperative for how the US sees itself, it may be that while America-China conflict over Taiwan is judged unjustified by both protagonists, it may still serve as a trigger to challenging American supremacy in Asia.

Undoubtedly, a nation's culture has a major bearing on its decision making in confronting threat. Culture is that set of purpose and assumptions and the values and attitudes driving them, with the written and unwritten beliefs and practices that define a group's or nation's identity. It is relevant in decision making when the explicit rules do not apply. "Of all of the factors involved in military effectiveness, culture is perhaps the most important." [205]

Now, Australia is anxiously watching the arms race and China's intensive weaponisation of the South China Sea, after many years of relative peace and quiet.[206] Great attention is being given to accurately and appropriately assessing the threat posed.[207] The PRC effectively claims the entire South China Sea as its own territory, ignoring counter claims of historical fishing rights and international waters by governments of the Philippines, Vietnam, Singapore and Malaysia and Indonesia. It has erected structures from small platforms to complete airfields and support facilities on contested islands and outcrops, and routinely has hundreds of vessels operating in the region. There are frequent conflicts with opposing forces, with coercive and reckless manoeuvres as well as small arms fire and water cannon. Hundreds of People's Armed Forces

---

[205] Mansoor, P. R and Williamson, M. (eds.) (2019). *The Culture of Military Organizations*. Cambridge University Press, p. 3.

[206] Roggeveen, S, (2023). The *Echidna Strategy: Australia's Search for Power and Peace*. La Trobe University Press, Collingwood.

[207] Hamilton, C. & Ohlberg, M. (2020). *Hidden Hand: Exposing how The Chinese Communist Party is Reshaping the World*. Melbourne, Hardie Grant.

Maritime Militia (PAFMM) "fishing boats" are armed and combat ready with payloads of drone swarms. These constitute a significant grey zone threat to the free passage of ships in international waters.[208]

Various scenarios are being imagined and "war-gamed", "just in case". China claims its rise is peaceful and its intentions are harmonious, yet its actions appear to be distinctly hostile and coercive to its neighbours. "Xi has designated the United States as the enemy of everything he stands for. Xi aspires to Chinese global domination in a world made safe for dictatorships."[209] If war is based on deception, as Sun Tzu claimed, how accurate and appropriate is Australia's threat assessment? Perhaps more to the point, even if our threat assessment is accurate, what should we do about it? With a tenth of its economy and a tenth of its armed forces Australia is in no position to win a conventional exchange of gunfire with China. It could never be a "fair fight". What possible effective strategy can we employ to deter China yet at the same time affirm that we want to live in peace and trade our goods and products to mutual advantage? Episodic presence may not be enough for deterrence.

Perception and Learning

The process of perception is critical in understanding the wider process of threat assessment. It is said that 'if the only tool you have is a hammer, you tend to see everything else as a nail.' The point is that perception actively involves the previous experience of the perceiver as well as the objective features of the perceived. If learning is defined as the relatively permanent

---

[208] Thornburg, K. (2022). Responding to drone swarms at sea. *Proceedings*, December. pp. 36-41.
[209] Tsang, S. and Cheung, O. (2024). *The Political Thought of Xi Jinping*. Oxford University Press, Oxford. UK.

change in behaviour consequent on experience, then the act of perception fundamentally involves a re-examination of what learning from past experience might be influencing the present process.

This act of perception that is the beginning of the process of threat assessment thus invites consideration of its early elements of stereotyping and heuristics that shortcut the judgment process. If a nation already has a negative apprehension of the supposed hostile intent of a potential adversary, it is likely that the perceived threat profile accorded to it will be raised.

Similarly, if a nation has experienced an exceptional event in its history from which it has "learned", such as the tragic lack of preparedness of the American military that contributed to the world-changing event of Pearl Harbour in 1941, then its estimation of its likely vulnerability will be affected. Also affected will be the extent to which it will go in preparing its forces for any potential attack in the future, based on its assessment of the threat posed by a perceived adversary. It relies on the judgment of later history whether an underestimation has led to disaster or overestimation has allowed expensive and unnecessary expenditure of a nation's resources.

Inertia and hubris in the assessment process

After decades of relative peace, the Royal Navy in the late Victorian era had evolved into a culture of regulators rather than rat catchers. "They thought they were good, but in ways that mattered, they were not. They thought they were ready for war, but they were not".[210] Too often in military history, the threat posed by an enemy has been underrated – a serious

---

[210] Gordon, A. (1996). *The Rules of the Game: Jutland and British Naval Command.* John Murray, London. P. 594.

and fatal error in world wars, and in Korea, Vietnam and Afghanistan. Perhaps it will always be our downfall. Admiral Dönitz refused to believe that the Allies could have broken his Enigma code, and so he persisted in using it, needlessly costing Germany hundreds of U-boats and their crews. It is sobering to recall the famous last words of the American Civil War General John B Sedgwick, at the battle of Spotsylvania in 1864: 'They couldn't hit an elephant at this dist...'.

The dark humour of quoting Sedgwick's last words should not trivialize the recurrent tendency in the military to underestimate the intent and competence of one's enemy.[211] The British underestimated the Japanese in Singapore in 1940. The Americans refused to believe they could be attacked at Pearl Harbour in 1941. The bewildered French failed to take seriously the Viet Minh artillery at Dien Bien Phu in 1954. The French left Indochine and the French government fell. The Americans failed militarily against the North Vietnamese and departed Vietnam in 1973.

One would have expected that by now, humility in the light of history would have encouraged both caution and preparedness. These lessons from the past are relevant in the present. Historically the British, the Russians, and more recently the Americans and Australians, have all departed Afghanistan in anything but triumph. All point to a fatal tendency to underestimate enemy threat.

In late 2021 the West railed against the Russian buildup of forces along the border with the Ukraine but maintained the comforting delusion that war in Europe was scaremongering. Thousands of combat deaths on both sides and the destruction

---

[211] Dixon, N. (1976). *On the Psychology of Military Incompetence*. Aldershot., Jonathon Cape.

of large areas of the Ukraine in 2022-24 have shown that our threat assessment was wrong. Those lacking insight who later said "we didn't think Putin would actually invade" need to reflect on the cost of their complacency. A sensible glance at his history should have warned us that his "special military operation" was a euphemism for an unprovoked and illegal invasion in which hundreds of thousands would die.

Some of this may be ascribed to inertia, the simple force that encourages us to maintain a steady course and speed when confronted by changed circumstances, because to do otherwise requires more effort. Some may be due to hubris, that more complex phenomenon of over-estimating our own abilities so as to maintain or enhance our self-image. The inherent appeal of the frontal assault for the military commander hungry for heroic reputation has historically been a contributor to ill-advised strategy and costly tactical failure.

All this ought to encourage threat assessors to begin the process of threat assessment with a careful self-examination of personal and organisational motive and purpose, and in the light of lessons to be learned from transparent if uncomfortable history. Inertia and hubris, when unguarded against, always hover overhead, and stand ready to degrade decision making. In 2024, American urging of restraint on a vengeful Israel as it brutality killed thousands of Palestinians under the carefully worded guise of "dismantling Hamas" will likely receive deserved criticism for catastrophically misguided threat assessment. No one can condone what Hamas did on 7 October 2023, but proportionality cannot justify the genocide of Gaza. Ironically Israel's actions appear to replicate what it decried the Nazis for doing to Jews in the ghettos in 1940 Poland. The lesson is that threat certainly needs to be assessed seriously but also realistically. We need to keep asking if submarines are really critical, and not just desirable.

Conclusion

This section has argued that the process of threat assessment should be underpinned by the psychological processes of perception and learning. Understanding the roles that this play, and the detractions presented in inertia and hubris, offers a constructive encouragement to take threat assessment very seriously. All our lives depend on it. Our nation's future will depend on it.

Bibliography

Alden, J. D. (1979). *The Fleet Submarine in the US Navy: A Design and Construction History.* London: Arms and Armour Press.

Ballantyne , I. (2019). *Undersea Warriors.* New York, USA: Pegasus Books.

Ballantyne, I. (2013). *Hunter Killers.* London, England: Orion.

Bergmann, K. (2021, October). A decision of enormous consequences taken with little analysis. *Asia Pacific Defence Reporter*, pp. 12-14.

Blair, C., & Blair, C. (1997). *Hitler's U-Boat War: The Hunters 1939-1942.* London: Weidenfeld & Nicholson.

Brenchley, F., & Brenchley, E. (2001). *Stoker's Submarine.* Sydney, NSW, Australia: Harper Collins.

Briggs, P. (2023, August 23). Mandating Australian Industry content for the AUKUS SSNs. *The Strategist.*

Campbell, G. (1937). *My Mystery Ships.* London: Hodder and Stoughton.

Carruthers, R. (2012). *The U-Boat War in the Atlantic vol 1 1939-1941.* Barnsley, South Yorkshire, UK: Pen And Sword.

Clancy, T. (1984). *Hunt for the Red October.* Annapolis, Maryland, USA: Naval Institute Press.

Cohen, E. A., & Gooch, J. (1960). *Military Misfortunes: The Anatomy of Failure in War.* New York: The Free Press.

Bibliography

Creswell, W. (1907). A Letter to the Minister of Defence. In *National Archives of Australia* (p. MP178). Canberra, ACT, Australia: Commonwealth of Australia.

David, S. (1997). *Miliary Blunders.* London: Constable.

Davidson, P. (2024). *Submarine!* Brisbane, Australia: Connor Court.

Dixon, N. (1976). *On the Pychology of Military Incompetence.* Aldershot: Jonathon Cape.

Dornan, P. (2010). *Diving Stations.* Barnsley, South Yorkshire, England: Pen & Sword Books Ltd.

Dunlop, D. (2023). A Wake-up call for Canada: Rethinking our Arctic Submarine policies. *Australian Naval Review.*(2), 58-68.

Dupont, A. (2024, February 3-4). A Game of High Stakes on the High Seas. *The Weekend Australian*, p. 33.

Enigma machine. (2023, 8 8). Retrieved from en.wikipedia.org/wiki/en:Museo_Nazionale_Scienza_e_Tecnologia_Leonardo_da_Vinci

Evans, M. (2023). The Eye of the Storm: Future Warfare in the Indo-Pacific and its implications for Australia. *Australian Naval review*(1), 22-30.

Evans, R. J. (2020). *The Hitler Conspiracies: The Third Reich and the Paranoid Imagination.* London: Allen Lane.

Fisher, J. A. (1919). *Records.* London: Hodder and Stoughton.

Fluckey, E. B. (1992). *Thunder Below!* Urbana and Chicago: University of Illinois Press.

Foster, J. (2006). *Entombed but not Forgotten* (1 ed.). Loftus, NSW, Australia: Australian Military publications.

Frame, T. (1992). *A History of Australian American Naval Relations.* Rydalmere, NSW, Australia: Hodder and Stoughton.

Franklin, G. (2015). *Britain's Anti-submarine capability 1919-1939.* London: Routledge.

Friedman, N. (2009). *Network-centric Warfare: How Navies Learned to Fight Smarter Through Three World Wars.* Annapolis, Maryland, USA: Naval Institute Press.

Friedman, N. (2019). *British Sumarines in Two World Wars.* London: Pen & Sword Books.

Gannon, M. V. (2010). *The Epic Story of the Allies' Defeat of the German U-Boats in May 1943.* Annapolis, MD, USA: Naval Institute Press.

Goldrick, J. (2014). Buying time: British Submarine Capability in the Far East 1919-1940. *Global War Studies, 11*, 8-24. doi:http://dx.doi.org/10.5893/19498489.11.03.02

Gordon, A. (1996). *The Rules of the Game.* London: John Murray.

Gorton, J. (n.d.). *The Age.*

Hamilton, C., & Ohlberg, M. (2020). *Hidden Hand: Exposing How the Chinese Communist Party is reshaping the World.* Melbourne: Hardie Grant.

Hanson, V. D. (2001). *Carnage and Culture: Landmark Battles in the Rise of Western Power.* New York: Anchor Books.

Hanson, V. D. (2020). *The Second World Wars.* New York: Basic Books.

Hardman, P. (2023, May). Maritime Trade is Essential to the Indo-Pacific. *Proceedings*, pp. 10-11.

Hennessy, P., & Jinks, J. (2015). *The Silent Deep: The Royal Navy Submarine Service Since 1945.* London, England: Allen Lane.

Hodges, A. P. (2014). *Alan Turing: The Enigma.* Princeton, NJ, USA:

Bibliography

Princeton University Press.

Holmes, W. J. (1979). *Double-Edged Secrets: U.S Naval Intelligence Operations in the Pacific during World War II.* Annapolis, MD, USA: Naval Institute Press.

Jeremy, J. (2022, August 3). *Submarines for the RAN going Nuclear. Technical Presentation to the Royal Institution of Naval Architects.* Retrieved May 17, 2023, from youtube/W6blo6tY2EU

Jones, D., & Nunan, P. (2005). *U.S. Subs Down Under 1942-1945 Brisbane.* Annapolis, MD, USA: Naval Institute Press.

Kemp, P. (2003). *Midget Submarines of the Second World War.* London: Caxton Editions.

Kennedy, P. M. (1983). *The Rise and Fall of British Nava Mastery.* Basingstoke: MacMillan.

Kerr, J. (2021, November). Which submarine will Australia build? *Australian Defence Magazine.*

Lambert, A. (2008). *Admirals: The Naval Commanders who Made Britain Great.* London: Faber and Faber.

Lee, B. (2019). *Right Man, Right Place, Worst Time: Commander Eric Feldt, His Life and His Coastwatchers.* Brisbane: Boolarong Press.

Lockwood, C. A. (2018). *Sink 'Em All.* Middletown, Delaware, USA: The Rocket Press.

Longstaff, R. (1984). *Submarine Command: A Pictorial History.* London: Book Club Associates.

MacIntyre, D. (1956). *U-Boat Killer.* London, England: Wiedenfeld.

Mackay, R. F. (1973). *Fisher of Silverstone.* London: Clarendon.

Mahan, A. T. (1890). *The Influence of Sea Power upon History 1660-*

1783. Boston: Little Brown and Co.

Mansoor, P. R., & Williamson, M. (2019). *The Culture of Military Organizations.* Cambridge, UK: Cambridge Universsity Press.

Marder, A. J. (1966). *From the Dreadnought to Scapa Flow: The Royal Navy in the Fisher Era 1904-1919.* London: Oxford University Press.

Miller, E. S. (2007). *War Plan Orange: The US Strategy to Defeat Japan (1897-1945).* Annapolis: Naval Institute.

Moffitt, R. (2023, September 13). As an island nation, why do we accept such a weak navy? *Financial Review.*

Moffitt, R. (2023, August 3). *Corvettes are not an option for Australia.* Retrieved August 10, 2023, from RowanMoffit://www.aspistrategist.org.au/author/rowan-moffitt/

Mole, D. (2020). Nuclear power for Submarines. In T. Frame (Ed), *An Australian Nuclear Industry Starting with Submarines?* Redland Bay, QLD, Australia: Connor Court.

Morison, E. E., & Morison, E. E. (1960). *Turmoil and Tradition: A Study of the Life and Times of Henry L Stimson.* Boston: Houghton Mifflin.

Nance, C. (2023, May). China's Great Plan, Coming to a Country Near You. *Quadrant,* 35-37.

O'Kane, R. H. (1977). *Clear the Bridge: The War Patrols of the USS Tang.* New York: Presidio.

O'Kane, R. H. (1998). *Wahoo: The Patrols of America's Most Famous WWII Submarine.* New York: Ballantine Books.

Pacey, B. (2012, November). *Sub Judice: Australia's Future Submarine.* Retrieved 2023, from Kokodafoundation.org.

Bibliography

Padfield, P. (1984). *Dönitz The Last Fuhrer.* London, England: Panther.

Parry, D. (2022). *Perisher: Its Evolution 1917-2017 and the Submarine Commanding Officer.* London: Kings College.

Ranft, B. (1977). *Technical Change and British Naval Policy 1816-1939.* (B. Ranft, Ed.) London, England: Hodder and Stanton.

Ray, M. (2023, August 8). *U-Boat.* Retrieved from www.britannica.com/technology/U-boat: www.britannica.com/technology/U-boat

Regan, G. (2001). *Geoffrey Regan's Book of Naval Blunders.* London, England: Carlon Group.

Robinson, P. (1999). *HMS Unseen.* London: W. F. Howes.

Roggeveen, S. (2024, June). Australia Needs a Military Alliance with Indonesia. *Australian Forein Affairs*(21), 6-27.

Ross, D. J. (2022). *The World's Greatest Submarines: An Illustrated History from 17th Century to the Present.* London: Amber Books.

Scott, P. (2023). Australias's Submarine Capabiity - Enduring Characteristics, Emerging Features. *Australian Naval Review*(1), 40-51.

Scott, P. (2023). *Running Deep: An Australian Submarine Life.* North Fremantle: Fremantle Press.

Seal, G. (2013). *Century of Silent Service.* Brisbane, QLD, Australia: Boolarong Press.

Seal, G. (2014). Finding the Lost Submarine: The Mystery of AE1. *Journal of Australian Naval History, 5*(1), 53-70.

Sebag-Montefiore, H. (2004). *Enigma: the Battle for the Code.* London: Wiley.

Sewell, K., & Priesler, J. (2007). *All Hands Down: The True Story of* the Soviet Attack on USS Scorpion. San Rafael, CA, USA: Gallery Books.

Shackleton, D. (2022). *The Hunter Frigate: An assessment.* Canberra: ASPI.

Simpson, G. W. (1972). *Periscope View.* London: MacMillan.

Sloan, G. (2019). the Royal Navy and Organizational Learning - The Western Approaches Tactical Unit and the Battle of the Atlantic. *Naval War Clllege Review, 72*(article 9). Retrieved from https://digital-commons.usnwc.edu/nwc-review/vol72/iss4/9

Sontag, S., Drew, C., & Drew, A. (2000). *Blind Man's Bluff.* Ingram Publisher Services US.

Sternhell, C. M., & Thorndike, A. M. (1946). *Antisubmarine Warfare in World War II. Operations Evaluation Group Report no. 51.* Washington DC, USA: Office of the Chief of Naval Operations, Navy Department. Retrieved August 8, 2023, from Retrieved from the Library of Congress, <www.loc.gov/item/2009655248/>

Stevens, D. (. (2001). *The Royal Australian Navy* (Vol. III). South Melbourne, Victoria, Australia: Oxford University Press.

Stewart, C. (2023, March 11-12). High Reward , but High Risk. *Weekend Australian*, p. 38.

Stimson, H. L., & Bundy, M. (1947). *On Active Service in Peace and War.* New York: Harper and Brothers.

Sturma, M. (2006). *Death at a Distance: The Loss of the Legendary USS Harder.* Annapolis, MD, USA: Naval Institute Press.

Sweeney, M. (2023, March). Submarines Will Reign in a War with China. *Proceedings, 149/3/11441*, pp. 21-25.

Tsang, S., & Cheung, O. (2024). *The Political Thought of Xi Jinping.* Oxford: Oxford Universiy Press.

Bibliography

Tyler, P. (1986). *Running Critical: The Silent War, Rickover, and General Dynamics.* New York, USA: Harper & Row.

Van der Vat, D. (2004). *Stealth at Sea: The History of the Submarine.* London : Wiedenfeld & Nicholson.

Werner, H. (1969). *Iron Coffins.* London: Arthur Barker.

White, M. (1992). *Australian Submarines: A History.* Canberra: Australian Government Publishing Service.

White, M. (2015). *Australian Submarines: A History* (2nd ed., Vol. 2). St Kilda, Australia: Australian Teachers of Media.

Woodward, S. (2003). *One Hundred Days.* London: Harper Collins.

Woolner, D., & Yule, P. (2008). *The Collins Class Story: Steel, Spies and Spin.* Port Melbourne, Victoria, Australia: Cambridge University press.

About the Author

Dr Paul Davidson BSc (Hons) BD DPS MBA PhD DBA was a National Serviceman and Flight Lieutenant in the RAAF in the late 1960s and as a psychologist in DEPAIR, RSTT Wagga (1969), and Instructor in QUNISQN (1969-72). In 1970, he had his first contact with submarines on the Antisubmarine warfare course at AJASS in HMAS Albatross and was posted to 10 SQN (SP2H Neptune ASW aircraft) in Townsville. He left the airforce in 1973 to study in Britain, where he was attached to the RAF, and then went on to a teaching career as a Clinical Psychologist and Senior Lecturer in Psychological Medicine in Otago University Medical School (1976-88), New Zealand.

In 1989-90 he became CEO of a health service provider company with 650 staff, and then a university business school academic in Brisbane (QUT), for 30 years. During those years he was seconded by his university to teach Management (Organisational Behaviour and HRM) for five years in the RAN Staff College in HMAS Penguin (1995-2000), and to the Defence Materiel Organisation (DMO) in Canberra. In 2004, he completed a second doctorate based on research in professional military education. From 2005 to 2012 he taught project management to Royal Dutch Shell engineers in Europe, Asia and the USA, before returning to lead the Master of Business in HRM program at QUT in Brisbane (2013-16). He retired from his university professorial appointment at QUT and was invited to laterally transfer from the Airforce Reserve into the Navy Reserve in 2017, with the rank of Commander, to lead a two year Defence Review of Submarine Commanding Officer training. This was followed by a year's fulltime service as an Instructor in the Directing Staff in the Australian Command and Staff Course in the Australian Defence College in Canberra (2019).

Subsequently, still in uniform, he spent three years as research director in Warfare Innovation Navy, principally engaged in robotics, autonomous systems and artificial intelligence. He undertook Organisational Reviews of Warfare Innovation and Information Warfare Branches. He has published papers on professional military education and organisational design, and several widely recommended textbooks on his academic specialty of management. Retiring from the Navy and returning to Brisbane in late 2022, he now continues his interests in military and especially submarine history and strategy.

Index

Aboukir 35
AE1 22, 76, 181, 182
AE2 16, 22, 38, 39, 76, 181, 182, 183
Air Independent Systems 9, 25
Aircraft carrier 11
Afrika Korps 99
Akula class 211, 213
Albacore 146
American submarine development 56
Antisemitism 47, 51, 66
ASDIC 28
Astute class 213, 241
ASW 29, 43, 84, 109, 113
Attack class 214
Atrocities 19
Auchinleck, Claude 100
Authoritarian 69
Ardent 80
Ark Royal 87, 97
Argonaut 57
Astoria 155
Astute class 189
AUKUS 9, 214, 217
Australia 20
Australian Submarine Service 37
Australia 147
Austria 18
Athenia 74, 75, 78, 90
Atomic bomb 72
Azorian 177
B-24 Liberator 117
Balao class 58, 151, 159

Balme, David 92
Barb 161
Battle of the Bismark Sea 145
Battle of Britain 85
Battle of the Coral Sea 141
Battle of Midway 142
Battle of Leyte Gulf 146
Battle of the Philippine Sea 146
Battleships 17, 57,74
Barracuda class 215, 216
Barracuda 57, 203
Barrow-in-Furness 21, 22
Bayley, Lewis 32
Beazley, Kim 195
Belgium 18, 70
Bismark 62, 97, 119, 168
Beresford, Lord Charles 22
Besant, Thomas 181
Black May 119
Blamey, Thomas 140
Bletchley Park 88, 89, 107, 125
Blitzkreig 52, 82
Borneo 8
Bosnian Serb 18
Britain 20
Brisbane 151, 152, 154 , 185
British 18, 31
British development 55
Bowfin 138
Briggs, Peter 284
Brown, Tim 281

Brownshirts 66
Brümmer-Patzig, Helmut 41
Bulldog 91
C3 27
C-class submarine 21
Campbell, Gordon 33
Canberra 155
Casablanca 116
Catalina 117
Cavalla 146
China 176
Cold War 8, 30
Columbia class 176
Conqueror 175
Convoy system 36, 108
Chief of Navy 9
Chinese Submarines 242
Christie, Ralph Waldo 513
Churchill, Winston 34, 68, 105, 108, 116,
Clark, Mark 116
Cressy 35
Creswell, William 21, 181
Collins class 181, 192, 193, 197, 201, 202, 203, 238
Collins, John 147, 153
Collins 196
Conte Rosso 133
Corbett, Julian 222
Courageous 80
Cruiser rules 53, 111, 137
Czechoslovakia 82
Diesel-electric power 11
D class 34

Deakin, Alfred 21
Dechaineux, Emile 147
Dechaineux 197, 202
Deloraine 136
Desant, Thomas 38
Design and strategy 58
Denmark 18
Deterrence 23
Dönitz, Karl 61, 73, 74, 79, 86, 103, 110, 121, 123, 126, 130
Dreadnought 148, 240
Dudley, Michael 67
Dunbar-Nasmith, Martin 87
Dunkirk 82
Dunne, Michael 198, 295
Edward, Prince of Wales 95, 96
Eisenhower, Dwight 116
Electric Boat Company 21
Einsatzgruppe 69
Empress of Britain 83
Enigma 27, 60, 87, 88, 89, 93
Falklands War 12
Farncomb 196, 201
Feldt, Eric 157
Ferdinand, Archduke 18
Fisher, Jacky 17, 19, 20, 23, 34, 55
Flower class 84, 118
Fluckey, Eugene 156, 161, 162, 165
Foch 45, 49
France 70
French 18, 67, 246
Fredendall, Lloyd 100
Fremantle 151, 152
Freyberg, Bernard 102

Index

Gato class 30, 137, 151, 159, 160
George, Duke of Kent 96
Getting, Frank 184, 185
German High Seas Fleet 30
German U-boats 60
Gilmore, Howard 157
Gorton, John 187
Glomar Explorer 177
Grayling 149
Great War 21
Growler 157
Gneisenau 80, 97, 182
Goebbels, Joseph 65
Göring, Herman 68, 79, 155
Gotland class 25
Guadalcanal 143
Greece 70
Griffin 144
Growler 157
Haig, Douglas 45, 70
Hamman 136
Hammond, Mark 287
Hanson, Victor Davis 50, 71
Hartenstein, Werner 109
Hawke, Robert 190
Heads 76
Hitler, Adolf 47, 49, 51, 52, 63, 64, 74
HFDF 113
Hindenberg 66
Hirohito 166
Hobart class 229
Hogue 35
Hood 97, 168
Holland, John Phillip 20

Hornet 140
Horton, Max 87
Howard, John 199, 200
Hudspeth, Kenneth 120
Hunt, George 133
Hunter class 223
Hunter Killer 13
Hiryu 142
I-5 136
I-26 136
I-124 136
Imperial Germany 18
India 175, 247
Iwo Jima 147, 166
J class 54, 183
Japan 71
Japanese submarines 61, 135, 247
Jews 65, 66
K-137 177
Kaiser 18, 44, 46, 64
Kaga 142
Katoomba 136
King, Ernest 98, 106, 109
Kriegsmarine 50, 73, 165, 174
Kretschmer, Otto 103
Kristallnacht 66
Kokoda track 141
Kursk 178
Lend Lease Act 106
Lemp, Fritz-Julius 74, 90, 92
Lethality 22
Laconia 109, 110
Lithgow 136
Lexington 141, 150, 154

335

Llandovery Castle 41
Lloyd George, David 45
Lockwood, Charles 153
Los Angeles 210
Lowenberg 90
Ludendorrf, Erich 44, 46, 47
Luftwaffe 85
Lusitania 40, 41, 54
Lüthe, Wolfgang 129
MacArthur, Douglas 140
Mahan, Alfred Thayer 57, 106, 148, 222
Malta 73, 94
Martindale 61
Messerschmidt 109, 68
Mesudiye 37
Miers, Anthony 112
Midway 142, 154
Morshead, Leslie 99
Morton, Mush 155, 156
Munchen 90
Mussolini, Benito 86
Mystery patrols 8, 189, 190
Mystery ships 32
Nationalism 19
Narwhal 57
Nautilus 78, 149, 172
NATO 8, 175, 178
Nelson, Lord 19
New Zealand 116
Nimitz, Chester 33, 140, 149
Netherlands 70
Norway 70
November class 173
Nuclear propulsion 8

Nuclear ballistic missiles 11
Nuclear-powered boats 24
Nuclear-powered fleet 9
O class 55, 184
O'Kane, Richard 156
Oberon class 171, 188, 189
Ohio class SSBN 29, 210, 237
Okinawa 147, 166
Operation Barbarossa 98
Operation Drumbeat 103
Operation Torch 100
Ottoman empire 46
Orwell 122
Orion 189, 190
Oxley 55, 184
Otama 189, 191
Otway 55, 184
Ovens 190
P-class 57
Pacific Theatre 134
Panzers 82
Parry, David 275
Paukemschlag 103
Paulus 69
Peace 65
Pearl Harbour 71, 150, 159
Periscope 9
Perisher 9, 43, 184, 265
Pétain, Philippe 44, 67
Petard 107
Plan Orange 57, 149
Platypus 188, 189
Poland 67, 70
Polaris 173

Index

Pound, Dudley 35
Prien, Gunther 78
Prince of Wales 139
Prinz Eugen 97
Propulsion 24
PLA(N) Fleet 228
Q-ships 32
Queen Elizabeth 80
Queen Mary 80
Raeder, Erich 73, 79
Rakuyo 161
Richthofen, Manfred 45
Rickover, Hyman 172, 209
Reparations 65
Repulse 139
Rodney 97
Röhm 66
Romania 47
Royal Navy 8
Royal Oak 78
Rubis class 175
Russia 70, 175, 248
S class 56
SSN 26
SSBN 29
Saipan 146
Sammut, Greg 292
Saratoga 136, 144
Scharnhorst 80, 182
Scott, Peter 302
Sea-bed cables 12
Sea control 23, 174
Sea denial 23, 174
Sealion 161

Schepke, Joachim 103
Schnorkel 25
Shackleton, David 198, 199
Shaw, Norman 184
Sheean 201
Shōkaku 141, 160
Short Sunderland 118
Singapore 139, 249
Sensors 27
Snort air intake 9, 25
Skipjack class 177, 178
SONAR 28
Somali 89
Soryu 142
SOSUS 29
Speed of submarine 33
Spitfire 69
Strategy 24
Strategic bomber 11
Stoker, Henry 39, 181
Stormtroopers 66
Sturgeon 158
Submarine War 30, 42
Submersibles 24
SSK 24
SSN 16, 26
Swordfish 177
T-class 56
Taiwan 205, 206, 207
Tambor class 58
Technology development 52
Tench class 58, 151
Thresher 177, 178
Tirpitz 62, 158, 185

337

Tobruk 99
Torpedoes 29, 150
Torpedo boats 73
Torpedo data computer 59
Toxic leadership 69
Trafalgar class 176, 241
Triton 173
Trump 186
Turing, Alan 92
Type VII 25, 61, 74, 75, 78, 127
Type IX 77
Type XXI 78
Typhoon 173
U-29 78
U-30 90
U-43 129
U-68 73
U-81 99
U-86 41
U-99 129
U-110 91
U-139 39
U-156 109
U-505 77
U-559 107
U-boats 76
Ultra 89, 133
Unity class 132
Upholder 133
USSR 8, 18
Unrestricted warfare 31, 32
Unterzeeboots 31
Vanguard 239
V-boats 57

Vendetta 100
Versailles 50, 60, 71, 72
Vichy 67
Vincennes 155
Vietnam 8
Virginia class 210, 219, 230, 235, 256, 257
VLS 29
Voyager 100
Wahoo 155
Walker, Johnny 109
Waller 197, 200
Wanklyn, Malcolm 133
Wasp 144
Waterhen 100
WATU 113
Weddigen, Eduard 35
Werner, Herbert 124
Whiskey class 173, 174
White, Hugh 217
Wilson, Arthur 22
Wilson, Woodrow 44
Withers, Thomas 138
Wolf pack 80, 81, 118, 120, 154
Wrens 113
X-craft 122
Yorktown 136, 141, 142
Yugoslavia 48
Zuikaku 141

www.ingramcontent.com/pod-product-compliance
Lightning Source LLC
Chambersburg PA
CBHW070013010526
44117CB00011B/1555